DISCARDED

The Gulf, Energy, and Global Security

The Gulf, Energy, and Global Security

Political and Economic Issues

edited by
Charles F. Doran
Stephen W. Buck

Lynne Rienner Publishers • Boulder & London

The map of the Gulf region is based on a map published in James A. Bill and Carl Leiden, *Politics in the Middle East* (Glenview, Illinois: Scott Foresman, 1984), and is used by permission of Harper Collins Publishers.

Published in the United States of America in 1991 by
Lynne Rienner Publishers, Inc.
1800 30th Street, Boulder, Colorado 80301

and in the United Kingdom by
Lynne Rienner Publishers, Inc.
3 Henrietta Street, Covent Garden, London WC2E 8LU

© 1991 by Lynne Rienner Publishers, Inc. All rights reserved

Library of Congress Cataloging-in-Publication Data
The Gulf, energy, and global security—political and economic issues / edited by Charles F. Doran and Stephen W. Buck.
    p. cm.
Includes bibliographical references and index.
ISBN 1-55587-254-9 (cloth)
1. Petroleum industry and trade—Political aspects—Persian Gulf Region. 2. Persian Gulf Region—Politics and government. 3. World politics—1985–1995. I. Doran, Charles F. II. Buck, Stephen W.
HD9576.P52G85   1990
338.2'7282'09536—dc20   90–9100
                                                                                                 CIP

British Cataloguing in Publication Data
A Cataloguing in Publication record for this book
is available from the British Library.

Printed and bound in the United States of America

The paper used in this publication meets the requirements
of the American National Standard for Permanence of
Paper for Printed Library Materials Z39.48–1984.

To Alphonse DeRosso

without whose vision this study
would never have been undertaken

Contents

	List of Tables	ix
	Foreword *Lucius D. Battle*	xi
	Map of the Gulf Region	xiii
1	Introduction: The Gulf 2000 Project *Stephen W. Buck*	1
2	US Energy Interests in the Gulf in the 1990s *Edward N. Krapels*	13
3	Charting the Unchartable *John W. Limbert*	27
4	Iraq in the Year 2000 *Phebe Marr*	49
5	Arms and the Gulf: The Gulf Regional Arms Race to the Turn of the Century *Michael Collins Dunn*	69
6	Saudi Arabia in the 1990s: Plus ça change . . . *David E. Long*	85
7	The Gulf Cooperation Council: The Smaller Gulf States and Interstate Relations *Joseph Wright Twinam*	107

8	A New Soviet Role in the Gulf? *Shahram Chubin*	131
9	The European Community and the Gulf *Philip Robins*	153
10	Japanese-Gulf Relations Toward the Year 2000 *Ukeru Magosaki and Yasumasa Kuroda*	173
11	Gulf Security in Perspective *Charles F. Doran*	189
	Epilogue *Charles F. Doran*	209
	Chronology *G. Wade Wootan and John Schembari*	211
	Bibliography	221
	The Contributors	227
	Index	229

Tables

2.1	Oil Reserves and Production in Persian Gulf Countries, 1988	16
2.2	OPEC Members with Owned Downstream Interests	22
9.1	Gulf Oil Imports as a Percentage of Total Imports, 1986	157
9.2	Net Oil Imports into Major EC States Importing Gulf Oil	158
10.1	Japan's Trade with the Middle East	176
10.2	The Share of West Asia in Japan's Trade	177
10.3	Japanese Energy Consumption	184

Foreword

Lucius D. Battle

As the prospect of a cease-fire emerged in the Iran-Iraq war, there was a strong temptation to put the Persian Gulf area aside for the moment and to consider the greatest conflict in that area in recent history to be finished. Even for Middle East specialists, the Gulf seemed to wane in importance: the flow of oil seemed assured as Iraq and Iran began to lick their wounds and repair their war-damaged economies.

In 1987, a consultant to the Middle East Institute, Alphonse DeRosso, began to discuss the urgent need for a longer-term look at US interests in the Gulf; he thought we should analyze those interests through the year 2000, and try to understand how they might be affected by possible developments during the decade of the 1990s. Growing out of these discussions came his proposal regarding the need for a serious study of US, Western, and Japanese interests in the Gulf, which resulted in this volume. Mr. DeRosso worked out a conceptual framework for the project, and he persisted in pursuing financial support from various foundations.

A preliminary discussion took place in 1989 at a day-long meeting in which experienced representatives of oil companies as well as academicians specializing in the field participated. Later, authors were selected for their expertise on the various topics considered important for the study. In April 1990, the Middle East Institute and the Johns Hopkins University School of Advanced International Studies hosted a conference in Washington, D.C., bringing together these authors and more than 150 other members of the academic, government, business, and diplomatic communities to discuss and analyze events in the Gulf.

We have assembled some very interesting papers. It was more difficult to anticipate future trends than we realized, but we take pride in what we have done. Whatever the outcome of the current crisis in and around the Arabian peninsula, the Gulf is with us today in a very different form than was the case only a few months ago. We must turn our attention, intelligence, and thoughts—our policy-determinative processes—to the Gulf on a long-term continuing basis, recognizing that change—sudden and perhaps dangerous—is always possible in this region. This book will be useful to many scholars, and to policymakers who need to follow and study the area and who need background and information for making decisions.

I am very grateful to the late Al DeRosso for his initiative, his energy, and his persistence. I am particularly grateful to the MacArthur Foundation for providing us our initial grant, and to the Exxon Corporation, the Pennzoil Company, the Committee for Energy Policy Promotion (Japan), and Ruane, Cunniff & Co. for additional funding. Warm appreciation is extended to Charles Doran and Stephen Buck, the coordinators of the project and editors of this volume.

I also wish to thank the Middle East Institute staff: Christopher Van Hollen, Andrew Parasiliti, and Kristina Palmer, who were actively involved in all aspects of the conference and publication; Robin Surratt of the *Middle East Journal,* who provided valuable editorial guidance; and MEI interns John Schembari, David Gordon, Mark Dennis, and Wade Wootan, who assisted in arranging the conference and preparing research support materials.

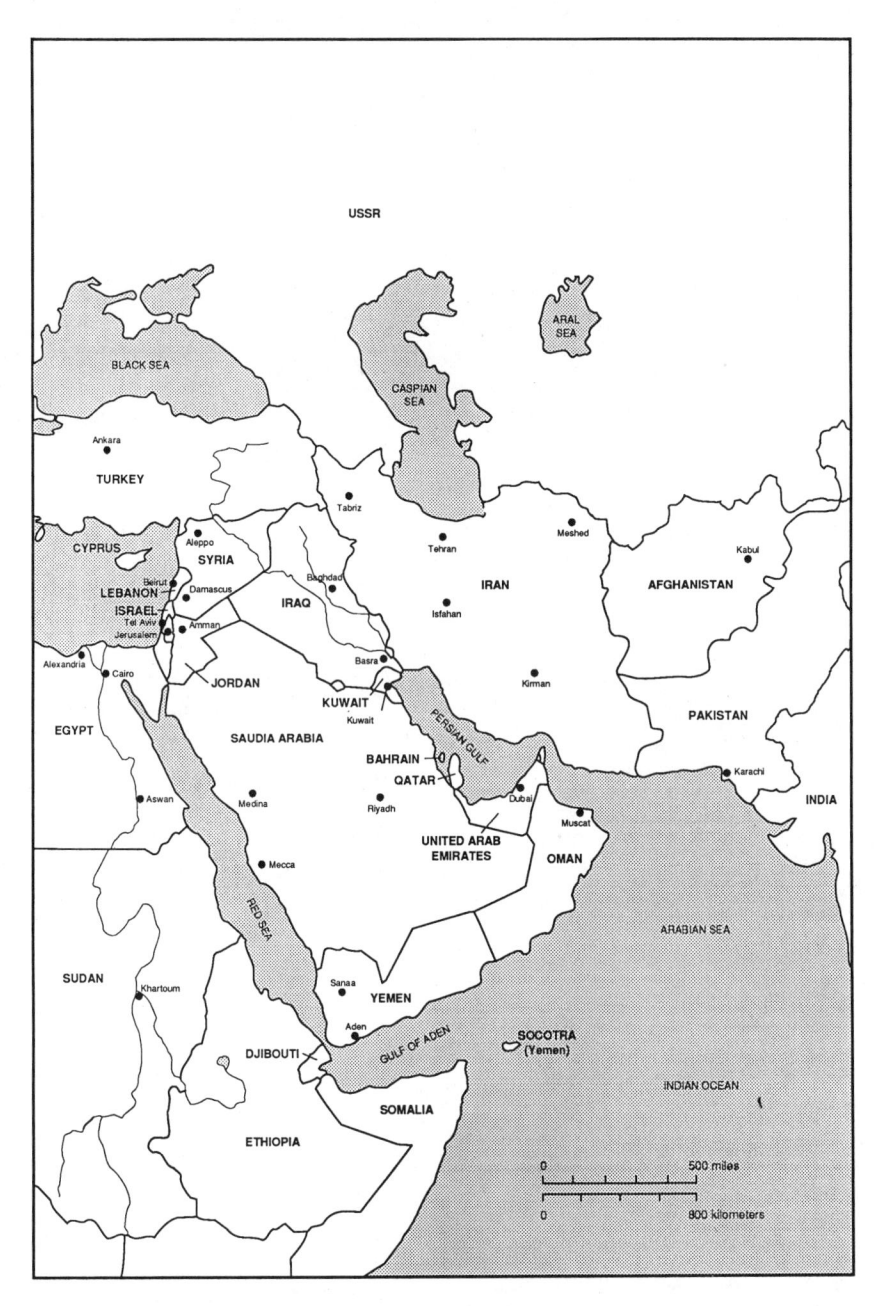

The Gulf Region

1
Introduction: The Gulf 2000 Project
Stephen W. Buck

Gulf security is important to the West. Equally important is stability for moderate governments seeking to export oil on the world market. Buyers and sellers need each other. But sometimes interests differ, not only between individual buyers and sellers of crude oil, but among the sellers themselves. Given the means to violence in the Gulf area, and the number of unresolved conflicts, the way politics impinges upon economics in the region requires careful assessment.

A review of the prior decade provides an instructive first step in understanding the problems confronting Gulf energy and security policy in the coming decade. (Readers who wish to insert "Persian" between "the" and "Gulf" are welcome to do so.)

In 1980, Americans were transfixed by the hostage crisis, and a US president was to go down in defeat largely because of it. The shah, the lynchpin of our so-called two-tier policy in the Gulf, had been overthrown, and the Soviets had invaded Afghanistan. Khomeini and Islamic fundamentalism seemed grave threats to our remaining friends in the area, as did the outbreak of the Iran-Iraq war. As the decade progressed, complacency that the war would be confined to bloodletting between equally nasty regimes gave way to concern that it would spill over onto international shipping and Gulf Cooperation Council (GCC) members. US agreement to reflag Kuwaiti tankers led to the ultimate deployment of forty-five US and thirty-five allied naval vessels in the area and a major debate in Congress over US involvement. Iranian support for terrorism and hostage-taking led directly to Irangate, Ronald Reagan's worst crisis and a continued embarrassment for his successor.

Viewed against this backdrop, the decline in attention to the Gulf at the beginning of the 1990s is striking. Khomeini is gone, and his brand of Islamic revolution appeared to be much less of a threat to the region than had been feared. The Iran-Iraq war had stopped, and with it the tanker war and the threat to shipping in the Gulf. (Indeed, some argued that the continued flow of oil from the Gulf during the height of the tanker war showed that no matter what, the world will get its oil from the Gulf and, therefore, not much attention has to be paid to the region.) With the Soviet withdrawal from Afghanistan and *glasnost*, the Soviet threat to the area commanded scant attention.

How quickly events in the Middle East reverse policy! It was this ever-growing complacence about energy and security in the Gulf that prompted the Gulf 2000 project. From the perspective of April 1990, the task of this introduction was to warn policymakers of the dangers of such complacence:

> In short, the Gulf has gone from front to back burner. This may be understandable in the near term, but we in the United States ignore or downplay this region at our peril. While developments in the Gulf in the 1990s may be less dramatic than in the previous decade, the trends in the region and in international markets bearing on the region could well turn out to have more profound implications for Western and US interests than anything that occurred in the 1980s.

The dramatic turn of events in the Gulf since August 1990 has changed complacency to urgency, and is accelerating movement in new directions for the coming decade. But the lesson remains: How quickly events in the Middle East reverse policy.

Nature of the Project

The purpose of the Gulf 2000 project was to formulate and analyze (1) more and less likely courses of political and economic development for each of the nations bordering on the Gulf and (2) the probable interactions among themselves, the United States, and other leading actors. Policy options were to result. We identified nine topics, and chose an expert on each topic to write a paper for the project. Professor Doran prepared a set of four possible scenarios for the authors to consider, modify, or reject in coming to their own conclusions about the security situation in the Gulf during the 1990s from the vantage point of their own topic.

One scenario stressed stability. It argued that "the governments are exhausted by the eight years of fighting between Iraq and Iran." They would now focus upon economic development and reconstruction, a task that would "require considerable political stability at home and in their foreign relations" and "divert them from major confrontation."

A second scenario stressed the theme of ideological radicalization as an outgrowth perhaps of "accelerated economic and social change." In this scenario, "both the possible incidence of major domestic violence and instability, coupled with the possible emergence of regimes less hospitable to cooperation in the short term than the present Gulf governments, could cause problems for US interests in the area."

A third scenario emphasized the possibility of increased regional political instability. In this view, the Iran-Iraq war was not so much settled as "temporarily suspended." Moreover, renewed war in the Yemens might spill over into Saudi Arabia or Oman, and technological advances might enable Iran to directly attack Arab oil fields in the latter part of the decade. It also posed a possibility of more immediate concern: "A quarrel now not foreseen but troublesome in concept would be that between Iraq and Kuwait or Iraq and Saudi Arabia. In the 1960s the British presence saved Kuwait. Could the US presence do so in the 1990s? At least one observer has come to the 'stark conclusion' that 'both the GCC and the United States may have to consider Kuwait expendable in the event of either an Iranian attack or a Soviet assault' (J. E. Peterson, *Defending Arabia*, 1986). Iraq might have to be added to this list of Kuwaiti opponents difficult to deter."

Fourth, the authors were asked to consider a scenario whose principal characteristic stressed neither stability nor instability "but a new more difficult international political climate," possibly stemming from the Soviet Union or from some other source exogenous to the region itself, in which "the terms of American access to the Gulf region are being redefined" and "American interests are allowed to suffer."

These scenarios were to be treated as suggestive rather than restrictive, and as the base for simultaneous occurrence rather than as strict alternatives. The various authors responded to the challenge with far-reaching and farsighted analysis of the future possibilities and likely trends on their topics.

While this project began more than a year prior to the Iraq invasion of Kuwait, all of the chapters encompass this event in their analysis. The policy conclusions and recommendations in the final chapter of the study, formally presented to the Washington policy community several months prior to the crisis, cover the decade as a whole and seem as valid today as at the time they were first drawn. In that chapter, bracketed inserts update those conclusions, and an epilogue has been added to highlight the implications of the Kuwaiti crisis for the long-term Gulf situation.

In brief, the organizers of the project came to believe that the Gulf was going to become, with a high probability of occurrence, a source of major policy predicament for the United States and its allies in the last decade of the twentieth century.

Iraq, Iran, and the Arms Race

Iraq

Of all the developments and trends discussed in this study, probably the most significant regional development is the emergence of Iraq as the predominant power in the Gulf and the Fertile Crescent. A few years ago US policymakers might have laughed at such a prediction. With its Kurdish problem and majority Shiite population dominated by a radical, Arab nationalist, Sunni regime, Iraq was considered unstable internally and a threat to the moderate regimes of the Arab world. But it was not the region's preeminent power. With the outbreak of the Iran-Iraq war, Iraq's oil production plummeted, Iran reversed roles with Iraq as occupier, and by middecade planners were worrying whether Iran's "final offensive" would succeed, with catastrophic consequences not only for Iraq but the whole Arabian peninsula.

It did not happen. The Iranian lines melted away before the Iraqi spring 1988 offensive, and Khomeini had to accept defeat and a cease-fire with well-equipped, battle-experienced Iraqi forces in the region. Throughout the war, Iraq had access to better equipment than Iran, particularly planes and tanks. It aggressively developed its own military-industrial capability, continued many development projects, and ensured that compulsory education continued throughout the country. To quote the original paper by Phebe Marr, "By the year 2000, Iraq may outstrip Egypt as the Arab world's largest military and industrial producer.... For the coming decade, Iraq will be the most powerful nation in the Gulf and possibly the most important military power in the Arab world.... There is every evidence that the Iraqi army will acquire and develop more high tech weaponry to maintain a military edge over Iran.... Iraq's main competitor in the shifting Gulf power balance—Iran—will not be able to match Iraq militarily by the year 2000."

In terms of internal stability, Iraq is in a much stronger position than before the Iran-Iraq war. The razing of Kurdish villages, forced resettlement of Kurds in more easily controlled urban and lowland areas, and resettlement of Arabs into formerly Kurdish territory raises significant human rights questions that are likely to trouble US-Iraqi relations for years to come. Deplorable as these actions may be, it is likely, as Dr. Marr indicates, that these actions give Iraq "firm control over its Kurdish border with Iran for the first time since the founding of the state."

If the Iran-Iraq war proved one thing, it is that the majority of Iraq's population, the Shia, are Iraqi first and Shiite second. They did not heed Khomeini's call. Instead, they constituted 70 percent or more of Iraq's ground forces. During the war, President Saddam Hussein downplayed Arab nationalism in favor of an Iraqi amalgam, drawing on 5,000 years of Iraqi history. The war integrated the Shia into the Iraqi state. At the same time, the "self-policing" nature of the Iraqi polity, based on a well-justified fear of Iraq's all-pervasive security apparatus, became even more effective, as Iraqis rallied around Saddam in a war of national survival. The 1989 National Assembly elections and talks of eventual moves to a multiparty system suggested that Saddam realized the need to open up the system. However, there is no significant, organized internal opposition. Hence, barring a successful assassination attempt, the likelihood of Saddam's being president of Iraq in the year 2000 is high, and of the authoritarian system now in place remaining essentially unchanged even higher. Speculation that the stability of Iraq's leadership might make it easier to deal with Iraq, despite continued concerns over human rights problems, has been proven wrong.

Besides its battle-hardened military, Iraq's power in the region is based on its oil wealth. Iraq's oil reserves are estimated to be second only to Saudi Arabia's. By constructing pipelines through Turkey and Saudi Arabia and a strategic north-south pipeline enabling switching of oil export flow as needed, Iraq effectively dealt with the cutoff of its oil exports through Syria and the Gulf. The consensus in April 1990 was that Iraq would maintain this flexibility while expanding exports through the Gulf. With large reserves, enhanced pipeline capacity, a developed oil infrastructure, and the potential to increase production and export capacity to well beyond 5 million barrels per day, Iraq should become the Gulf's second-largest producer after Saudi Arabia over the next decade. This would ensure it an increasing say in OPEC councils and increasing importance on the world oil scene.

Even with a larger population, Iran may not overtake Iraq because its oil reserves are less. It may have difficulty even maintaining present levels of production. Iran's population growth may, to quote Dr. Marr, "be a liability, not an asset, to economic development." Thus, Iraq's economic and military superiority "have already shifted the balance of power in the Gulf and the Fertile Crescent in Iraq's favor."

Iran

Venturing predictions about Iran ten years hence is much more difficult than for authoritarian Iraq. However, the very factors that make for such uncertainty lead to some important conclusions about Iran's future.

John Limbert convincingly shows that a relatively small clique has retained power in Iran since the beginning of Khomeini's revolution. They have also argued endlessly over paths to be taken—"revolution in one country" versus exporting it abroad, more central control of the economy versus letting the private sector have its way, bringing in needed foreign expertise and capital versus going it alone, for example. Khomeini made a point of letting such factionalism flourish; indeed this was probably a method of governing. His legacy is that severe infighting continues as of this writing and is likely to do so for some time. As Dr. Limbert says, "Without Khomeini, no one has the last word."

Thus, the few dozen leaders who developed factionalism to an art form under Khomeini are likely to string out the end game, devoting all their energies to political survival and little to reconstruction or long-term planning. The spectacle of the Salman Rushdie affair's destroying months of Iranian effort to woo European countries back is likely to be repeated as hard-liners fight the so-called pragmatists. In the meantime, the economic and military reconstruction Iran desperately needs is likely to be delayed. Dr. Limbert concludes that "the current regime has been incapable of taking the decisive political steps necessary to restore the Iranian economy." There is little to indicate that this will change anytime soon.

Indeed, the history of the Islamic Republic to date could easily justify the conclusion that the various factions in the leadership will lurch between conflicting policies for the coming decade. If this happens, it is hard to envisage Iran's being able to make significant progress in economic and military reconstruction, since such action would require consistency in policy over time. If the hard-liners triumph, "self-reliance" and "export of the revolution" will mean further deterioration of infrastructure, isolation, and economic and military decline. Even if the "pragmatists" prevail, their consolidation of power is likely to be marked by costly fits and starts as the hard-liners fight rearguard actions and the pragmatists bow and weave to avoid charges of betraying the revolution.

What this all adds up to is an Iran that will be lucky indeed to have dug itself out from under the destruction of war and neglect by the year 2000. For the Soviets and others, Iran may retain the aura of being the "strategic prize" in the region because of its location, size, and population. But in reality, Iran will be weak, unstable, and beset by problems to the year 2000, and most likely beyond. Indeed, its very population growth (expected to reach 100 million by 2010) may be a liability as oil reserves inevitably decline. In the power equation of the Gulf, Iran is no longer first, and there is little likelihood that this will have changed by the turn of the century.

The Gulf Arms Race

The present "no war–no peace" standoff between Iran and Iraq only encourages the already existing arms race. Iran never could match Iraq's planes and tanks during the war, and at the end of the war it lost massive amounts of equipment, particularly tanks. At the moment, Michael Dunn notes, "Iran's major suppliers remain countries like China and North Korea, whose equipment is by no means comparable to Iraq's French and Soviet aircraft and tanks." Iran cannot hope to acquire equipment to match Iraq's unless the West or the USSR suddenly prove willing to sell massive amounts of equipment, which Iran will not be able to afford in the near future.

Iran's procurement problems will not, however, lead to any slowdown in the arms race. To quote Dr. Dunn, Iran's "population, strategic location, and the fact that it will remain a political question mark for some time mean it will be the benchmark against which its neighbors judge their military arsenals *even if Iran were to prove the best of neighbors,* though the latter is a highly unlikely prospect."

Although the fighting has stopped, the 1980–1988 Iran-Iraq war has left the Gulf a much more dangerous place. The nature of arms in the region has changed qualitatively—and for the worse. During the war, both sides used chemical weapons and intermediate-range ballistic missiles. Despite international treaties, nothing was done to effectively stop such use. One of the most troubling legacies of the war was to widely publicize the efficacy of chemical weapons. It now appears that both sides are developing capabilities to arm their missiles with chemical weapons, and developing biological weapons. Iraq's fear of Iran's three-to-one demographic edge makes it likely that Iraq will try to pursue the nuclear option, even though this runs the risk of another Israeli preemptive strike.

Even if the United States were in the arms supply game, it would be unlikely to have much of an effect on the introduction of the most troublesome weapons in the area, such as intermediate-range missiles and chemical weapons. Despite US efforts to interdict the sale of precursors for chemical weapons, local production is well advanced and stopping supply from all sources extremely difficult. Although the INF treaty bans US or Soviet production of medium-range missiles altogether, this does not stop the Chinese, who have supplied the Saudis with missiles, nor other Third World suppliers, such as Brazil and Argentina, which are actively engaged in missile production projects with Egypt and Iraq. "It is likely," Dr. Dunn concludes, "that the suppliers of new technologies, those which may contribute most to the destabilizing side of the arms race, will be the newer arms merchants of the developing world, not the US, USSR or Western Europe.... Increasingly, the arms race will be one conducted independently of the US. Yet ironically, the long-term stability of the Gulf continues to be one of the US' most important strategic concerns."

Saudia Arabia and the Other Gulf Cooperation Council States

Saudi Arabia

The good news is that the Saudis have weathered a decade of war, threats, and economic downturn well, and the prognosis for internal stability is good. David Long demonstrates that the Saudis do not have to fear for their fundamentalist credentials; their Wahhabite system is just as radical and fundamentalist as revolutionary Iran's, perhaps even more so. Hence Khomeini's message is not a threat. The strong family base of Saudi society is likely to mean continued political stability based on social stability.

The bedrock of US-Saudi relations from a Saudi perspective has always been security and a shared opposition to communist inroads. With a small population and vast resources spread over a large area, the Saudis looked to the United States as their ultimate security guarantee, with the litmus test of US commitment being its ability to provide arms.

As Dr. Long notes, "for years, Saudi Arabia has been taken more or less for granted by Western policymakers." Whether such an outlook contributed to the conditions facilitating the takeover of Kuwait is problematic. Certainly, the aftermath of that takeover has changed the relationship between the kingdom and the Western states profoundly. Not only its external relations have been affected. Its exposure to Western values and individual citizen contact may have altered the traditional fabric of its society irreversibly.

According to Professor Doran, in terms of its foreign policy, Saudi Arabia has had to confront a bitter truth: Arab friendship is not able itself to offset the pressure of hostile nationalism. Similarly, alone Saudi Arabia is unable to defend itself. The GCC is as much a burden and responsibility for Saudi Arabia in security terms as it is a source of common defense. Thus Saudia Arabia must find the outline of a new set of alliance relationships internal to the region, and perhaps external to it. That is one of the principal conclusions that follow from the Kuwait takeover.

The Gulf Cooperation Council and the Smaller Gulf States

Four members of the GCC (Saudi Arabia, Kuwait, the United Arab Emirates, and Qatar) account for roughly half of OPEC's production capacity, two-thirds of OPEC proven reserves, and close to half of proven world reserves. Thus when the GCC block is united on oil policy, it carries enormous weight in OPEC councils. As non-OPEC oil supply diminishes, the clout will only grow. Sometime before the year 2000, Joseph Twinam concludes, it is likely "growing demand for Gulf oil will absorb the present excess capacity in the GCC states as well as in Iran and Iraq. At this point a significant and expensive effort to expand GCC production capacity might be necessary if sharp upward pressure on world oil prices is to be avoided.... How the GCC coordinates production and pricing policies is likely to become increasingly critical to world economic health and broad US interests as the year 2000 approaches."

The outlook for the smaller GCC states appears good. Their populations are small, but this makes it easier for rulers to keep in touch, and for economies to ride out slumps in oil prices. This said, some long-term trends and present problems bear watching. Two-thirds of the populations of Kuwait, Qatar, and the United Arab Emirates are foreign. Some are truly temporary workers, but others, such as Palestinians, are longtime "resident aliens," who are going to grow more strident in demanding equal rights. Some could import the political problems of their homelands into the Gulf. Their presence poses a significant long-term internal security problem, "a time bomb that will tick into the twenty-first century."

The smaller GCC countries, particularly Kuwait and Bahrain, can congratulate themselves on having weathered Khomeini's revolution and subversion promoted by Iran in their indigenous Shiite communities. However, this has not been without cost, particularly in terms of shunting Shia aside to "nonsensitive" positions and generally making them feel untrusted. Over time, Shiite-Sunni animosity may grow, undermining the social fabric in some of these countries.

Oman does not have a Shiite problem, but as Ambassador Twinam aptly puts it, newly educated Omanis are coming home looking for work in "a land still notable for the influence of the foreign adviser and the dominance of non-Arabs in the commercial sector." More than thirty years after King Hussein retired Glubb Pasha, Omani officers still find themselves reporting to British officers. It seems unlikely that they will accept this for another decade. Kicking the "foreign habit" is likely to prove crucial to Oman's long-term stability. Whether those in control can bring themselves to do this with sufficient speed remains to be seen.

Outside Powers and the Gulf

A New Soviet Role in the Gulf

In the 1970s, the Gulf remained largely a Western preserve, even after the withdrawal of the British. Soviet involvement was largely with the then peripheral states—Southern Yemen and radical, rejectionist Iraq. The Soviet invasion of Afghanistan reinforced the image of the USSR as aggressive and looking for targets of opportunity.

By 1989 exclusive Western influence in the region had virtually ended. Kuwait was no longer the lone GCC state to have relations with the USSR.

Soviet diplomats and Saudi officials had met in Riyadh and elsewhere, and formalizing of already well-established contacts appeared only a matter of time. The acute sense of rivalry with the United States had diminished as Soviet national security came to be seen as less reliant on sheer force and more on diplomacy, and as the Soviets began to look at the region to their south less as an area of targets of opportunity and more as one of damage limitation.

As Shahram Chubin notes, Soviet policies toward the region will continue to be determined by the "nature of its central relationship and competition with the United States." By 1989 Soviet foreign policy as a whole had been radically revised, with significant implications for its role in the Gulf. This does not mean that the USSR will not be alert to opportunities to profit at Western expense. But it does mean that the Soviets are likely to find more of a convergence of interests with the United States than they have in the past. If the region remains relatively tranquil, the Soviet reaction, as Professor Chubin points out, is likely to be one of "relief and encouragement," since the Soviets want a quiet backyard as they get on with dealing with their own major internal problems.

This said, the Soviets will continue to devote major attention to the Gulf. If their own oil production flags, they will have to turn more to the world market and ultimately the Gulf in the 1990s. If, as appears likely, Western and US dependence on Gulf oil increases significantly in the late 1990s, then for the USSR the region will become an important source of leverage on the United States.

The most likely pattern for US-Soviet relations in the Gulf will be, in Professor Chubin's apt phrase, one of "competitive cooperation." The USSR is likely to share a sense of relief with the United States if the region remains tranquil. The USSR is likely to see political radicalization as conjuring up as many problems as opportunities. Indeed, in May 1989 the USSR agreed to discuss possible cooperation on terrorism with the United States because of concern about the spread of subversive activities within the USSR itself.

If it continues, a more benign, damage-limitation Soviet approach may open up significant opportunities for US-Soviet cooperation in the Gulf. There would be costs to the United States in a region previously considered a Western preserve, but the benefits are worth exploring and will be discussed further in Chapter 12.

As Professor Doran warns, whether the lofty ideals expressed in President Bush's September 1990 speech on Kuwait regarding a new international order founded on US-Soviet cooperation come to pass, it is an architecture whose success vis-à-vis Gulf stability is still quite untested. Surely Soviet internal economic and political reform has ensured a benign response to such a US overture. Ideological mellowing and even abandonment has also contributed its share to cooperation. At base, neither the United States nor the Soviet Union wants massive unrest in the Middle East, although the means chosen to offset that unrest and the distance each government is willing to travel in terms of cost to achieve stability may differ substantially in Washington and in Moscow.

European Community Countries and the Gulf

Throughout the Iran-Iraq war, EC countries, particularly West Germany, maintained significant trading relationships with Iran, and West German Foreign Minister Hans-Dietrich Genscher made a special effort to develop relations with Iran. The Iranians were hence surprised when the EC, including West Germany, reacted so strongly to Khomeini's death threat against Rushdie. Although many EC countries have returned their ambassadors to Tehran, the relations of these countries with Iran may take a bumpier course than expected in response to continued Iranian provocations, particularly Iranian-supported terrorist actions.

Similar actions regarding Iraqi military attachés and their families during the Kuwait crisis suggest the unease of relations between the countries of the Middle East and the West. What strikes the observer is how in one moment of history, Iran becomes the regional archenemy; in the next, it is Iraq. Governments formerly ostracized as "terrorist governments," like Syria, become instant allies in the cause of Gulf stability.

Professor Doran notes that European relations with countries external to the Continent have not been so flexible since the nineteenth century. Perhaps the new coalitional change and flexibility within the Gulf region is a forerunner of coalitional changes at the global level as well. France and the United Kingdom appear to be more fully participant in these regional reorientations than, for instance, Germany, with its unification worries and its preoccupation with Ostpolitik. Even the flow of arms sales seems to move with fits and starts in a way that has had few precedents in the post–World War II period. US sales to the region begin to look more like those of France and the United Kingdom. US congressional restrictions on use and third-country transfer still play some part in the contracts. But the fact remains that the arms sales were something of a bonanza to the European countries, offering potential revenue in tens of billions of dollars, and are a measure of their increasing role in the region.

Japan and the Gulf

The chapter by Ukeru Magosaki and Yasumasa Kuroda leads to some interesting conclusions on Japan's relations with the Gulf states in the next decade. Japan is already somewhat of an anomaly in the area, since it is a giant economically yet appears to eschew a political role. The authors conclude that it is out of the question that Japan will play any sort of military role in the area, either with forces or arms sales. Even the provision of so-called dual-use items is likely to be constrained given the Toshiba scandal. Indeed, the authors argue that lack of any military involvement, including arms sales, "gives Japan credibility in peace attempts in the region."

Certainly Japan's "neutral" position and its extensive oil purchases from Iran enabled it to maintain a dialogue with that country through the Iran-Iraq war. In the postwar period, because of Iran's economic difficulties and Iraq's greater oil reserves, Iraq's oil exports to Japan may grow rapidly. This could help solve Iraq's festering debt problem with Japan and lead to more balance in Japan's economic relations with Iran and Iraq.

Because of the yen's appreciation, Japan's exports to the Gulf have declined. Japan's imports of oil from the Gulf have jumped in the last two years, and it appears likely that Japan will become increasingly dependent on Gulf oil in the 1990s. This will make the Gulf the only area with which Japan experiences a trade deficit.

Japan's foreign policy establishment appears to believe that the "highest priority" must be given to the "development and maintenance of political stability" in the Gulf—"a necessary condition for the continuous flow of oil to Japan." Some may argue with this premise, since oil flowed to Japan without interruption at the height of the tanker war in the Gulf. Whatever the case, if Japanese policymakers believe the "security of supply" argument to be important, one can wonder whether an essentially "economic" foreign policy, divorced from the political-military, can be considered sufficient to the task. As Japan's dependence on the Gulf grows, it is likely to have to become more involved in the region than it has in the past.

This introduction to the various chapters suggests something of the complexity confronting US foreign policy in the Gulf in the next decade. In the final chapter of this book, Charles Doran places all of this analysis in the larger policy context. The United States and its allies face a far greater security dilemma in the Gulf region than was perceived in the immediate aftermath of the Gulf War. Iraq's annexation of Kuwait was one consequence. Professor Doran examines what to do about the situation and the larger security problem.

Note

The views expressed in this chapter are those of the author and should not be construed as representing the policy or position of the US Department of State or the US government.

2
US Energy Interests in the Gulf in the 1990s

Edward N. Krapels

US dependence on Gulf oil will almost certainly rise to very significant levels in the 1990s. This prospect raises several central questions for students of international affairs in general and of the Middle East in particular. The first is whether the US government will allow this trend toward high dependence on Gulf oil to continue for much longer. After all, it has only been a decade since oil import dependence was part of an energy problem President Jimmy Carter portrayed as the "moral equivalent of war" and only less than two decades since Arab countries imposed an oil embargo on the United States.

If it does not act soon to contain rising dependence, the next question will be whether that dependence will give rise to a new era of US-Arab relations, or be managed by the oil-security mechanisms of the past. If the former, we could be living at the turn of the century in a substantially different environment, one in which mutual commercial interests are likely to be much more influential in shaping overall US Gulf policy, in which certain important industrial relationships (e.g., Saudi-Texaco) are centerpieces of nations' foreign affairs.

The Energy Outlook

There have been hundreds of efforts, over the years, to develop effective oil and energy forecasting tools. The results have been humbling. At the beginning of the 1980s, governments and oil companies alike made enormous misjudgments about the development of oil supply and demand in the decade ahead. The 1990s may be equally surprising.

With these experiences, one can best talk about the future of oil supply and demand in the broadest terms. The most conventional view is that a fairly stable relationship between economic growth and energy and oil exists. If that energy-oil growth relationship in the 1990s were to be one to one, the 1990s would resemble the 1960s, with annual oil-demand growth of as much as 3 percent. That is unlikely, because it would result by the year 2000 in an unsustainable demand of up to 70 million barrels per day, almost 20 million barrels per day more than the 1989 level.[1] At the other extreme, if the 1990s turn out to be a decade of chronic recession or a decade in which oil conservation measures decouple GNP growth from oil growth, oil demand at the end of the century may be little if any higher than it is today.

Whether world oil demand grows quickly or slowly, in other words, does not depend only on the rate of global economic growth. It also depends on the incentives to increase energy efficiency—to substitute other factors for energy and oil. These incentives diminished with the oil price decline of 1986 but are likely to increase in the wake of Iraq's invasion of Kuwait. In the absence of government action, these incentives would remain weak, and thus global economic growth would carry with it higher energy growth in general and higher oil use in particular in the 1990s than it did in the conservation-minded early years of the 1980s. Thus, governments play a central role here: An aggressive program to impose excise taxes on energy and oil products could restrain even further petroleum product demand in industrial countries and could limit surging demand in developing countries.

It is surprising, given oft-stated concerns about oil-demand growth, that the governments of leading industrial countries have not taxed oil products more heavily as the price of crude oil fell during the 1986–1988 period. As we get deeper into the 1990s, however, the oil-demand increases that began in the late 1980s could well *generate* a governmental reaction, specifically, large new taxes on the transportation fuels that are an increasingly significant component of oil demand and, less prominently, on the use of oil as a heating and industrial fuel.

On a global basis, the most important excise tax question in oil is whether the United States will increase its federal gasoline tax and, if so, by how much. Beginning in 1986, considerable support developed in favor of a gasoline tax. There is a rule of thumb that each penny per gallon of tax imposed would raise $1 billion per year in US tax revenues. Given that a gasoline tax would favorably affect the US fiscal deficit, would ameliorate concern about the effects of oil consumption (and more generally hydrocarbons) on the environment,[2] as well as concern about the effects of higher oil-import demand on national security,[3] it seems likely that a larger gasoline excise tax will be imposed sooner or later.

Important as US transportation fuels demand is in the global oil market, it has not been the source of the most impressive growth in the global demand for motor fuels. US gasoline demand did not increase at all in 1989, whereas gasoline demand in South Korea increased by more than 10 percent. As their oil import bills increase (and especially if unexpectedly higher oil prices cause those bills to increase more rapidly than forecast by financial authorities), even the fast-growing developing countries of the Pacific Rim may decide to increase further their already high petroleum excise taxes.

In the early 1990s, in other words, there will be a relationship between higher oil demand (and imports from Persian Gulf members of OPEC) and a policy reaction by still-wary governments of importing states. Thus, the higher demand is in the next few years, the greater the reaction (i.e., the higher the taxes) to the ultimate detriment of oil-demand growth rates later in the 1990s.

The other major uncertainty about oil demand in the 1990s is whether problems in the nuclear industry and increased concerns about the impact of coal use in the environment will drive some of the electricity generation market back toward oil.[4] Even a partial return to using mothballed or to building new oil-fired electricity generation to meet incremental electricity demand could raise the demand for oil by millions of barrels per day. A wholesale return to oil due, for example, to a nuclear power disaster in a country like France would be an energy shock of the first magnitude.

While a shock of such magnitude is unlikely, it does raise the general issue of what will drive oil-consuming nations' energy policy in the 1990s. In the 1970s and early 1980s, one can say that governments were preoccupied with oil supply and price security as a result of the embargo of 1973–1974 and the Iranian revolution of 1979–1980. The policy attitude was "anything but insecure oil." Since then, oil-producing states have become better integrated into the world economy and the likelihood of a deliberate embargo is no longer taken as seriously. The threat of super-wealthy oil producers jeopardizing the world financial system with their petrodollar surpluses is also a thing of the past.

Energy security in the 1990s will be defined in two contexts, one favorable to oil and one unfavorable. The first is that an increasing number of countries appear to be moving toward an "anything-but-nuclear" energy posture. If that attitude continues to spread, and if governments do not develop other non-oil alternatives (for example, natural gas), oil may enjoy a renaissance in the electricity generation sector. In the same vein, concern about global warming is creating "anything-but-coal" attitudes among environmentalists, and this may also help get oil back under the burners of electric utilities.[5]

If this drift back to oil as a result of disenchantment with nuclear and coal energy does happen, it is likely to be relatively short-lived. In terms of adverse effects on atmospheric pollution, oil is better than coal,[6] but it is worse than all other sources. The need to develop environmentally benign sources of energy will hurt oil's share of the market. The world will increasingly value alternatives to oil, not only in electricity generation but also in transportation. Given this value, it is reasonable to expect some technological surprises that either burn oil more cleanly or use something other than oil (for example, natural gas or electric batteries) to power automobiles and other vehicles. The movement toward substitutes for oil (and also toward ever-more efficient vehicles) was slowed by the decline in the price of oil, thus tax policy will have to be changed to restore incentives that in the early 1980s were moving people away from oil.

The conclusion of this brief survey is that governments will play a critical role in shaping the demand for oil in the 1990s. In choosing between oil-demand scenarios, therefore, it seems unlikely that the high-growth scenario will be *allowed* to manifest itself for many more years. Governments will tax and tax and tax to keep petroleum consumption near the low-growth path in the mid- to late 1990s.

"Forecasting" global oil supply is, like forecasting demand, a difficult art. The heart of any global oil supply is an assumption that the most reserve-rich Gulf countries (see Table 2.1) will no longer feel a need to wage all-out campaigns for market share. Saudi Arabia tried such a campaign in 1986, and it drove oil prices down to single-digit levels.

Table 2.1 Oil Reserves and Production in Persian Gulf Countries, 1988

	Reserves (billion barrels)	Production (thousand barrels per day)
Saudi Arabia	170	4,555
Iraq	100	2,090
Iran	93	2,310
Kuwait	92	1,270
United Arab Emirates	96	1,650
Subtotal	551	11,875
Rest of the world	366	50,320
Major Gulf countries as a percentage of world total	60	19

Source: British Petroleum, *BP Statistical Review of World Energy, July 1989.*
Notes: 1. World total includes the centrally planned economies.
2. Saudi and Kuwaiti figures include Neutral Zone.

The world oil supply picture, therefore, can be seen in terms of the output of non-OPEC countries (who usually produce all they can) and the amount left for OPEC. In the 1970s the global "call on OPEC" ultimately reached 30 million barrels per day. In the 1980s non-OPEC production rose and demand fell, causing the amount required from OPEC to plummet to as low as 16 million barrels per day, precipitating the oil price collapse of 1986.

Non-OPEC supply in the 1990s is likely to range between 21 and 25 million barrels per day, leaving the rest of global oil demand to be satisfied by OPEC. With that kind of non-OPEC supply estimate, what the call on OPEC in the 1990s will be depends on one's view of demand.

In a scenario of low oil demand, demand for OPEC oil should rise from about 20 million barrels per day in 1989 to at least 22 million in 1995 and further to 26 million in 2000. This contained growth in demand is well within OPEC's capacity to supply, which is expected to increase to about 35 million barrels per day sometime in the 1990s. This outlook, therefore, does not require OPEC, especially the Persian Gulf members, to produce at or even near its expected capacity. To the contrary, in this case there will continue to be a substantial amount of shut-in oil production capacity in the world, and all other things held equal, one would expect this to keep oil prices from rising very rapidly. Moreover, if a recession occurs in the early 1990s, one would expect strong downward pressure on oil prices.

In a more bullish oil-demand scenario, the demand for OPEC oil could exceed 25 million barrels per day in the early to mid-1990s, rather than at the end of the century. In that case, demand for oil would come very close to OPEC's productive capacity. When this has happened in the past, prices have increased sharply. Whether, in the face of rapidly rising demand, such a tight supply-demand situation develops depends on how quickly the "big five" Persian Gulf OPEC members expand their production capacity. The resource base of these countries is so large and the costs of production so low that they *could*, if they chose, expand production capacity quickly enough to meet even the very high demand of a high-growth scenario without a major increase in oil prices.

In the final analysis, it is difficult to subscribe to the high-growth view of oil demand because a global economic slowdown is highly probable in the early 1990s, because consuming countries are likely to impose defensive tax increases to cool down oil-demand growth, and because increasing concern about the environment will prevent the oil market from recapturing a substantial share of electricity generation.

Indeed, a more bearish oil price scenario seems more plausible, especially if 1990 and 1991 turn out to be slow-growth years. A recession would probably cause the demand for OPEC to decline for the first time since the mid-1980s. Given that the Persian Gulf OPEC members' production capacity will be substantially higher in the early 1990s than it was in the mid-1980s (because of the repair of Iraqi and Iranian production and export facilities), such a reduction in demand for its oil would put OPEC members under considerable pressure.

Traditional Versus Innovative Responses to Rising Energy Dependence

OPEC oil will almost certainly be more important in the 1990s than it was in the 1980s. Whereas the 1980s was a decade of steady decline in OPEC's production and market share, the 1990s will be a decade during which there are likely to be more years of growth than of decline in OPEC production. To be sure, a recession in the 1990s would cause demand for OPEC oil to slow or perhaps even to drop, but unless we face an entire decade of economic stagnation, or unless there are truly breathtaking technological breakthroughs like cold fusion, the demand for OPEC oil in 2000 will probably be substantially higher than it was in 1988.

How oil-importing nations like the United States react to this depends to some extent on their domestic politics and on the politics of oil-supplying countries. We should distinguish traditional from innovative policy responses to the reality of higher oil trade on both sides. The traditional US response in some quarters of the body politic is to raise the specter of new oil embargoes and disruptions and to promote protectionist measures like import tariffs and domestic production subsidies. Similarly, the traditional response in some OPEC countries is to convey the impression that trade is a zero-sum game in which OPEC was victimized during the 1980s. The two traditional views are mutually reinforcing: The more offensive one is, the more offensive the other becomes.

Will OPEC be OPEC in the 1990s? Or can its members transcend OPEC's traditional, narrow, zero-sum focus and fashion a new strategy to maintain a secure place for oil in the world economy? We will consider the ability of OPEC members to find a new path first and then assess how OPEC members' behavior is likely to be perceived among importing countries.

One must begin by acknowledging that the oil policies of all states are always subject to what could be called the "political security veto." That is, when an oil-exporting or -importing state is under an imminent security threat, oil policy is totally subordinated to foreign policy. This was true for OECD countries in the 1970s as it has been for Persian Gulf OPEC members in the 1980s. In the case of the crisis in the Gulf, US foreign policy was being driven by US need for oil. Under more tranquil national security conditions, however, OPEC oil policy has been dominated by members' financial conditions: When all OPEC members are rich beyond their expectations (as occurred in 1973–1975 and again in 1979–1981), their willingness to cut production jointly to support prices goes up; and when all OPEC countries are poor beyond their expectations or face a calamitous price decline, as they did in 1986, they again may all be willing to cut production to restore higher prices.

OPEC Coalitions and Saudi Oil Price Preferences

In conditions between the feast of 1979 and the famine of 1986, however, the principal oil-exporting countries typically compete in efforts to dominate world oil markets. Thus, between 1975 and 1980 there was a continuous contest for control over OPEC's pricing policy between the "price hawks" (usually Iran and Algeria) and the "price doves" (usually Saudi Arabia). From 1982 to 1985, while Iran and Iraq were preoccupied by their war, the Saudis held sway, acting as swing producer to maintain high oil prices. From 1986 to 1989, the United Arab Emirates, Iraq, and Kuwait produced in excess of their OPEC quotas in spite of constant Saudi exhortations for all members to behave themselves and occasional Saudi threats (usually in the form of placing production in excess of quotas in storage near importing areas) of a repetition of the price collapse.

By the end of the 1980s, only Kuwait and the UAE had become price doves that were willing, within the limits of their abilities, to keep prices below $20 per barrel. Saudi Arabia was edging up to the moderate camp, as evidenced by its behavior in the June 1989 OPEC meeting, where it would join Indonesia, Venezuela, and Nigeria in support of moderately higher prices.

The character of OPEC in the 1990s is already being shaped by shifts in its coalitions. Saudi King Fahd in the spring of 1989 indicated that he wanted the price of oil to rise to above $20 per barrel. The Kuwaiti oil minister appears to oppose this move. These most recent shifts in OPEC coalitions appear to have more to do with financial exigencies than with the security threats that were so prominent in the 1980s.[7]

Many OPEC members began the 1980s with budgets swollen by the experiences of the 1970s and with revenues swollen by the crisis of 1979. They enter the 1990s with budgets pared down as a result of the price collapse of the mid-1980s and with revenues just beginning to recover from that experience. With that behind them, it is likely that most governments perceive their current budgets and current levels of oil revenues as being quite austere.

Given this austerity, countries with some shut-in production capacity (Saudi Arabia, the UAE, and Kuwait at the top of the list) will still have in the 1990s the choice between maximizing revenues by producing higher volumes at a lower price or lower volumes at a higher price. In 1989 Saudi King Fahd began to send signals that he was becoming more interested in higher oil prices. With stronger global oil demand, it appeared that the Saudis believed they could aspire to the $18 per barrel price that had seemed impossible only a year earlier.

Due to the absence of an overriding political or security concern, in other words, Saudi Arabia has changed coalitions largely in response to its financial requirements and its vision of the oil market (specifically, the short-, medium-, and long-term elasticity of demand to price). If we assume that, after nearly a decade of relative austerity, the Saudi government believes it cannot shrink the budget deficit any further with spending cuts and that it cannot enhance revenues via the "go-for-volume" policy of 1985–1986, then it will be increasingly interested in (if not desperate to) increase revenues with higher prices. Saudi oil-pricing policy is increasingly dominated by *short-term* financial requirements.

In this view, with the Saudis in the moderate camp, the UAE and Kuwait (assuming its future autonomy as a state) will dominate prices until demand reaches the point where they are producing all they want. Kuwait and the UAE can historically be characterized as price doves. In the case of Kuwait, such a characterization can be justified by the repeated statements of Kuwaiti officials endorsing lower prices for the sake of promoting oil's long-term market share.[8] An Iraq in combination with an annexed Kuwait would not have these preferences. Moreover, Kuwait has acquired an oil-marketing network that allows it to earn revenues from all phases of the industry, from production to marketing: Kuwait Petroleum is the closest that any OPEC company has come to being a modern version of a "major" oil company.

If Kuwait and the UAE are the only price doves, at what point will demand for OPEC oil increase beyond their ability to satisfy it? Their combined shut-in capacity at the end of the 1980s was about 2.7 million barrels per day. They will increase their capacity by an additional 1.8 million barrels per day by the end of the century, providing incremental production capacity from 1990 levels of about 4.5 million.

Whether this is sufficient to maintain prices in their (presumed) price range of under $20 per barrel depends on the world's incremental demand for OPEC oil. Bearish oil scenarios show that incremental demand rising by only 4 million barrels per day in the 1990s.

In more conventional oil supply-demand scenarios, however, the incremental demand for OPEC oil rises by some 7 million barrels per day by 2000. In this case, prices are likely to slip beyond the grasp of the price dove coalition. Moderates will have to increase production, which presumably they would not do without an increase in prices. In even more bullish scenarios, demand for OPEC oil could rise by more than 10 million barrels per day in the 1990s, outstripping even the capacity of the moderates. Oil prices would then rise to the levels the price hawks desire.

That brings us to the crux of the traditional versus innovative policy response issue. Kuwait Oil Minister Ali Khalifa has more than once advocated an innovative oil policy, which is that OPEC's oil-rich members see to it that oil prices remain stable in the $18–$20 per barrel range. Such a policy, if backed up by a Saudi-Kuwaiti accord, would do much to defuse the energy-security concerns in defensive importing countries like the United States and Japan. Such a policy would be the oil equivalent of the change in the Soviet bloc, and, again in oil terms, it would be similarly disarming.

Such a bold and innovative policy of oil price and supply stability, however, is beyond the means of Kuwait alone to implement. Saudi Arabia would obviously be an essential participant. The leadership of Saudi Arabia must be torn, however, between the desire to participate in a price stability policy on the one hand and a "take-the-money-and-run" policy on the other. There is little doubt that during the 1990s the Saudis will have an opportunity to let oil prices rise, even to the $26 per barrel level mentioned by King Fahd in 1989. If they do so, however, they will have succumbed again to the traditional OPEC short-term behavior. Such behavior, and the oil price increases it *enables* to occur, will provoke a defensive reaction (a renewal of the retreat from oil) from oil-importing countries.

Reintegration of World Oil as an Innovative Response to Dependence?

Before 1980, the traditional US response to higher oil-import dependence was alarm and a policy push to increase domestic oil production and decrease oil consumption. In the 1980s, however, the US government was engaged in a most innovative policy. Even though it became clear in 1986 that US oil-import dependence would rise again, a laissez-faire oil security policy relying almost exclusively on the strategic petroleum reserve (SPR) has been in force.

As the reality of substantially greater oil-import dependence has become clearer and clearer, so the unease with this laissez-faire policy has grown stronger, at least in some quarters. There have already been numerous calls for a reinvigorated traditional oil security policy.[9]

Thus far, the Bush administration has held the course of its predecessor. But not entirely. Several new and fairly innovative variations on traditional policies are under discussion. For example, the US Department of Energy is studying the possibility of building up the SPR more rapidly by *leasing* oil from exporters, and negotiations have taken place with Saudi Arabia, Kuwait, Mexico, and others.[10] If such a policy comes to fruition, the United States would be leasing oil from the very countries against whose oil disruptions the SPR was originally designed.

The Reagan-Bush laissez-faire oil security policy could be derailed, however. A substantial oil shock would probably cause a groundswell of support for subsidies for domestic oil production (if not for a gasoline tax) that would pull back US demand for imported petroleum. Such a pullback could make the crucial difference, turning the bullish prospects for global oil demand into bearish ones.

Those who desire the 1990s to be a decade of high oil-demand growth and increased OPEC oil exports, therefore, should consider additional mechanisms whereby the present innovative open-market policies of the Bush administration can survive the 1990s, mechanisms that either protect supply and price stability or that protect importing countries from economic damage should supply stability be impossible to maintain.

One such mechanism that could bring OPEC (and especially Persian Gulf) countries closer to their customers is reintegration of the world oil industry. In his February 16, 1989, Oklahoma speech, Saudi Oil Minister Nazer made the argument that vertical integration by oil exporters in general and Saudi Arabia in particular will enhance both supply security and price stability:

> The growing US dependence on imported oil can either be viewed only as a political threat to energy security, or it can be seen as a great opportunity to enhance cooperation and integration in the global energy business.... [Our] joint venture [with Texaco] ... is an important link in favor of reintegration of the oil industry for efficiency purposes.... We expect to make more downstream joint venture arrangements around the world.... If we succeed, independent [US] producers will be the first to enjoy the fruits of market stability.[11]

Table 2.2 presents a review of the countries with the most notable efforts to integrate downstream. The more prevalent type of downstream integration by OPEC members has been the type of joint ventures made by the Saudis with Texaco, the purchase of smaller refining companies as Venezuela has done in the United States, or purchase of parts of the networks of major companies as Kuwait did with Gulf's European interests.

Of all the OPEC members, only Kuwait and Venezuela can be said to have created a vertically integrated company that is able to dispose of a significant share of the country's crude oil exports. Saudi Arabia began early with its joint venture refineries with Mobil and Shell at Yanbu and Jubail. Those refineries, however, are based in Saudi Arabia, making them seem like a somewhat halfhearted move downstream. The Saudis' venture with Texaco, in which they purchased a 50 percent interest in Texaco's eastern US marketing network, is more along the lines of what Venezuela has done, but neither has been as aggressive as Kuwait, with its policy of 100 percent ownership of its downstream assets.

Table 2.2 OPEC Members with Owned Downstream Interests

	Integrated Export Volume (Mb/d)	Integrated Venture
Saudia Arabia	200–300	1. Joint export refinery ventures with Shell (Jubail, about 100 mbd in exports 1988) and Mobil (Yanbu, about 140 mbd in exports).
	300–600	2. Star Supply, joint venture with Texaco.
Kuwait	1,000+	Kuwait Petroleum Company is now a fully integrated multinational oil company that typically disposes of all of Kuwait's exports and sells products in Europe under its own trademark (Q8). KPC entered the European market by purchasing the facilities of Gulf Oil.
Venezuela	1,200	Petroleos de Venezuela owns 1.12 mb/d of foreign refining capacity: 1. F.R. Germany: 140 mb/d 2. Sweden: 20 mb/d 3. Belgium: 8 mb/d 4. US: 640 mb/d 5. Curaçao: 320 mb/d
Abu Dhabi	0	The Abu Dhabi Investment Authority has purchased a 10 percent share of Spanish refiner CESPA and a 5.5 percent share in France's CFP.
Libya	100–350	The Libyan Foreign Investment Company reportedly bought in 1986 a majority shareholding in Italian independent Tamoil.

Sources: Petroleum Economics, Ltd, *Crude Oil Disposals: Fourth Quarter 1988*, and John Roberts, "The Gulf, Integration, and OPEC: Overseas Downstream Activities" (Boulder, CO: International Research Center for Energy and Economic Development, Occasional Papers No. 4, no date given).

Beyond the Saudi-Kuwaiti-Venezuelan "big three," the other OPEC members had done very little, as of late 1989, to get on the integration bandwagon. Countries like Libya have engaged in what could be called "poor man's integration." It made deals in which foreign refiners processed crude oil on behalf of the Libyan state oil company, which in turn sold the products into the world market. The most extreme variation of "poor man's integration" is simply to cut crude oil prices to levels at which unintegrated or independent refiners would have to buy it.

Is vertical integration the innovative response to the increased flow of oil between the United States and the Gulf oil-producing countries? Should the United States encourage Saudi Arabia, Kuwait, and others to buy refining and marketing assets as a positive security gain? Should Washington oppose such integration as raising the security risk? Or should it be indifferent on the grounds that there is no connection between the level of Gulf investment in US oil and the stability of imported oil supply and price?

These are questions that merit further study. A good preliminary argument can be made, however, that the positive political effects of the new producer–oil company "combines" will be complicated, if not obliterated, by a critical problem in the reintegration process. That problem is that the process begun by the oil-exporting countries is likely to result in partial, rather than large-scale, downstream integration. This may actually *enhance* competition among oil-exporting countries and thus promote rather than mitigate downward pressure on oil prices. As long as only a few of the more sophisticated oil-exporting countries integrate, the other producers frozen out of those segments of the market will have to compete harder for what is left over. In so doing, of course, they may well cause international oil prices to weaken.

The extent of the reemergence of the vertically integrated oil market in the 1990s also depends on the reactions of governments of oil-importing countries. By early 1989, moves downstream had focused on certain European countries (West Germany in particular) and on the United States. Japan was distinctly inhospitable to OPEC efforts to purchase Japanese refineries or start joint marketing ventures. In one of the most publicized clashes between governments over oil, the British and Kuwaitis tangled over the latter's efforts gradually to purchase more than 25 percent of the shares of British Petroleum. As the Kuwaitis' shareholding increased, the British government became increasingly more vocal about its opposition to having the agent of a foreign government control such a large portion of the shares of one of Britain's most important companies. The Kuwaitis ultimately sold the bulk of their BP shares. The British government took pains to assure Kuwait that it would have opposed such a large shareholding in BP by *any* foreign government.

The BP-Kuwait row does not appear to signal a general industrial nation prejudice against the acquisition of downstream assets by oil-producing countries. With the exception of Japan and, less forcefully, France and Italy, most industrial countries are open to these acquisitions. The United States, somewhat surprisingly in light of its oil-protectionist history, has made very little fuss about Saudi and Venezuelan incursions into the US oil-refining and -marketing businesses.

Conclusions

Would this tolerance survive a period of oil stress? One cannot be sure. On matters of great national interest, which oil becomes when prices and supplies are seriously disrupted, laissez-faire policies can be summarily suspended if not terminated. If the oil-exporting countries of the Gulf desire long-term markets in the United States for their raw material, they are well advised to prevent such a period of oil stress if at all possible.

If that seems like a one-sided bargain, if the burden of guaranteeing stability that is on the oil exporter seems unfair, it is important to remember that by virtue of its sheer size the United States is a monopsonist in the world oil market. If sufficiently provoked, it can theoretically, but at high political cost, return to its traditional policy of near self-sufficiency in oil. To be sure, such transitions take time. The 1980s illustrated, however, just how quickly OPEC as a group could lose half of its market: It took only the five years between 1980 and 1985.

Bringing this all back to the question with which this argument began, what are US energy interests in the Gulf in the 1990s? There is little doubt that US oil-import dependence will rise. There is little doubt that, for at least a few more years, that rise will not cause the Bush laissez-faire policy to be abandoned. There is little doubt that oil-exporting countries may, if they choose, pursue downstream integration with little opposition. All of these things combine to give the United States a continued interest in the resources, nations, and peoples of the Gulf. It is clear that the United States will continue to regard the strategic defense of oil-exporting countries against outside threats as one of its primary military missions.

There is also no doubt that, in spite of the size of the SPR, by letting import dependence increase dramatically the United States is contributing to a rise in the likelihood of oil supply and price disruptions that are "internally caused," i.e., from conflict between or within important oil-exporting countries. Having lived through several of oil's boom and bust cycles, however, we also know such disruptions are not fatal. Moreover, we know they cause anti-oil reactions, retreats from oil that are extremely painful to the economies of the still poorly diversified oil-exporting countries. Thus, there would appear to be in the 1990s a fairly balanced relationship between the United States and the Gulf: Access to the world's biggest reserves of oil supplies is important to one; access to the world's biggest oil-consuming market is important to the other.

Notes

1. It is usual practice in oil forecasts to exclude the centrally planned economies, and this convention will be followed in this chapter. It is clear, however, that the pace and extent of change in the Soviet bloc is such that their energy and oil futures will also be affected. For the sake of this analysis, however, no effort has been made to include such major changes. One might expect higher energy and oil demand from some East European countries (e.g., East Germany), but this may be offset by lower growth in others (e.g., the Soviet Union).

2. After the very hot summer of 1988, the question of whether "global warming" was occurring as a result of hydrocarbon and other emissions became an increasingly prominent part of the public policy discussions in the United States. Oil use (and hydrocarbon combustion generally) releases sulfur and nitrogen oxides, carbon dioxide, carbon monoxide, lead, and organic compounds into the atmosphere. Oxides, retained in

the atmosphere until released as "acid rain," have come to the fore as an international public policy problem because one nation's combustion becomes another's pollution. Carbon dioxide and other pollutants may impede infrared radiation from escaping the atmosphere, thus causing global warming.

3. The Reagan administration released a study in 1987 that argued that although rising import dependence did raise national security concerns, those concerns could be dealt with by existing policies, specifically the strategic petroleum reserve. See US Department of Energy, *Energy Security* (Washington, DC: US Government Printing Office, 1987). For a critique of that study, see Edward N. Krapels, "Revitalizing US Oil Security Policy," *SAIS Review* (Summer 1989).

4. Beginning in late 1988, nuclear power sector reversals became apparent in a number of countries. They ranged in severity from Italian and Swedish rejection of any growth in nuclear power capacity to nuclear maintenance problems in Japan that increased oil demand by 200 to 300 thousand b/d.

5. Coal represents an entirely different sociopolitical problem than nuclear energy for coal-producing countries like the United States, Germany, and the United Kingdom. Politically powerful coal miners' unions are likely to get governments to fund clean coal rather than abandon coal to low-sulfur fuel oil or natural gas.

6. How much better depends on what kind of oil and coal. Most crude oil has some sulfur in it, and in the environmentally conscious 1990s, low-sulfur oil should command an ever-larger premium over coal and high-sulfur oil.

7. The formation of OPEC's dominant coalition—Saudi Arabia, the UAE, and Kuwait—was precipitated in the mid- to late 1980s in the first instance by the regional political and security context created by the Iran-Iraq war. In the 1970s, the political and security context had been shaped by Arab-Israeli-US relations, but these receded into the background in the 1980s as a result of the Camp David Accords and Arab disunity about how much to invest in a resolution of that dispute.

Gulf Arab concern over Iran's revolutionary threat to the legitimacy of their Sunni and familial regimes united the three principal oil powers in the Gulf Cooperation Council, which under the duress of the imminent Iranian threat became a forum not only for discussing security issues but also for coordinating Saudi–Kuwaiti–Abu Dhabi oil policy in advance of OPEC meetings. An external political threat, in other words, caused otherwise competing countries to develop greater policy coordination on a range of issues than would normally be the case.

When the Iran-Iraq cease-fire was agreed upon in 1988, some of the fissures in the Saudi-Kuwaiti-UAE relationship began to emerge. In a manner reminiscent of the relationships between European countries in the nineteenth century, the shift in the intra-Gulf balance of power toward Iraq that the cease-fire represented caused the other Gulf powers to become more wary of the threat Iraq posed to their security. Kuwait's and Abu Dhabi's response was to explore tentatively better relations with Iran, while Saudi Arabia sought to contain Iraq's ambitions with a nonaggression agreement in early 1989. For more on the Saudi-Iraqi maneuvers of 1989, see Charles Snow, "King Fahd on Tour: Non-Aggression in Baghdad," *Middle East Economic Survey* (April 3, 1989): C3.

8. See Ian Seymour's interview with Kuwaiti Minister of Oil Ali Khalifa al-Sabah in *Middle East Economic Survey* (March 27, 1989): A2–A3.

9. See, for example, Daniel Yergin, "Energy Security in the 1990s," *Foreign Affairs* (Fall 1988): 110–132.

10. US Department of Energy, *Report to the Congress on Alternative Financing Methods for the Strategic Petroleum Reserve,* February 1, 1990.

11. Hisham Nazer, "The Need for Stability and Predictability in the Oil Market."

3
Charting the Unchartable: What Next for Iran?

John W. Limbert

Islam is no fun.
—Imam Khomeini

Predicting events in Iran is an iffy business. Many who tried during the last ten years have regretted the effort after predicting the imminent collapse of the Islamic Republic or the moderation of its policies. Political figures, too, have misread Iranian events. Jimmy Carter saw his administration paralyzed and his political career ended because he and his advisers misunderstood the signals from Tehran. Even the seemingly invulnerable Ronald Reagan found it hard to shrug off the fact that a group of clerics in Tehran had outwitted the members of his inner circle and had shown how inept were his best and brightest.

Iranians themselves misread or ignored the omens in their own revolution. As Shaul Bakhash wrote, "They loved the revolution not knowing it would not love them back." Many well-educated and sophisticated people who shouted "long live Khomeini, death to the shah" in the excitement of 1978–1979 believed an Islamic republic would create something better than the monarchy. That republic, they hoped, would reassert Iran's national identity and dignity after centuries of humiliation. At the same time, they expected to continue enjoying prosperity and the benefits of the existing social system minus the shah's authoritarian rule and the gross excesses of his family and courtiers. They convinced themselves that, with the shah gone, the nationalist heirs of Mohammad Mossadegh—mostly devout and open-minded men—would rule in association with popular and progressive religious leaders. Those few who had listened to Khomeini's speeches or read his books refused to believe he meant what he said about Islamic government. They knew him only as someone who had dared to criticize the shah when others were silent. The *fact* of criticism was enough: Its substance did not matter.

Why were so many people who should have known better consistently wrong about Iran? The Islamic Republic in its first ten years lurched unpredictably from one extreme to another, confounding expectations of consistent, predictable behavior based on national interest. In the Islamic Republic yesterday's black is today's white. One day all shout, "War, war, until victory," and the next day Iran accepts a cease-fire with Iraq. One day Iran proclaims a policy of normal relations with all countries based on mutual respect; the next day it attacks diplomatic premises, holds hostages, and proclaims that international law is a fraud, a superpower tool to dominate small nations.[1] One day Britain returns its representatives to Tehran after long negotiations; the next day the Islamic regime turns on the British government and condemns a British citizen to death for writing a book that was said to be blasphemous.

Seeds of Revolution

The Collapse

In the mid-1970s the shah and his system seemed all-powerful. In January 1978 Iran was, according to President Carter "an island of stability in a turbulent region." Bolstered by the windfall of high oil prices after 1973, the shah invested heavily in new roads, power plants, industries, ports, housing, and telecommunications. The shah also spent large sums on modern weapons, although he had few foreign enemies. Iran had settled its disputes with most Arab countries, even traditionally hostile Iraq. It had cordial relations with the Soviet Union, China, and other communist countries. At home, the monarchy had little to fear from organized opposition. Small groups of urban and rural guerrillas undertook isolated bombings and assassinations, but the authorities, often with help from local inhabitants, captured, imprisoned, and killed most of the attackers.

What brought down the shah's system were its own imbalances. The spectacular revenue figures concealed problems that eventually undermined the monarchy's bases of power. Government oil revenues, for example, rose from $2.3 billion in 1972 to $18.5 billion in 1974. The fifth development plan (1973–1978) provided for spending $69 billion compared to $8.3 billion in the fourth plan (1968–1972). Almost all Iranians benefited in some way from this new wealth, but some benefited much more than others. A few could afford to fly to London and Paris to shop, while others had to stand in line to buy onions. Although most Iranians had more money, their daily lives became increasingly unpleasant as shortages and power cuts became regular events. In the meantime, shiploads of imported goods rusted and rotted in the ports because there was no transport to move them.

Bazaar and Boutique

These problems would normally have made people complain, not revolt. The new wealth, however, exacerbated divisions within Iranian society, which split into antagonistic cultures of bazaar and boutique. The former accused the latter of imitating the worst features of foreign life—pornography, extreme fashion, and moral indifference. The latter, in turn, ridiculed the values of the bazaar as superstition and ignorance.[2]

The shah, for his part, simply ignored the values and traditions of most of his subjects and pretended that the Islamic component of Iranian culture did not exist. The culture of the bazaar never liked the monarchy's statist and secular policies. What was more dangerous to the shah, however, was that professionals and intellectuals, perhaps given courage by newfound prosperity, were unwilling to support the regime that had helped create their well-being. When the crisis came in 1978–1979, teachers, doctors, lawyers, and journalists either stood on the sidelines or shouted for an Islamic republic that, ironically, had no place for them and their values.

The shah had stayed in power for decades by manipulating the clerical and anticlerical forces in his country. To the former, he presented himself as their best defense against the threat of atheism, communism, and the alien ideologies of the West. To the latter, he presented himself as heir to his father's secular policies and a barrier against the powerful forces of "black reaction"—the clerical obscurantism that had blighted the lives of earlier generations and had kept Iran backward for centuries.

These tactics had been effective. When the bazaaris rioted in June 1963, after Ayatollah Khomeini's arrest in Qom, university students remained quiet while the army shot down rioters in the streets. Similarly, disturbances at Iranian universities throughout the late 1960s and 1970s found no support from the bazaars, which heard the students talking of Marxism and the alien experiences of Cuba, Vietnam, Algeria, and Palestine. As long as these scare tactics worked, the authorities were free to deal with each group of opponents separately.

Khomeini as National Savior

By 1978, however, the Iranian political scene had changed, and the shah could no longer divide and frighten potential opponents with the specters of Marxism and black reaction. The most militant clerics, including Khomeini and his followers, had been implacably hostile to the monarchy for a long time, attacking it for cooperation with Israel, corruption, close relations with the United States, and "un-Islamic" practices in culture, justice, commerce, and education. But by 1978 the monarchy's support among both moderate clerics and the secular middle class was drying up. As disturbances continued, the shah confronted a new, hostile alliance of his traditional clerical enemies and members of Iran's Western-oriented intelligentsia who demanded freedom of expression, an end to arbitrary police powers, and a multiparty system.

By itself, the religious opposition would not have defeated the shah. It took the support of the middle-class constituency of Mossadegh's old National Front—professionals, civil servants, students, and teachers—to ensure the success of the revolution. In 1978 simultaneous outbreaks in mosques and bazaars and in the modern sector of the economy—banks, newspapers, the oil industry, and government offices—meant serious trouble for the government. When employees at customs and the banks struck, they paralyzed Iran's import-based economy. When oil workers struck, they cut off supplies of fuel and heating oil and stopped government income from crude oil exports. These strikes also inflicted crippling psychological damage by persuading many Iranians that the shah's regime had lost its grip.

Members of the educated Iranian middle class decided that the revolution would proceed, with or without them, under Khomeini's banner. Many members of this class, which in fact had the regime at its mercy, joined Khomeini's call for an Islamic republic that had no interest in their demands for free expression and had declared war on their social values. Sa'id Amir Arjomand states the case as follows:

> Against this background, one is astounded by the behavior of Iran's sizable new middle class, the class that could be expected to assume the nation's political leadership by virtue of its educational and economic resources. How can one comprehend that this unprepared middle class could not think beyond the instant gratification of regicidal vengefulness and rise to the most elementary of the long-term political calculations? Why, instead of wringing concessions from a desperate Shah and a frightened military elite, did they choose to become subordinate allies of a man who treated them with haughty contempt and rejected their principles of national sovereignty and democracy? How can one account for the abject surrender to the clerical party of one after another of the feeble, middle-class based political factions: liberals, nationalists, and Stalinist communists alike?[3]

The New Oligarchy

Masters in Their Own House

The coalition that made the Iranian revolution agreed on only one thing: The shah must go. But few members of that coalition knew what would follow. All believed the Islamic republic (whatever it was) they were demanding would be better than the monarchy, steeped in corruption and given to bombast. Many revolutionaries had heard the teacher Ali Shari'ati's (d. 1977) call to abandon the alien ideologies of nationalism, capitalism, or Marxism and return to a true Iranian, Islamic "self." Students, teachers, women, bazaar merchants, clerics, and others all marched for an Islamic republic that would, they convinced themselves, reassert that self and make Iranians once again masters in their own house. Two questions remained unanswered: Which Iranians would be masters and in what sort of house?

After the shah's downfall, it turned out that only Khomeini and a small group of followers had the answer. Only they had a clear idea of what they wanted for Iran. Their political vision, although not complete in all details, was far more coherent than anything offered by their rivals. They not only had a vision of a harsh and strident Islamic republic, they had the determination to make that vision a reality at any cost.

The Ruling Elite

In the last weeks of the monarchy, the revolutionary leaders, clerical and secular, had formed a "revolutionary council" ostensibly to oversee the transfer of power from Prime Minister Shahpour Bakhtiar's cabinet to the provisional government of an Islamic republic. Once the shah was overthrown, however, Premier Mahdi Bazargan's provisional government remained a cipher while the revolutionary council, dominated by an inner circle of powerful clerics, became the only effective government of Iran. Within a few months after the revolution, the key figures of the council—Mohammad Beheshti, Seyyed Ali Khamene'i, Abd al-Karim Mousavi-Ardabili, and Ali Akbar Hashemi-Rafsanjani—had become the nucleus of an inner circle of twenty-five to thirty clerics, joined by strong friendships forged in seminaries, the shah's prisons, and in exile. This inner circle, with allies from outside the clergy, became the powerful network that has ruled the Islamic Republic for eleven years. The network has been strong enough to survive assassinations, civil disturbances, economic setbacks, international isolation, and a disastrous war. It may also be strong enough to survive well beyond Khomeini's death.

Other members of the victorious revolutionary alliance had expected their clerical allies, once the shah was overthrown, to give up politics and return quietly to their mosques and schools. Clerics, they believed, should leave running the state to those who spoke foreign languages and understood the complex worlds of high technology, international finance, and diplomacy. The clerics, however, made short work of their former coalition partners and moved easily into secular politics and administration. They first wrote the constitution of the new theocratic state and took control of its legislature, judiciary, armed forces, foreign policy, and propaganda machine. As for their mosques, they converted them into centers of political power that eclipsed ministries and other secular institutions. In every Iranian town the Friday prayer leader became the power center that replaced the governor, the police chief, and their military commander.

Most members of this network were little known outside Iranian clerical circles. A key figure was Ayatollah Beheshti, deputy speaker of the first Council of Experts, member of the original revolutionary council, and secretary general of the Islamic Republican party (IRP). A skillful and well-educated politician with little history of opposition activity, Beheshti in 1979 organized the informal ruling network into the IRP. Following his death, IRP leaders continued to dominate the ruling elite, but without Beheshti's leadership the party apparatus atrophied. In 1987 its activities were suspended indefinitely.[4]

Notably absent from this inner circle are the most senior religious leaders of Iranian Shia—the "sources of emulation" (*maraje'-e-taqlid*). Many of these senior clerics were uneasy with Khomeini's idiosyncratic version of Shiite Islam, the militancy of his followers, and their innovations in law and practice. As a result, the most powerful figures of the ruling inner circle are second-rank clerics who have pushed aside their more conservative elders. After a power struggle in Shiraz, for example, the militant Ayatollah Abd al-Hossein Dastgheib, with support from younger seminarians, bested his more conservative rival, Ayatollah Baha al-Din Mahallati. In Mashhad, Jojjat al-Eslam Va'ez-e-Tabasi became all-powerful in Khorasan at the expense of the senior

Ayatollahs Abdollah Shirazi and Hassan Tabataba'i-Qomi. In 1979 Khomeini made Va'ez-e-Tabasi his personal representative in the holy city and guardian of its shrine; in 1990 he still held both these posts.

Hanging (Opposites) Together

Despite the loss of many members to assassination—a June 1981 explosion at IRP headquarters killed Beheshti and over seventy other party officials—this network has held together since the first days of the Islamic Republic. It has done so thanks to its leaders' political skills, ruthlessness, and ability to organize gangs to command the streets and terrorize rivals. Members of this network have been able to put aside their individual differences and act decisively and brutally when threatened. In 1981 and 1988, for example, the group waged an efficient and savage war of extermination against determined Mojahedin-e-Khalq enemies. At the death of Khomeini in June 1989 it moved quickly to ensure a smooth transfer of power. In a highly symbolic gesture of unity, four key members of the elite—the leaders of the three branches of government and the prime minister—signed the first official statement issued after the announcement of the imam's death. And within twenty-four hours the Council of Experts had elected a new supreme leader.

Differences among the clerics of this network have not stopped them from taking concerted action against threats to their power. In times of crisis or sharp disagreement, all submitted to Khomeini's policy judgments and gave at least token obedience to his orders to preserve unity. Without specific instructions from the imam, however, those members responsible for a part of the government—justice, legislation, security, and so on—acted like feudal lords who recognized no authority but their own. There is, nevertheless, an underlying core of shared attitudes that has held the network together for more than ten years. All of its members have nearly identical views on six basic points:

1. Commitment to political activism for the clergy. Separation of religion and politics is anathema and contradicts the imam's beloved principle of *velayat-e-faqih* (political-religious leadership). These clerics see themselves as political and military leaders, using ceremonies such as Friday prayers as political-religious occasions for making major policy statements. Khomeini himself condemned those who advocated clerics' staying out of politics and would occasionally bend religious doctrine to the demands of militant, revolutionary ideology.[5]

2. Rejection of Iranian nationalism in favor of revolutionary Islam. In all but the most extreme cases, Iranian national interests will yield to the dictates of worldwide religious revolution. In the beginning of 1989, for example, when the regime was at odds with Turkey over the issue of head coverings of female university students, Iranian national interests would have dictated avoiding disputes with an important neighbor over such matters. Instead, ideology took priority. The regime has also discredited the memory of Iran's most famous nationalist

leader, Mohammad Mossadegh, and honored the memory of Ayatollah Kashani, one of his bitterest clerical opponents.

3. Distrust of bureaucracy, technical expertise, and traditional methods of statecraft. The regime has preferred ideological purity over professional competence. In the foreign ministry, for example, young, inexperienced ideologues (some of whom participated in the capture of the US embassy) have replaced trained professionals. Many highly trained specialists in medicine, aviation, and petroleum have left Iran to find work abroad, leaving technicians and mechanics to fill the gaps as best they can. Khomeini himself, in a February 1989 message, made it clear that Iranian specialists living abroad were welcome to return home only if they did not ask questions such as "Why did we fight the war?" or "Why did we say 'No East, no West'?"

4. Commitment to a "cultural revolution" in schools, families, and universities that will replace foreign and non-Islamic values with revolutionary Islamic principles. In the schools, authorities have purged staffs, textbooks, and curricula. Universities in general are mistrusted as places that must deal with alien ways of thought, and there are frequent changes of personnel. The regime still struggles to come to terms with traditional Iranian music and poetry. Attempts to suppress these forms of expression drove them underground for several years, but they reemerge whenever pressure is lessened.

5. Commitment to imposing, by force if necessary, strict "Islamic" standards of personal and social behavior. The authorities have attempted to regulate details of male and female dress and social behavior. Just as wearing Islamic coverings at universities was a sign of opposition to the monarchy, today wearing a necktie or a slightly stylish head covering is an act of political defiance, a rejection of this regime's values. In response, roving squads of zealots have enforced the regime's version of correct dress and behavior.

6. Commitment to a "no East, no West" foreign policy that has the declared goal of economic self-sufficiency and political independence. At times, however, this policy has come to look suspiciously like the traditional Iranian policy of "both East and West," i.e., playing off one superpower against another. In early 1989, when it appeared that a rapprochement with the West was proceeding, the uproar over Salman Rushdie's *Satanic Verses* brought a sudden reversal of policy and a visible warming of relations with the Soviet Union.

No More Parades, Thank You

Ten years after the revolution, despite many lurches and unexpected changes of direction, a system of sorts has taken shape. Although it is still too soon to know exactly what kind of Iran will emerge from the ferment of the revolution, many familiar patterns of Iranian history have persisted in new guises. For example, the Islamic revolution has loudly criticized despotic rule but has not changed Iran's ancient tradition of rule by a charismatic leader backed by religious legitimacy. The style changed, but the principle did not.

There is no going back to the days of the Pahlavis. Iran will eventually reject some or even most of Khomeini's vision of a pure, "Mohammadan" system, but his movement will still have drastically reshaped society. Whatever system emerges from the current turmoil, Iran in the year 2000—with its experiences of war, mass politics, and cultural revolution—will be very different from what it was in 1975. For the Iranian revolution has not only replaced one elite with another; it has shaken the foundations of Iranian political and social structures. Perhaps these changes are still not as profound as the most radical ideologues would like, but the upheavals of the revolution have gone farther in remaking Iranian society than many would have believed possible.

One important trend, and one that will continue, is the progressive disengagement of most Iranians from the political scene. The millions of Iranians who mourned for Khomeini are no longer participants in the political process. The era of mass politics is over. The ruling inner circle has grown smaller and tighter, and its workings more secretive. Within a day of Khomeini's death, in a closed session with no pretense of popular participation, the Council of Experts had elected President Ali Khamene'i the new supreme ruler. Having made its decision, the elite then organized public declarations of allegiance from revolutionary guards, military units, and the religious schools. But the million-strong marches and rallies and the noisy public debates that characterized the revolution and the early years of the Islamic Republic are no more. The ordinary citizen no longer participates in politics as he did during the exciting years of 1978–1982. In those years, political ferment, such as the arguments over the constitution, the hostage crisis, the battles against the Mojahedin-e-Khalq, and the campaigns against President Bani Sadr, Ayatollah Shari'at Madari, and others featured marches, rallies, petitions, and massive, orchestrated shows of public support. Such demonstrations are now neither sought nor offered.

In the future the regime will probably not even try bringing masses of supporters into the streets to back its policies. It has reached a tacit understanding with its citizens: We will not ask you to march or shout as long as you do not challenge our right to rule and make decisions behind closed doors. The citizenry, struggling with shortages, lines, and rationing, has lost interest in any political development that does not affect daily life. The phenomenon of mass politics has given way to indifference and rule by a secretive *nomenklatura*. When millions of ordinary Iranians mourned publicly and emotionally for Khomeini, they did so outside the political process. They wept for him as they would for Imam Hossein—not as political participants but out of deep emotional and religious ties.

This public apathy and disaffection about politics in general will not, in the short term, threaten the survival of the Islamic Republic. For decades, most Iranians remained indifferent to the shah, who apparently preferred them that way. The Islamic Republic now prefers its citizens standing in lines for cheese, soap, and tires instead of marching for or against this or that policy. If they come to the street, let them come for a funeral: Better the ordinary citizens stay out of politics altogether, except when the regime needs them for a halfhearted cheering section.

Such a system will survive as long as there is no focus of popular opposition, the ruling elite remains united, and political disputes do not become public questioning of the foundations of the Islamic Republic—i.e., the forbidden "hundred whys" of Khomeini's February 1989 message. Today it is difficult to see any opponents having enough organization and support to threaten the ruling network. The monarchists have no stomach for street fighting and neighborhood politics. The nationalists and communists are no match for the regime's goon squads of *hezbollahis* who drove the National Front from the Tehran streets in 1979. The Mojahedin-e-Khalq have devoted followers and are well organized, but their ideological mix of Islam and socialism has so far had little appeal to most Iranians. Many bazaaris prefer the current regime's corruption, inefficiency, and brutality to the utopian promises of the Mojahedin. The Islamic regime, for all its faults, has strong ties to Iran's private sector. It has persecuted individuals, not classes, and most people wanting to leave Iran have been allowed to do so. The Mojahedin, however, could be an uncompromising Iranian Khmer Rouge, which eliminates "class enemies" en masse in pursuit of some egalitarian, pseudoreligious utopia.

For the moment, Iranians may have tired of the search for perfection. Bad as it is, this regime is the devil they have come to know. Iranians have always seen government as an affliction—it takes your money in taxes and your sons for the army. But for centuries Iranians have softened the harshest officials and their rules by bribes and hypocrisy. In that sense, the Islamic Republic, even with its apparent rejection of Iranian cultural and historical traditions, has acted within the limits of national experience. Some influential friends and relatives, a beard, a set of worry beads, a few well-chosen Arabic phrases, and the correct style of dress puts one in harmony with the prevailing mood. Good relations with and payments to the local neighborhood security committee ensure that private parties are not disturbed by visits of morality squads seeking cards, musical instruments, or other evidence of depravity. The Mojahedin, however, frighten many Iranians because their young and idealistic leaders may be impervious to the usual blandishments and temptations that, for centuries, Iranians have used to preserve their way of life and national identity under appalling political conditions.

The Usual Suspects Rule at Home

Since the revolution, this ruling network has consolidated its power. It has dealt ruthlessly with numerous enemies: Soviet-backed Marxists, Maoists, nationalists, monarchists, ethnic separatists, the Mojahedin-e-Khalq, the conservative and traditional clerics who opposed Khomeini's political activism on theological grounds, and quixotic individuals such as former President Bani Sadr and Foreign Minister Sadq Qotbzadeh. When the regime had almost destroyed itself in the war against Iraq and in desperate attacks on the US Navy in the Persian Gulf, this network could reverse Iran's "war, war until victory" policy and have Khomeini himself endorse a cease-fire.

The Iranian ruling elite is not suicidal: Martyrdom is fine for individuals, and the leaders never hesitated sending thousands of young men to die on the fronts. But by the summer of 1988 the ruling network, with Hashemi-Rafsanjani as acting supreme commander of the armed forces, knew that it could not both continue the war and remain in power. Faced with conflicting goals, the inner circle chose survival and convinced Khomeini that preserving the revolution required accepting a cease-fire with the detested Saddam Hussein.

In the case of Ayatollah Hossein Ali Montazeri, designated successor to Khomeini, the ruling network had to deal with a political threat. Montazeri himself was never a part of the ruling circle. Although respected for his personal modesty and his long friendship with Khomeini, Montazeri was out of his depth in Iranian clerical politics. He lacked the political skills and ruthlessness to be one of the elite, which tolerated Montazeri only as long as he was content to be a jovial figurehead, the loyal Gabby Hayes (in the memorable characterization of one US journalist) of the Islamic Republic. When he began to take himself seriously and publicly question the wisdom of the Islamic Republic's harshest policies, he became dangerous and had to go. Many individuals within the ruling elite probably agreed with Montazeri that inept leadership had made Iran an international pariah, famous for terrorists and executioners, at a time that the country desperately needed friends; that an Islamic government should rule by tolerance and forgiveness as well as by executions and whippings; and that such a government should not harass its citizens over trivial questions of personal behavior. But Montazeri was an outsider, and an outsider should follow his script. When he refused to do so, he became a threat to the ruling elite, which convinced Khomeini his old friend had to be removed.

We're Still Collegial, Rah, Rah, Rah!

Khomeini Supports the Elite

As long as Khomeini lived, he supported this ruling elite against criticism of outsiders such as Montazeri or Mahdi Bazargan, insisting in return that its members keep their ideological and personal disputes within limits. He also demanded absolute obedience to his causes and obsessions—such as anti-Americanism, Lebanon, and the campaign against Salman Rushdie and his book—even if those obsessions disrupted both Iran's domestic economy and its foreign policy.

Within the ruling circle, Khomeini maintained a rough balance among competing political factions. His usual method of solving a problem was to submit it to a commission of his close associates he knew would act according to his wishes. Although preferring to stay above the day-to-day battles of government, in the most important cases he would intervene directly to lay down the law. He did so, for example, in July 1988 to endorse the cease-fire with Iraq and again in February 1989 to condemn those who spoke of mistakes, who criticized Iran's confrontational foreign policies, who questioned the wisdom of applying harsh justice against opponents, and who questioned having continued the Iran-Iraq war for eight years. At that time, he also turned on a favorite target, the liberal nationalists, and said, "As long as I live, I will never let them have a role in the government."

This ruling circle of twenty to thirty clerics, supported by younger followers and secular allies, will, barring some unforeseen upset, continue to control Iran's political life for the next five to ten years. It was resilient enough to withstand the loss of key members and demonstrated remarkable powers of survival during the first ten years of the revolution. With Khomeini gone, it will continue to rule.

The Rulers Make the Rules

This group has written the rules designed to keep itself in power. It wrote the original constitution of a theocratic Islamic republic in 1979—humiliating the nationalists in the process. In April 1989, two months before his death, Khomeini appointed some of the most powerful members of the group to a twenty-five-man commission to redraft Iran's fundamental laws with specific instructions to examine: (1) supreme leadership (i.e., succession to Khomeini), (2) centralizing executive authority, (3) centralizing judicial authority, and (4) organizing Iranian radio and television.

The membership list of this commission was a who's who of the Islamic Republic's elite: In addition to then President Khamene'i, Prime Minister Mousavi, Parliament Speaker Hashemi-Rafsanjani, and Supreme Court Chief Justice Mousavi-Ardabili, the commission included Ayatollahs Jannati, Mahdavi-Kani, Meshkini, and Hojjat al-Eslam Mousavi-Kho'iniha. Other important members were Ayatollahs Azari-Qomi Bigdeli and Yazdi, and Hojjat al-Eslams Emami-Kashani, Nuri, Tavassoli, and Karroubi.[6]

All these figures were survivors, veterans of the revolution and the Islamic Republic's political wars. They had held key positions from the first days of the revolution, and many had been active in religious opposition politics for fifteen years before that. Their offices gave them control of the media, culture, clerical organizations, Friday prayers, security apparatus, courts, the military and revolutionary guards, and major economic institutions. Directly or indirectly, they dominated all centers of political power.[7]

Even Khomeini's death did not interrupt this commission's work for long. Moving quickly, it rewrote the Iranian constitution in a way that tightened the elite's grip on power. Their revised constitution was approved in a July 28 combined referendum and presidential election. Thanks to the commission's efforts, Iranians can look forward to another ten years of collegial rule by the same group that has held power since the revolution.[8]

Hard Times Ahead: Rebuilding Without Leadership

If the ruling elite is going to retain power, it must begin to rebuild Iran's shattered economy. But an effective reconstruction program means unpleasant choices for the authorities: Either bring back Iranian specialists or hire large numbers of Westerners. Doing either will force the regime to moderate both its strident rhetoric and harsh social legislation. Unless it does so, the regime will have to entrust reconstruction to undertrained people incapable of building and running a sophisticated economic system.

In the short term, the authorities may try to finesse these choices by seeking cooperation with the Soviet and Eastern European partners in economic reconstruction. Such agreements have the attraction of using Iranian gas, which is otherwise burned, to earn hard currency and of allowing the authorities to avoid facing the sensitive issues of economic cooperation with Western countries denounced as sworn enemies of the Iranian revolution. Recent agreements with the Soviets, however, will address only a small part of Iran's rebuilding needs. These agreements call for Iran's spending about $6 billion in hard currency over fifteen years, yet independent studies estimate Iran will need at least a $100 billion for its reconstruction.

The Iranian economy will remain paralyzed unless the government can make the political decision to seek Western help and bring back its own trained specialists.[9] Because of war damage, mismanagement, and neglect, Iran cannot produce enough of anything to fulfill domestic demand. Too much money chasing too few goods has caused devastating inflation and collapse of the Iranian rial, worth (in June 1989) about one-twentieth of its prerevolution value against the US dollar. Domestic industry is operating at less than 40 percent capacity because there is no foreign exchange to buy machinery and raw material and no one in authority to authorize purchase of even cheap and simple spare parts. Much of the foreign exchange available goes to imports of foodstuffs, weapons, and finished goods, such as vehicle batteries and tires, which do nothing to revive domestic production. Reportedly, much of what the government imports finds its way into private warehouses, where it remains while speculators wait for the rial to fall and prices to rise.

The regime faces two alternatives, but has so far lacked the will and organization to do either. It must arrange foreign financing for imported machinery and raw materials, or it must relax controls over the private sector, restore control of factories to private owners, and allow them to use foreign exchange to import what they need. Without leaders capable of taking such rational economic decisions and without some apparatus to carry them out, most Iranians will continue to face a life of shortages, inflation, and a worthless currency. Iran can today produce about 3 million barrels per day of crude oil. After filling domestic needs, about 2.5 million barrels are available for export. Income from the sale of that much production should finance the base of a carefully planned reconstruction program. With such an income and without any important foreign debt,

Iran, if it needed to do so, could also borrow abroad to finance rebuilding its power plants, transportation network, refineries, ports, cities, and industries.

Undertaking such a program, however, needs a political environment in which "economics" is no longer a dirty word and in which managers know they can consider factors such as return and profitability without facing accusations of being counterrevolutionary. Instead of encouraging Iranian industry to meet domestic needs, some officials have urged selling factories to families of war dead, a socially admirable idea that will probably not do much to increase production. Seemingly incapable of reviving Iranian industry, the authorities have allocated hard currency to the importation of new buses, for example, instead of spending much less importing the equipment and raw materials needed to restart Iranian bus factories. For reasons of political prestige, Iran is determined to complete the Iran-Japan Petrochemical Company plant at Bandar Khomeini.[10] In a traditional political environment, the Iranians would cut their losses and salvage what they could from the project. Today, however, the authorities insist on completing a useless project at an estimated additional cost of $2 billion.

An Iran Without Khomeini

Rule by Visions

As long as Khomeini lived, his visions dominated Iran. No one could openly question his "Mohammadan system," his version of the seventh-century Islamic state ruled from a mosque in Medina by a combination prophet, prime minister, judge, and military leader. Those within the ruling elite who understood Khomeini's visions could manipulate them skillfully for factional and individual political gain. When the imam attacked the United States, all shouted, "Death to America." When he denounced clerics who questioned his political activism, the elite turned against some of the most-respected figures of contemporary Shiite Islam such as Ayatollahs Shari'at-Madari, Baha al-Din Mahallati, and Tabataba'i-Qomi. When he launched one of his periodic crusades against the "liberals," goon squads would trash newspaper offices and attack women whose coverings did not meet standards.

In his remarkable will, read by President Khamene'i in the first days after the imam's death, Khomeini described his absolutist political vision in detail. This document is Khomeini at his most feisty and defiant. He bequeathed Iranians a legacy of endless confrontation with those at home and abroad who incurred his enmity. In addition to his usual curses on the United States, he insulted the Saudi ruling family and the leaders of Jordan, Egypt, and Morocco. He wrote this document in order to keep Iranian politics on the disorderly but single-minded path he had laid down. The will is vintage Khomeini: He regrets nothing and apologizes for nothing. If he could, he would continue to lead Iran from his grave.

The Dwarfs Remain

Without Khomeini, however, these visions may not survive for very long. Few members of the inner ruling circle have his total commitment to principles. If they do, they lack the charisma and power to force others to accept them without question. If only to stay in power, they will have to make the compromises with reality that Khomeini always rejected. Nor can any of his disciples replace Khomeini as chief of the theocratic state he designed. When Beheshti, Hashemi-Rafsanjani, and others wrote the Islamic Republic's constitution in 1979, they based the state on Khomeini's unique vision of Islamic government, giving the new state a political-religious leadership (the famous *velayat-e-faqih*) that only Khomeini could assume. His death ended that institution in its original form. None of his adept political allies has his religious stature as a Shiite source of emulation, and none of the senior religious figures has unerring political instincts and ability to sense a popular cause.

With Khomeini dead, the inner circle will have to reorder its original arrangements. The same elite, plus or minus a few members, will continue to rule in his name for a few years at least. His picture will still appear everywhere; his name remain on streets, squares, and towns; and his sayings be used on appropriate occasions. The same people will still control the key institutions of Iranian life: security, justice, education, culture, administration, trade, and law-making.

So what will change? The leaders will have the power of their government posts, but without the stamp of religious legitimacy that Khomeini's support once conferred. The Islamic Republic will still have collegial rule, but without a final arbiter. The Iranian *nomenklatura* will lose its anchor and its legitimizer. Khamene'i, Hashemi-Rafsanjani, and their colleagues are skillful politicians but can be little more than trustees of Khomeini's legacy. President Khamene'i's new title of "leader" (even with his promotion to ayatollah) rings hollow without the addition of Khomeini's grandiose titles of "political-religious leader of the community" (*imam-e-ommat*), "founder of the Islamic republic," or "hope of the deprived of the world." The system may continue for a few years, but it will lack any final, incontestable authority that can restrain ideological and personal competition. Authority will be divided among a clique of strong-willed individuals who will have no outside force—only their collective survival instinct—to impose limits on their disagreements.

Three Possible Directions

Divided authority, however, does not necessarily mean anarchy. It means only that power struggles will go farther than they did when Khomeini was alive to pronounce final judgment on contentious issues. There are three possible outcomes:

1. A Lebanon outcome: violent clashes between competing political factions. As happened in the first years of the Islamic Republic, these clashes may

have ethnic overtones. If not controlled, they could lead to the central authorities' losing control over areas such as Kurdestan, Baluchestan, or even important cities in the Persian-speaking heartland.

2. The status quo: continued political paralysis. Infighting may not become violent, but it could paralyze a government. If no individual or faction achieves a clear victory, Iranian politics will become a setting for permanent struggle among members of the elite such as occurred between 1941 and 1953, between the departure of Reza Shah and his son's coup against Mossadegh. In such a case the leaders will devote all their energies to political survival and make none of the difficult decisions needed to rebuild a shattered economy or bring Iran back into the world community.

3. An Iraq or Syria outcome: emergence of a clear winner or group of winners. Having defeated their rivals, the victors would be able to impose a particular ideology on Iranian political life.

The first outcome is the least likely. The second is more likely, but will, by paralyzing the political system, prevent the government from taking any but the most immediate and emergency measures to repair the economic damage from years of war and neglect. The third is the most likely outcome but leaves unanswered the question of the orientation of any centralized regime.

The Search for Moderation: King Log or King Stork?

Observers have classified members of the Iranian leadership as "ideologues," "pragmatists," and "moderates" and have tried to predict their behavior based on which individuals have the upper hand. But the outlook of Khomeini's successors is better determined from their acts than from labels that are often based on misperceptions and wishful thinking. If the new leaders are going to reorient Iran on a less ideological course, then we should look for signs of change in the following crucial areas:

Culture: What happens to traditional Iranian music, which has been driven underground by clerical extremism?

Economy: Does the government establish orderly relations with foreign companies in order to undertake a serious reconstruction program?

Foreign policy: Does the government cut its ties to foreign extremist groups, perhaps using economic necessity as the excuse? Does it end gratuitous media attacks on foreign neighbors and leaders?

Personal status: Can the authorities limit the activities of domestic vigilantes who have tried to enforce their own version of correct Islamic dress and behavior?

Many Iranians are hoping the third outcome will end today's endless political disorder and improve their daily lives. The reasoning is that almost any government that speaks with one voice and carries out a consistent policy will be better than the current system of lurches and swings. Iranians have lived with brutal and arbitrary governments for centuries, and even a harsh regime that ensures security and enforces the same set of rules every day will be easier to deal with than the current system. At the moment, yesterday's friend is today's enemy; yesterday's respected clergyman is today's nonperson; and North Korea is presented as an ideal friend of an Islamic state with a "no East, no West" foreign policy.

If Iran eventually speaks with one voice, however, there is no guarantee that the voice will be a pleasant one. The most optimistic view is that the new leaders in Tehran will concentrate on Iran's internal economic difficulties, take a more reasoned view of the country's national interests, and control revolutionary excesses of fringe groups. Such an outcome would mean no more hostage-taking, terrorism, and gratuitous attacks on other states and their leaders. At home it would mean ideology would have to yield to economic reality and the authorities would have to concentrate on matters other than enforcing conformity to their version of Islamic dress and behavior.

But such a happy outcome is by no means a certainty, and Iranians may end up trading King Log for King Stork. A new Iranian leadership may unite, but not necessarily around policies that we consider reasonable. Whoever takes control may be as tenacious and uncompromising as Khomeini was on the need for permanent confrontation and may insist on executing the provisions of the imam's will in every detail. New leaders may continue to enforce strict social legislation, believing, like Khomeini, that if Iranians' instinctive hedonism is allowed the slightest room to breathe, it will inevitably get the better of their religiosity and lead them to forget martyrdom and self-sacrifice in pursuit of worldly delights.[11] If the current regime, for example, can present North Korea as a model of a revolutionary state, then a future Iranian government may decide that its citizens need Pyongyang's style of discipline. In that case, today's bureaucratic feudalism and paralysis will appear benevolent in retrospect.

US Interests: What Might Work

Better and Worse

The Iranian revolution has been analyzed, explained, debated, clarified, dissected, and rationalized ad nauseam. Many analysts were wrong because they considered the Iranian revolution the result of some US policy failure or because they let wishful thinking get the better of their judgment. In fact, from a US point of view, events have turned out both better and worse than expected: Iran did not become a Soviet base in the Middle East; Iran did not become a police state like Iraq; Iran has a government of sorts that provides a minimum of daily security; Iran did not make a suicidal attempt to close the Straits of Hormuz and stop the flow of oil from the Persian Gulf; nor did the Islamic Republic imitate the Khmer Rouge and murder a third of its own population.

On the other hand, the revolution bitterly disappointed many foreign sympathizers by not creating an Iranian social democracy with an Islamic veneer.

Although thoughtful and cosmopolitan Iranians, watching their country from abroad, have repeatedly predicted the imminent end of revolutionary fury and the emergence of more open-minded values, the absolutist spirit of the revolution continues to thrive. The republic still pursues the ideal of a revolutionary Islamic state no matter what the consequences to its people and the rest of the world. The regime has delighted in outraging world opinion and has, as a matter of principle, resisted accommodating itself to standards of international political behavior or the demands of the international marketplace. It does what it must to survive, but no more.

If Iran faces another decade of uncertainty, what does that mean for the United States? First, events of the last eleven years should have taught us some caution.[12] We should avoid basing our predictions and policy on muddled knowledge of events in Iran and on the basis of how things *ought* to be there. Khomeini, for example, *ought* to have been another Gandhi; Hashemi-Rafsanjani *ought* to be a moderate; and the Mojahedin-e-Khalq *ought* to be an organization of Islamic Titoists. Wishing or believing these things, however, will not make them true.

An Iranian Event in an Iranian Setting

We can begin by understanding the Iranian revolution as an *Iranian* event. Whatever the origins of today's Iranian revolutionary Islam, it differs radically from the religion practiced elsewhere in the Islamic world. What Khomeini and his followers have done is to create a new church, a new version of religious truth, and add it to a long list of Iranian-based heresies—a list that stretches from the Manicheanism of pre-Islamic times through the Babi/Bahai movement of the nineteenth century.[13]

In today's chaotic aftermath of the Islamic revolution, we must see events in their Iranian setting. Much of the controversy surrounding Ayatollah Montazeri, for example, originated in the mid-1970s in an obscure doctrinal dispute within the Iranian clergy over the correct interpretation of the uprising of Imam Hossein. In a similar fashion, the capture of the US embassy in 1979, the anti-Saudi campaigns leading to the pilgrimage riots of 1987, and the uproar over British author Salman Rushdie's *Satanic Verses* in 1989 had little to do with the United States, Saudi Arabia, or Rushdie and the United Kingdom. All originated in convoluted power struggles inside Iran—power struggles that remained largely hidden from outsiders.

Anti-American for How Long?

Competing factions in the Islamic Republic have found anti-Americanism a useful tool in political infighting. When a policy is obviously bankrupt and when all else fails, one can always get a crowd to shout, "Death to America!" Rival groups on both left and right have struggled to outdo each other in the violence of their anti-American rhetoric. In the early months of the Islamic Republic, leftist groups, including the Mojahedin-e-Khalq, beat the anti-American drum the loudest and joined religious extremists in order to sabotage the provisional government's attempts to maintain normal relations with Washington.

The Islamic Republic may continue its anti-American policies for years to come. Many Iranian political figures have built their careers, both before and after the revolution, on that policy, and they will not abandon it quickly or easily. But the same politicians have also survived by following shifting winds wherever they blow, and when anti-Americanism is no longer useful to mobilize political support, the leaders will give the crowds a new slogan to shout and order them to forget yesterday's slogans.

The Iranian leadership will rationalize such a shift by arguing that a "mature revolution" has nothing to fear from normal relations with any foreign state, even a superpower. Some Iranian politicians were tentatively making such an argument just after Iran's acceptance of UN Resolution 598, but the seed fell on rocky ground at the time. Whenever the new government does decide to reverse the imam's beloved anti-Americanism, it will justify the change on the basis of political maturity and on the need to restore economic ties and settle outstanding disputes over property, hostages, and other matters.

Under such conditions, the United States will need the patience not to react to every new twist of the Iranian political scene. We must stand back, watch, and listen. The revolution will swing this way or that depending on the course of events in Tehran. France, Germany, Turkey, and Britain were recent victims of these swings, and as long as the political struggle for control of the Islamic Republic continues unresolved, the United States and other foreign countries will be a convenient and popular target of competing factions.

All Radicals, All Moderates

Temporary shifts in the political winds should not mislead us. Nor should we be drawn into a fruitless search for Iran's ever-elusive "moderates." We should watch not only the political fortunes of this or that politician but what the Iranians say and do. There are few fixed positions in today's Iran. According to the direction of the political winds, today's moderate is tomorrow's radical and vice versa. To paraphrase Thomas Jefferson (a most unlikely source), they are all moderates; they are all radicals. Today's radical will become surprisingly reasonable when it suits his purpose to do so.

We should not repeat the mistake of dealing with powerless figures who happen to speak a language familiar and pleasing to Western ears. In 1979–1980, Bazargan, Qotbzadeh, and Bani Sadr, for example, spoke words we wanted to hear. But despite their nominal posts, they were unable to translate intentions into deeds. If we deal with anyone in Iran, we should deal seriously with the Mahdi Karroubis, the Mohammad Yazdis, the Mahdavi-Kanis, and other individuals or groups who can speak for the ruling elite and make good on their promises. We may need to deal with some tough, unsavory characters, but if they are strong enough, it will not matter whether we call them moderate, radical, pragmatic, or anything else. The combination of their self-interest and power should deliver the goods.

What Matters and What Does Not

All we need ask is a minimum of decorum: no attacks on embassies or diplomats, no public advocacy of terrorism, no kidnapping, and no overt attempts to overthrow neighboring regimes. It may matter to Iranians, but it matters little to US foreign policy whether Iranian women have to wear raincoats, pantsuits, or headscarves or whether Iranian men may wear neckties. Of course we would like to see "Islam with a human face" in Tehran, but what concerns the United States is that Iran have a government that (1) seeks normal relations with the United States and is prepared to act as a responsible member of the international community, and (2) speaks with one voice instead of veering from extreme to extreme according to the fortunes of political warfare in Tehran.

For the United States the policy, not the policymaker, is important. It will make no difference whether a "pragmatist" or an "ideologue" ends Iran's international isolation and brings it back into the community of nations. If the policy is acceptable, we can live with either.

One last suggestion: The United States may inadvertently reinforce the most strident anti-Americanism within the Islamic Republic by overreacting to provocation. A stony silence (what the Iranians call *qahr*) even to the most absurd statements is the best reaction. An act of overt hostility, of course, should meet a correct and firm response. But too much verbal recrimination will give the victory to the smaller adversary who has succeeded in provoking the giant. The United States should avoid shouting contests with the Islamic Republic. Since the revolution, the leaders of the republic have made absurd claims about Iran's importance to the United States and about how the Islamic revolution has shaken the US system to its very roots. US overreaction to Iranian provocation only feeds those leaders' sense of self-importance and implicitly confirms their claim that a small, weak, underdeveloped Islamic nation has been able to manipulate and frustrate the policy of a much larger and stronger adversary. Even worse, the leaders of the Islamic Republic will overreach themselves if they begin believing their own rhetoric about all-conquering Islam. Armed with illusions of invincibility, they could undertake some dangerous and foolish act in the international arena.

Something about Iran has made the United States—and other outsiders as well—lose its sense of judgment and proportion. As the late Justice William O. Douglas put it, "We are suckers for people who wear funny hats." Perhaps we can begin by admitting just how little we know about Iran and how wrong we have been in the past. From that beginning we can better deal with people who, since the revolution, have regularly done the opposite of what we believed they had to do. During that time the leaders of the Islamic Republic have steadfastly refused to be "responsible revolutionaries." Instead they have delighted in confrontation and in defying respectable international opinion.

When the leaders of the Islamic Republic finally settle on arrangements for their government, they may choose to adopt conventional methods of statecraft. But they may not. So far, by refusing to compromise, they have defeated monarchists, leftists, traditional clerics, and secular liberals. They may see no reason to abandon that successful formula for more flexible policies that we think they should follow. The Islamic Republic will, in any case, continue to make political and economic decisions on its own terms, not on ours. In dealing with that republic, the United States should be prepared to confront leaders who reject our notions of what is in Iran's interest and who follow policies based on logic of their own manufacture.

Notes

Portions of this paper have appeared, in slightly different form, in my *Iran: At War with History* (Boulder, CO: Westview Press, 1987). The opinions are entirely my own and do not reflect the views of the US government.

1. The Turks, for one, must wonder just what constitutes normal relations with Iran. Both countries recalled their ambassadors in March 1989 after Iran had criticized the Ankara government for banning Islamic dress on female university students. Two months later, with a straight face, the Iranian deputy foreign minister, on a visit to Turkey, could say that "Iran believes in the indisputable policy of non-interference in other countries' internal affairs" (Radio Tehran, May 26, 1989).

2. In the 1970s, films of social commentary such as *Mohallel* and *Hakim-bashi* ridiculed many of the customs and values of the bazaaris. These films were great successes among the intelligentsia but were resented by traditional groups, which considered such works proof that the government had declared war against their values.

3. *The Turban for the Crown* (New York: Oxford University Press, 1988), p. 109.

4. Other important members of the ruling network include: (1) Hojjat al-Eslam Mohammad Mousavi-Kho'iniha., revolutionary prosecutor-general, member of Parliament, member of the twelve-man council for determining the interests of the system (Expediency Council), deputy chairman of the Association of Militant Clerics, formerly imam's representative for pilgrimage affairs; (2) Ayatollah Mohammad Reza Mahdavi-Kani, chief of the Tehran Militant Clergy Association, former minister of interior, temporary Friday prayer leader of Tehran; (3) Ayatollah Ahmad Jannati, former Friday prayer leader of Ahvaz, member of the Expediency Council, member of the assembly of experts to determine succession to Khomeini (second Council of Experts); (4) Hojjat al-Eslam Hashemi-Rafsanjani, president of the Islamic Republic (from August 1989), speaker of the Parliament, member of the Expediency Council, acting supreme commander of the armed forces, former deputy secretary general of the IRP, temporary Friday prayer leader of Tehran; (5) Ayatollah Ali Meshkini, Friday prayer leader of Qom, member of the supreme council of Friday prayer leaders, speaker of the second Council of Experts, chairman of the commission to amend the constitution.

5. In 1988, for example, he ordered Iranians to boycott the Islamic pilgrimage to Mecca rather than accept Saudi limits on the numbers and behavior of Iranian pilgrims.

6. (1) Ayatollah Ahmad Azari-Qomi Bigdeli, member of Parliament, chairman of the *Resalat* foundation and publisher of the Persian-language daily *Resalat*; (2) Ayatollah Mohammad Yazdi, deputy speaker of Parliament, member of the second Council of Experts, member of the Council of Guardians, member of the Expediency

Council (to resolve disputes between Parliament and the guardians' council), Islamic Republican party representative on three-man commission to resolve disputes between the IRP and President Bani Sadr (1981); (3) Hojjat al-Eslam Mohammad Emami-Kashani, member of Parliament, member of the Expediency Council, member of the Council of Guardians, member of the second Council of Experts, acting Friday prayer leader of Tehran, and justice minister; (4) Hojjat al-Eslam Shaikh Abdollah Nuri, the imam's representative in the Ministry of the Revolutionary Guard; (5) Hojjat al-Eslam Mohammad Reza Tavassoli, director of religious affairs in Khomeini's office; (6) Hojjat al-Eslam Mahdi Karroubi, deputy speaker of the Parliament, chairman of the Tehran Association of Militant Clerics (a rival of Mahdavi-Kani's Militant Clergy Association), the imam's representative on the bloody Mecca pilgrimage of 1987, chairman of the war victims' foundation.

7. Hashemi-Rafsanjani's brother, for example, is managing director of Iranian National Radio and Television. Meshkini's son-in-law, Mohammad Reyshahri, was minister of intelligence and security and former revolutionary prosector of the army. Reyshahri's deputy minister, Ali Fallahian-Khuzestani was chief of the special court that investigates the clergy. Karroubi's wife runs medical services at her husband's foundation and controls a large budget for buying medical supplies from abroad.

8. Two of the commission members have taken key positions in the new administration: Yazdi as chief of the judiciary branch (which replaced the previous High Council of the Judiciary), and Karroubi as speaker of Parliament, replacing the new President Hashemi-Rafsanjani.

9. There are signs that the government is interested in resuming serious talks with Western companies about reconstruction projects. So far, however, these contacts have been very cautious and limited to a few sectors, particularly the oil industry.

10. Eighty-five percent finished (at a cost to Iran of about $3 billion) when revolution and war stopped construction, the plant is obsolete and uneconomical in today's petrochemical markets. Originally scheduled for completion in 1979, it should have already repaid its investors.

11. Khomeini had a pessimistic, if perhaps realistic, view of his countrymen. He saw in each of them an equal mixture of extreme religiosity and extreme hedonism. The only way to bring out the former, in his opinion, was to suppress, by force if necessary, all manifestations of the latter. If the Iranian's love of music, wine, and beauty were allowed the slightest chance to express itself, it would soon dominate the religious side of his nature.

12. In the last year, for example, serious Iran-watchers have told us: Iran would never stop fighting Iraq while Khomeini was alive; Iran could stop fighting Iraq only while Khomeini was alive; Iran could improve relations with the United States only during Khomeini's lifetime; Iran would never improve relations with the United States while Khomeini lived.

13. Militant, messianic Shiism itself is not new in Iran. In the sixteenth century, the Safavids, a Turkish-speaking military-religious order based in Azerbaijan, imposed Shiism by force on a mostly Sunni population. The Safavids owed their victory to decades of covert missionary work and to the tenacity of devoted tribal warriors. Following the Safavid's example in the twentieth century, Khomeini's covert network with Iran's mosques and schools carried on a determined, underground struggle for decades.

4
Iraq in the Year 2000

Phebe Marr

Following its sudden invasion of Kuwait on August 2, 1990, Iraq faces an uncertain—even a potentially ominous—future. Iraq's economic health, its political stability, and its regional role depend on the outcome of the Gulf crisis, but no realistic outcome is likely to be more favorable for Iraq than that which it faced on August 1. Iraq possesses two assets that make it the predominant Arab power in the Gulf. First, it has the largest, best-equipped, battle-tried armed forces in the region as well as a growing edge in military technology. Second, its oil reserves, now estimated at 100 billion barrels, are second only to Saudi Arabia's. The Gulf crisis has put both the retention of this power and its future exercise at high risk. The imposition of UN sanctions has weakened Iraq's economy, already damaged by an eight-year war with Iran. Iraq's ruthless occupation of a neighboring Arab country has reduced, perhaps eliminated, its potential leadership role in the region, and the threat of war with a formidable array of international forces in the Gulf threatens Iraq with much physical and human destruction and subsequent political instability.

The range of crisis outcomes, from a peaceful negotiated settlement that might even result in a few marginal gains for Iraq to a damaging and destructive war that would leave the country in a shambles, make assessments of Iraq's future hazardous. However, some realistic parameters can be set on likely outcomes and the effects these would have on Iraq's future, economically, politically, and regionally. If the crisis ends peacefully with an Iraqi withdrawal from all—or almost all—of Kuwait, Iraq's potential for economic development and political stability, though greatly reduced from its precrisis status, is considerable, and it could still play a role, quite possibly a disruptive role, in regional politics. If the crisis ends in war, Iraq faces a bleak future. Its economic development would be set back at least a decade and possibly more; its state structure could be weakened, and a new regime would be likely, possibly bringing Iraq a new direction. With the need to rebuild, Iraq could not play much of a regional role and, indeed, could become prey to hostile neighbors. Iraq's resources and its human potential will survive the crisis, but as so often in the past, political management has dimmed its future and limited the realization of its potential.

The Economy

Any assessment of Iraq's economic growth is dependent on whether there is a military or a peaceful solution to the Gulf conflict. The outcome of a war scenario is easier to estimate. In any military conflict, the damage to Iraq's physical infrastructure is likely to be high. Air attacks could destroy much of its military-industrial complex, its refining and loading facilities, and its power grid, while airports, rail lines, roads, bridges, and telecommunications facilities would all suffer varying degrees of damage. Depending on Iraq's military response, its human casualties could also be high, further depleting its skilled manpower. Even a limited war would set Iraq's economic development back a decade, and possibly two. Although Iraq's oil resources guarantee its gradual revival, the task would be long and arduous and would probably require help from its neighbors. In the meantime, Iraq would be doomed to a decade of weakness and economic stagnation.

A peaceful outcome would have more ambiguous economic results. Iraq's economy was in serious difficulty before its invasion of Kuwait; indeed, economic problems played a major role in its decision to invade. Pent-up expectations of a war-weary population, reconstruction needs, continued high levels of defense spending, inflation, and annual payments on its war debt had created demands that Iraq could not fulfill from its own oil revenues, particularly in a period of declining oil prices. Debt payments and a development program too ambitious for Iraq's revenues had reached a crisis stage in Baghdad prior to August 1990. Without a new debt policy or a radical reorientation of spending priorities, or both, Iraq could look forward only to slow growth and continued debt payments. [1]

Iraq's invasion of Kuwait and the UN sanctions have made these development prospects far grimmer: The oil boycott is estimated to be costing Iraq $1.5 billion per month in lost oil revenues, at precrisis oil prices. Because Iraq has canceled its outstanding debt, its creditworthiness will be difficult to restore in the postcrisis period; indeed, its former creditors may demand repayment by other means before they are willing to do business. Iraq's treatment of its foreign work force—holding them hostage—will make it difficult to secure foreign skills in the future. And a degraded industrial establishment, deprived of spare parts and maintenance, will need repair. Meanwhile, Iraq's oil markets may be taken over by its competitors. And, in the aftermath of the crisis, the West is expected to clamp down on transfers of arms and technologies of various kinds, impeding Iraq's industrial development. In short, whatever Iraq's economic difficulties before the crisis, they have been magnified many times over, blighting its prospects for economic development for the remainder of the decade. The following analysis is based on Iraq's economic prospects under some kind of peaceful withdrawal from Kuwait. Where necessary, modifications will be made to take account of a war scenario.

Iraq's Oil Revenues

Iraq's prospects for development will hinge mainly on two factors: its potential for increased oil revenue and its perceived role in the regional and international community. Because of its oil resources, Iraq will attract some investment and technology from overseas, but further disruptive behavior will limit their flow. Prior to the crisis, Iraq was producing just under 3 million barrels per day, but its potential for increased production is significantly higher. In addition to Iraq's older Kirkuk fields, it has rich hydrocarbon deposits in Rumailah, Majnun, East Baghdad, and elsewhere, waiting for exploitation. Bringing in such fields could raise Iraq's maximum production to 6 million barrels per day by the end of the decade, or, more realistically, to a sustainable capacity of about 5 million—about half that of Saudi Arabia. [2]

Iraq has expanded its network of pipelines, enhancing its export capacity and flexibility. The offshore terminal at Mina al-Bakr, when fully restored, should be capable of exporting about 1.6 million barrels per day. Two parallel pipelines through Turkey can carry about 1.5 million, while the pipeline through Saudi Arabia to the Red Sea is capable of handling 1.6 million, a total of 4.7 million barrels per day even without the defunct pipeline through Syria (with a capacity of 1.2 million barrels per day), which could at least theoretically be opened if relations between Syria and Iraq improved. Additional offshore loading capacity in the Gulf at Khor al-Amayah, destroyed in the Iran-Iraq war, could, if restored, add another 1.6 million (its prewar capacity), and four offshore mooring buoys could add 1 million barrels per day. Iraq's strategic pipeline from Kirkuk to Faw allows it the flexibility to switch exports from the Mediterranean to the Gulf or the Red Sea depending on market conditions, and most of these systems could be expanded if finances became available or market conditions required it. [3]

There will be some constraints on the oil sector in the aftermath of the boycott. Wells, pumping stations, and other facilities will have to be brought on line after a period of neglect. The optimal figures given for Iraq's oil production capacity require bringing in wells in new fields. This will require extensive capital and foreign expertise that, even before the crisis, were not readily forthcoming due in part to Iraq's poor credit position and its flagging economy. These difficulties will be magnified in the wake of the crisis. In addition, Iraq may emerge from the boycott to find its markets captured by its competitors. Iran has reportedly signed long-term contracts with many of Iraq's previous customers. Lastly, even if Iraq is able to increase production and export capacity, market forces and Iraq's relations with other OPEC members are likely to be volatile, making increased revenues uncertain. A war that destroyed some oil production and export facilities in Iraq, Kuwait, and possibly Saudi Arabia would reduce supply and might push prices up, at least temporarily. Alternatively, an outcome that ends the boycott and brings Iraqi and Kuwaiti oil back on stream could reduce prices. This situation, however, could keep tensions high, as Iraq,

Kuwait, and Iran fought for market share.[4]

To make up for the effects of the boycott, Iraq will want to increase revenues by maximizing production or prices or both, a situation that may well bring it into conflict with other OPEC members. Indeed, the crisis is likely to be followed by severe competition over pricing and resource allocation between Iraq and its neighbors. Barring windfall profits, Iraq's oil revenues are likely to be modest indeed compared to its needs.

Iraq's Development Priorities

Iraq's development in the postcrisis era will depend not only on oil revenue but on its spending priorities. Prior to the crisis, Iraq had four main priorities: defense expenditures, reconstruction and growth investment, consumer imports to offset inflation, and debt repayment. A major cause of its economic difficulty was its emphasis on military expenditure, showcase projects, and nonproductive investments, such as the rebuilding of Faw and Basra, and mismanagement of debt repayment. Unless these difficulties are addressed, Iraq's recovery from the Iran-Iraq war and the effects of the boycott will be slow.

Iraq's Military Expenditures

Without a reorientation of Iraq's economy away from military expenditures and toward productive economic sectors, Iraq's economy is likely to suffer from continued international restrictions on its economic growth. In 1988, Iraq's military expenditures totaled an estimated $5 billion, approximately 40 percent of its export earnings.[5] In the year before the invasion of Kuwait, that figure was reduced only slightly. The occupation of Kuwait and the subsequent military buildup has been costly. Mobilizing, training, and feeding an army of well over a million men has not only devoured development funds but displaced workers from the economy, causing disruptions in factories, farms, and administrative structures. A war, of course, would raise these calculations astronomically.

Even before the invasion of Kuwait, Iraq's military buildup caused regional and international consternation. Iraq has acquired the largest stockpile of chemical weapons (CW) in the Third World, and there is ample evidence that it is striving for a nuclear weapons capacity.[6] In addition, as the December 1989 test of a projected space launch vehicle indicated, it continues to develop longer-range missiles. The arms race is expensive and constitutes a major drain on the treasury. The future of this industry has now been put in some doubt. A war would probably destroy most (although probably not all) of what has been built. A peaceful resolution of the conflict would surely bring intense international pressure for an arms control regime designed to cripple its development. Iraq's oil revenues will continue to make it a market arms merchants are not likely to ignore. In particular, Eastern European countries, in need of oil, may be interested in barter agreements exchanging arms and technology for oil. This factor may enable Iraq to elude constraints. However, Baghdad will face an acute choice between "guns" and "butter" as it seeks to rebuild its economy with fewer resources than it had prior to its Kuwaiti venture.

Iraq will also have to demobilize a large standing army—over a million troops. Even before the crisis, Iraq had some difficulty in absorbing soldiers demobilized in the aftermath of the Iran-Iraq war. A year after the cease-fire, about 200,000 to 300,000 (not an insignificant number) Iraqi troops were sent home; subsequent clashes between Iraqi and Egyptian workers indicated that the regime had problems in absorbing the ex-soldiers into the civilian economy.[7] Demobilization is, in turn, dependent on the pace of economic growth, not in high technology, but in labor-intensive industry.

Agriculture

If Iraq should shift its priorities away from military industries, what are the prospects for increased productivity in Iraq's non-oil sectors—especially agriculture and industry? Much will depend on political management and the regime's orientation, but based on past performance, the answers are not very promising.

Increased self-sufficiency in agriculture is a goal that has long eluded the government. A substantial portion of Iraq's foreign exchange is spent on food imports. In 1958, Iraq imported little food and exported some grain; by the early 1980s, food constituted 15 percent of all its imports.[8] The need to improve agricultural productivity and reduce agricultural imports impelled the government to move furthest and fastest with privatization in agriculture. State farms have been completely dismantled, and some experimentation has occurred with the removal of price controls on fruits and vegetables. Although these may have spurred production of some crops, improvements in overall productivity are likely to be limited. At least four major constraints limit agricultural productivity in Iraq:

First is water limitation. Turkey has started work on the giant Southeast Anatolian Project comprising thirteen hydroelectric and irrigation schemes on the upper reaches of the Euphrates and the Tigris. If the scheme moves ahead as scheduled (it is by no means certain that it will), Iraq's share of Euphrates waters could be reduced by one-third to one-half of the present volume by the mid-1990s.[9] Turkish utilization of the Tigris will probably not impact on Iraq for at least ten to twenty years, however. Iraq has also begun construction of canals and hydroelectric systems designed to divert Tigris waters into Euphrates channels to cover gaps in the Euphrates flow. Regardless of these schemes, however, the overall amount of irrigation water Iraq is likely to receive will diminish substantially.

A second constraint on agricultural productivity lies in the marginal productivity of soil in the south, where overirrigation and intensive agriculture over the centuries have depleted soil resources.[10] It would take enormous expenditures ($30,000 per hectare) to restore this area to fertility, and even that would produce only marginal benefits for the cereal culture that is the mainstay of the area.[11]

A third constraint is rural-to-urban migration. In 1950, roughly 70 percent of Iraq's population was rural; today 70 percent is urban. Some 30 percent of the work force is engaged in agriculture but produces only 15 percent of the GDP.[12]

To repopulate rural areas, Egyptians were encouraged to settle in Iraq and purchase land. Although the per capita income of farmers has improved, maldistribution of wealth in Iraq is still marked, with rural areas receiving poorer housing, schooling, health care, and other amenities. These factors tend to keep agricultural productivity low and push farmers into cities.

The fourth constraint is more intangible. Most of the farm population in Iraq has been tribal (rather than agrarian) in origin; Iraqis are not natural cultivators. Furthermore, recent urbanization has accustomed the population to a different and easier life-style. As a result, few Iraqis seem willing to challenge the desert.

Industry

What of industrial sectors? Before the war with Iran, non-oil industry produced only 7 to 8 percent of GNP and employed only about 10 percent of the population.[13] What are the prospects for growth in a postcrisis environment? Much will depend on a peaceful solution to the crisis. A war could destroy much of Iraq's industrial underpinning, especially its communications and transport sector and its power grid. It could also deplete manpower resources, possibly severely, setting Iraq's industrial sector back at least a decade.

A peaceful solution will make it possible for Iraq to build on its previous base despite some boycott-induced setbacks. These will be mainly felt in lack of spare parts, degradation of infrastructure due to lack of maintenance, and depletion of the skilled—mainly foreign—work force responsible for highly technical operations. Prior to the crisis, Iraq's industrial priority was heavy industry and export-oriented production. Production of its petrochemical, iron, steel, and fertilizer plants in the Basra area was being restored. Expansion of oil refineries and petrochemical plants, new truck, bus, and auto factories, and road and port expansion were all planned at the time of the invasion, although many of these projects had been temporarily put on hold due to lack of financing.[14] Both in civilian and military sectors Iraq has been moving toward building a high technology industrial base, including the development of skilled manpower.

The weakest link in Iraq's industrial development is light and intermediate industry aimed at import substitution. Such industries would broaden its industrial base, diversify the economy, reduce its dependence on foreign exchange, and, above all, help create jobs. While Iraq will probably make some progress toward these goals in the future, unless there is a change of direction in Baghdad, the progress is not likely to be substantial. Past performance, particularly during the oil boom of the late 1970s, when funds were available, showed little growth in these sectors.[15] Such industries are not visible symbols of power and prestige and count for little in international circles—factors that have always weighed heavily with the regime. There is another reason import substitution has not grown much: It is precisely in this area that privatization has the most to offer, but substantial private investment in industry requires a secure economic environment and a light government hand, circumstances that have not existed in Ba'thist Iraq. Without these features, private and mixed-sector enterprises are likely to languish.

Iraq will also face another constraint on its near-term economic development, one with social and political consequences as well—an inflation rate that was already 40 percent prior to the invasion.[16] Inflation has skyrocketed since the boycott, which has created an even greater shortage of goods. The Iraqi dinar has lost much of its value on world markets. Inflation, if it reaches critical proportions, could have a devastating effect on the middle class in Iraq, with significant social consequences for any regime. Such inflation could prove difficult to bring under control in a postcrisis environment.

How Iraq develops in a postcrisis environment will depend on the government in power and the direction it takes. If the Ba'th is still governing, if much of the economy remains in government hands, if it is driven by military requirements and a military economy that pulls investment away from the civilian sector, if most investment goes into large showcase projects rather than those that involve small and middling entrepreneurs, Iraq could end up with an economy based more than ever on oil and foreign markets and an overblown military that brings prestige but little prosperity. This option would have significant foreign policy ramifications (as discussed below). If, on the other hand, this government—or a new one—reorients the economy away from military expenditures and into medium and light industry, if it frees up the private sector and encourages outside help, Iraq has the potential for healthy economic development and diversification away from oil.

The Boycott Legacy

Even with more enlightened management, however, Iraq will have to confront serious economic problems resulting from the crisis. Following the international embargo joined by most of Iraq's creditors, Iraq canceled its debts, an act likely to have serious implications for its creditworthiness. Bankers may well be unwilling to advance loans and governments to guarantee them without a radical change in Iraq's fiscal policy, including financial disclosure and adherence to other internationally accepted banking standards. Even with changed behavior, Iraq may have to make restitution for the canceled loans or face prohibitively high premiums on new credit. A stagnating economy may also make Iraq a less attractive place for investment.

A second liability Iraq may face is the difficulty in acquiring foreign skills and technology. Iraq's treatment of foreign technicians as hostages has created widespread antipathy toward the regime, an antipathy likely to linger for a long time. Recruitment of qualified foreign personnel—still needed at top- and middle-management levels in Baghdad—is probably going to be difficult. Even more critical will be Iraq's access to Western technology. If Saddam Hussein and his regime remain, and if his military priorities are maintained, restrictions on arms transfers and on dual-use technology are likely. Without a change of regime or, at the least, a decided change in direction in Baghdad, these factors will hamper Iraq's postcrisis economic and technological development.

Domestic Politics

Two key questions must be asked of Iraq's domestic politics in the wake of the Gulf crisis. The first concerns the regime's survival. Is it likely to remain in power in a postcrisis environment, and, if it does, what sort of a regime is it likely to be? The second question concerns replacement of the regime. If it does not remain in power, what is likely to take its place, and with what implications for Iraq's stability?

The survival of the regime will depend on the outcome of the crisis and Saddam's own actions. Survival is more likely under a scenario of peaceful withdrawal than that of war. Even with a peaceful solution, there are outcomes that could make Saddam's longevity more, rather than less, secure. His lease on political life would be higher under a negotiated settlement under which he was able to gain some concessions than if he withdrew unilaterally and totally. If Saddam can keep some territory, such as the "tail" of the Rumailah oil field lying inside Kuwait and the islands of Warbah and Bubayan, he will be able to claim some tangible gains. A total withdrawal without any gains will put him at higher risk. For a regime that depends on a large psychological dose of "awe" to remain in control, over time, this could prove fatal. Whatever the rhetoric from Baghdad, such an outcome would be regarded as a failure at home and Saddam's competence and credibility as a leader severely questioned, particularly among the military on whom he relies for support.

Regime Survival

However, one should be wary of underestimating Saddam's resourcefulness or his capacity for survival. On at least two previous occasions—in 1975 when he made concessions on the Shatt al-Arab to avoid a war with the shah he would have lost, and in 1982, when he withdrew his troops to the international frontier after a resounding defeat by Iran—he has found ways to explain adversity to his people and survive.

If the regime of Saddam survives, it will be for several reasons. First, he has consistently demonstrated a will and a capacity to rule. After his more than two decades in power, half behind the scenes and half as president, most Iraqis find it difficult to conceive of Iraq without him. Indeed, the most notable feature of his presidency (assumed in 1979) has been an unprecedented concentration of power in his hands and a control over his population that is relatively unparalleled in the Third World. Second, Saddam has behind him a finely honed police state apparatus that he has shown himself willing to use, selectively but ruthlessly. Third, opposition organizations of all political orientations—communist, Kurdish, Shiite, and dissident pro-Syrian Ba'thists—have all been brutally but successfully eliminated inside Iraq. The leadership of these movements, as well as most of their supporters (numbering in the tens of thousands) are in exile in Turkey, Iran, Syria, and Europe. Last, most Iraqis have become so accustomed to Saddam's rule that few think in terms of replacement, although more may do so after the Kuwaiti venture.

There may also be some positive reasons Saddam may remain. He has succeeded in making himself the embodiment of some important Arab aspirations—a just settlement of the Palestinian problem, Arab independence from foreign control, and resentment of the wealth and corruption of the Gulf ruling families. The military, although indignant over concessions to Iran, may take consolation at retaining positions as the leading military power in the Gulf. And Iraq's ample oil resources will provide Iraq with an avenue to a better social and economic future, even if it may have to be postponed. Most Iraqis will recall the rapid economic and social progress made in the late 1970s under Saddam's leadership, with a relatively good record for wide distribution of wealth, the spread of education and wealth to rural areas, upward social mobility for the underprivileged, and a relative absence of corruption. They will not want to jeopardize this potential future through the political instability that would follow Saddam's overthrow.

If the regime survives, what sort of a future does the county face? In assessing Iraq's future, several developments bear watching. The most important is a generational change certain to culminate in the decade of the 1990s. Three distinct generations of leadership can already be identified. The first is Saddam's generation, the one in power. The formative years of this group were the late 1950s and 1960s, which were spent mainly underground in conspiratorial revolutionary activity. The harsh experience of these years, the constant instability engendered by military coups, and habitual use of violence to achieve political ends has shaped their outlook.[17] And it is this outlook of suspicion and distrust, and of a desire for stability at all costs, that has created the police state apparatus that is the backbone of the system. Time has mellowed these men, and the apparatus has become more sophisticated and less intrusive, but it is unlikely to disappear if this generation is maintained in power.

A second generation of leaders is already moving into positions of authority. These are men who came to maturity just before or after the party took power in 1968. Their memory of the pre-Ba'thist period is dim, and they take the stability of the regime for granted. Their most significant experience has been the peace, prosperity, and social mobility of the later 1970s, to which they would like to return. This group has greatly benefited from party rule—in education, upward social mobility, and in political privileges. Although their generation appears to accept the broad parameters of party ideology, its desideratum is pragmatism. They will react harshly to attempts to upset the system but will probably move it in a more pragmatic direction in response to economic and international pressures. Whatever the outcome of this crisis, regardless of the regime in power, this generation will be in control by the end of the decade.

A third generation is waiting in the wings. This is the age group whose most formative years have been spent at the front, or, in the case of women, waiting for their men to come home. Born or reared in the early years of the Ba'thist regime, they have no real memory of pre-Ba'thist Iraq, and their exposure to a non-Iraqi environment is virtually nonexistent.

The views of this generation are difficult to assess. It is possible that these young people have developed a greater sense of patriotism under pressure of war, but they may just as well have come home alienated and bitter over their lost youth. As yet this generation has no stake in the system and will acquire one, if at all, rather later in life. Thus far the war generation has exhibited a strong desire for normalization—marriage, career, and a "peace dividend" in the form of a better standard of living and some measure of freedom, especially the freedom to travel. If the system does not respond to their needs, they could become restive and attracted to ideas emanating from outside, especially those from Eastern Europe. These young people have fought successfully to repel an enemy at great cost to themselves, and they are likely to be far more demanding than their predecessors.

The Shia and the Kurds

The second development to consider in assessing Iraq's future is the issue of ethnic and sectarian integration. Will a weakened regime be able to control pressures from the Shia and the Kurds? In the event of a war, or a regime change, what role might they play?

The Iran-Iraq war provided several insights on the issue of ethnic and sectarian integration. On the positive side, the conflict went a long way toward laying Iraq's Shiite problem to rest. Shiite willingness to fight, with relatively few defections, has proved their basic loyalty to the Iraqi state, although they remain dissatisfied with their share of political power and social status.

In the past decade, however, the regime has taken several steps to remedy this situation. First, it has spent development funds in Shiite areas—on roads, schools, hospitals, and shrines and mosques. The massive rebuilding of Basra was, in part, a commitment to the Shia.

Second, the regime has made considerable strides in bringing Shia into the upper echelons of the political structure. In 1969, a year after the party came to power, there were no Arab Shia on the Revolutionary Command Council (RCC) or the Regional Command. By 1986, between a quarter to a third of the RCC and 44 percent of the Regional Command were Shia, and several of the regional party bureaus were under Shia.[18] Ironically, this trend may be partially offset by Shiite losses in the commercial sphere, which they traditionally dominated. The new moves toward privatization may disproportionately benefit those with regime ties—mainly Sunnis and Tikritis. If this trend continues, the Shia will have yet another cause for alienation.

Third, the regime has gradually shifted its ideological orientation in a direction more compatible with Shiite notions of nationalism. Iraqi patriotism, which appeals to Shia with deep roots in Iraq, has been emphasized; Shiite heroes, such as Ali, have been held up as models, and ancient Mesopotamian themes have reminded both sects of their pride in a common heritage.[19]

Despite these attempts at integration, Shia still have a well-developed minority psychology (despite their majority status), and sectarian bonding plays an important role in their lives. Their continuing marginality to the political process relative to Sunnis will persist in creating alienation among some.[20]

The Kuwait crisis has not been a divisive issue among Shia and Sunnis. Indeed, poor Shia from the southern region were reportedly among those who first went into Kuwait and pillaged, and some may have settled in Kuwait in the wake of the occupation. While they will be the losers in any withdrawal, they are more likely to hold that against the West than the regime. An Iraq greatly weakened as a result of a war would certainly tempt Iran to stir up Shiite sentiments once again, but this will prove difficult to organize from Iran. Iraqi Shia clearly indicated in the war with Iran that they preferred an imperfect Iraqi leadership to one that was Iran-sponsored or committed to Shiite messianism.

No such statement can be made about the Kurds. The Iran-Iraq war revived a Kurdish separatist rebellion, dormant since 1975. However, the two major Kurdish groups opposing the government, the Kurdish Democratic party (KDP), under Mas'ud Barzani, and the Patriotic Union of Kurdistan (PUK), under Jalal Talabani, have been so badly weakened that their ability to mount a serious opposition movement against the government inside Iraq is highly doubtful. By most estimates, including those of the Kurds themselves, it would take the best part of a decade to rebuild their forces and renew the struggle.

It is difficult to tell what the long-term outcome will be of Iraq's use of chemical weapons against the Kurdish population. Iraq's draconian resettlement measures, which have removed at least 500,000 Kurds from villages and towns bordering Iran to newly built settlements away from the frontier, have prevented smuggling of arms and other material from Iran but may have created new pockets of hostile Kurds inside of Iraq.[21] At the same time, the government is encouraging Arabs to settle in the north, the better to scramble a population that in some northern cities and towns is already mixed. Whether this effort will be successful remains to be seen. For the short to medium term, it has given Iraq firm control over its Kurdish border with Iran for the first time since the founding of the state. The reputed use of CW against Kurdish rebels in the north, however, has resulted in over 60,000 refugees who fled to Turkey. They and other Kurds situated in Europe constitute a permanently hostile group of exiles now organized as an increasingly effective pressure group against the Baghdad government.

Despite their setbacks, the Kurdish leadership has announced its intention of reviving its movement. Given the social and demographic changes in the north, any future opposition efforts may be urban rather than rural. The middle class is growing in Irbil, Sulaimaniyyah, and Kirkuk, as well as in smaller towns. This class could help dissolve ethnic solidarity in the north, as it has sectarianism among the Shia in the south. Or, alternatively, Kurdish nationalism could unite with the middle-class desires for more freedom and greater participation in government to give the regime continued trouble.

Any instability in a postcrisis Iraq would give the Kurds added impetus for unrest, although under the present regime that would be very difficult to carry out. A war, particularly one that resulted in severe damage and erosion of government institutions, would unquestionably provide the Kurds with an opportunity to be more assertive against the central government. Any new government, military or otherwise, would have to take the Kurds into account.

Regime Change

Despite his impressive survival record, Saddam has put his future at risk in the Kuwait crisis. Withdrawal would weaken his regime to an undetermined degree. To secure Kuwait, he has made concessions to Iran on the Shatt al-Arab, won after eight years of war and over 350,000 casualties. Withdrawal from Kuwait, especially complete withdrawal, could leave Iraq with the long-term economic costs of a foolish venture with nothing to show in return. Even if Iraq should acquire some territory from Kuwait, many Iraqis will question whether such concessions could not have been obtained by other means. Under changed circumstances, some individuals or groups may become emboldened to challenge Saddam.

In the event of war, the chances of the regime's survival are slim. A limited war that forces Iraqi military withdrawal from Kuwait but does not destroy the military could leave Saddam as the only man capable of rescuing the situation, but his legitimacy would be so damaged that his tenure would probably be short. A more devastating war, with heavy casualties and destruction of Iraqi facilities, would almost certainly take the regime with it, if not as a direct military casualty, then at the hands of some members of the Iraqi establishment or an irate population.

If the Saddam Hussein regime should be overthrown, what is likely to take its place? Much would depend on who initiated the change and under what circumstances. A war-induced change is likely to be more radical than one in peacetime. Because of the absence of alternative groups or structures, the most likely replacement to Saddam, should he be deposed, would be a member of the inner circle of Tikritis surrounding him or, more probable in the case of a coup, a dissident member of the Ba'th party or the military or a combination of both. Any such combination is likely to continue Iraq's current domestic policy—that of a secular, modernizing state based on a mix of Iraqi and Arab nationalism, although alternative leadership is more likely to have a stronger mix of pragmatists and possible reformers. Any successor regime, however, is bound to be weaker, and a struggle for power could well ensue. In such circumstances, the army could be expected to play a larger role in politics, as it attempts to hold the regime together, avoid political instability, and maintain the political integrity of the country.

If such a regime does emerge, it is likely to have the potential for a new direction. It might bring more pragmatists and technocrats into the inner circle, it could open the country to more outside influences, and it could strengthen rudimentary parliamentary institutions, which are at present in existence but ineffectual in the absence of free elections and candidate selection. However, any new regime is also likely to bring instability, since no successor to Saddam could replace his iron grip on the country. Indeed, if the military should succeed to power, the country could go through a prolonged period of political struggle, similar to that between 1958 and 1968, when four different changes of regime took place. In this case, Iraq's institutions, even its national cohesion, could be gradually eroded.

In the event of a war with substantial damage to the country, there is more likelihood of political upheaval. In this case, the past two decades of Ba'thist rule are likely to weigh heavily on the future. Lack of an organized opposition or an alternative cadre to take power, the absence of open discourse or habits of compromise among political groups, unrequited nationalist claims from Kurds, hostile neighbors in Iran and Syria, and a demonstrated inability of opposition groups outside the country to coalesce suggest that Iraq would slip into a period of political instability and weakness. Renewed army rule, possibly with considerable repression, and a revival of the Kurdish rebellion would be the probable outcomes.

Iraq's Foreign Policy

The greatest uncertainty of all in the aftermath of the Gulf crisis is Iraq's future foreign policy. Much of its international behavior during the past decade—its military aggression, its attempt to impose its leadership on its neighbors, and its inherent reliance on the use of force, are due to the ambitions and modus operandi of one man, Saddam Hussein. If he should go, these attributes of Iraqi policy would probably go with him. Few successors are likely to have such grandiose visions or, more important, the power or following to carry them out. But what if Saddam withdraws from Kuwait with his forces, and his political fortunes, intact? What can the region expect? Or alternatively, what if a war removes Saddam and destroys much of Iraq's military potential, leaving it weak and unable to defend itself adequately?

A war that substantially damaged Iraq's physical plant, defeated its army, and caused high human casualties is Iraq's most ominous future. Such an eventuality would not only leave Iraq with little or no international influence for much of the decade, it would also have an incalculable impact on its domestic stability. A defeated army, or one that is greatly depleted, would weaken the one institution most capable of preserving Iraq as a nation-state. If the war so devastated Iraq's army that it could no longer adequately perform domestic security functions, Iraq could slip into a situation similar to that in Lebanon.

A devastating war would also produce a regional power imbalance; it would leave Israel as the regional superpower and Iran with the potential to emerge, if unchecked in the course of the decade, as Persian Gulf hegemon. Such a situation would also leave Iraq prey to the machinations of its powerful neighbors, Syria, Iran, and possibly Turkey. All three could exploit Iraq's weakness by interfering in its domestic affairs, Iran among the Shiites, Syria among Ba'thist factions or various Arab nationalist and Kurdish groups. The Turks have unrequited claims to northern Iraq and ties to a minority of Turkish speakers in Kirkuk and northern Iraqi cities. (Turkey is unlikely, however, to stir up trouble among Iraq's ethnic minorities, because such actions could backfire by encouraging ethnic nationalism among its own Kurdish minority.) Lastly, a war that wreaked great destruction on Iraq would cause deep resentment toward the West, especially the United States, setting back US-Iraqi relations for at least another decade in a situation similar to Iran. And a war that greatly weakened Iraq would probably intensify, rather than relieve, Iraq's isolation, the source of much of its current international misadventures.

What of the alternative—a peaceful scenario in which Saddam withdraws from Kuwait and his military survives? Even in this case, Iraq would be in a weakened position and unable to play much of a regional role, at least initially. An international peacekeeping force would likely be left in Kuwait as a tripwire to prevent a repetition of the invasion, and the US military presence in the Gulf would probably remain, though at reduced strength. The international community, led by the United States, would likely attempt some sort of arms control and technology transfer to restrict Iraq's ability to develop weapons of mass destruction, although it is difficult to predict the effectiveness of such measures. Economic plans may also be put into effect to compel Iraq to shift from military to development priorities. These measures, together with a weakened economy and an unsavory international reputation, would inhibit Iraq's ability to play a major regional role, at least in the immediate aftermath of the crisis. But in the longer run, a gradually strengthened Iraq with an enhanced military capacity could emerge to constitute a considerable danger for the region, if unchecked.

All of the problems that beset Iraq prior to the invasion will remain. Iraq's straitened financial situation will make its need for development funds essential. The problems of access to the Gulf will remain to be negotiated with its neighbors, a revived Kuwait and a strengthened Iran. And Saddam's desire to play a dominant role in the Gulf and the Arab world will remain unrequited. Iraq will not only be weakened; it will be frustrated. This combination of factors might lead to a modification of policy, but, based on Saddam's past performance, it is far more likely to result in tensions, instability, and uncertainty.

Iraq and the Gulf

Iraq will have two chief concerns in its Gulf policy: secure access to and eggress from the Gulf, and an oil policy that will yield it high revenues and greater market share. If Saddam remains, a third aim can be added—desire to regain his status as the dominant force in the Persian Gulf and OPEC enforcer. All will be complicated by the crisis and the bitter feelings that will undoubtedly be left between Iraq and the GCC states, especially Kuwait and Saudi Arabia.

Secure access to the Gulf has been a key issue in Iraq's disputes with both Kuwait and Iran. Iraq is not likely to obtain this access through the Shatt al-Arab waterway during the first half of the 1990s. Although Iraq has struck a tentative agreement with Iran over division of the Shatt, the costs and technical difficulties of clearing the Shatt are formidable. Reliable estimates indicate that the task could take from three to five years and cost over $.5 billion.

At the close of the Iran-Iraq war, Iraq had already turned its attention to an alternative route through the Khor Abd Allah waterway, which separates Kuwait from Iraq. This would utilize its other port, Umm Qasr, about 97 kilometers from the Gulf. Before the crisis, efforts were under way to deepen this waterway and to increase the size and capacity of Umm Qasr by adding berths.[22] In time, these additions, together with offshore facilities to handle oil shipments, might have satisfied most of Iraq's shipping needs, but the need for dredging and expansion is expensive and inconvenient.

Not surprisingly, Iraq's development of Umm Qasr shifted the focus of its concern for Gulf access to Kuwait. Iraq not only had a boundary dispute with Kuwait over the Khor Abd Allah channel (Iraq wanted the border drawn on the Kuwaiti shore; Kuwait, in the center of the channel), but, in addition, Iraq wanted possession of two Kuwaiti islands at the entrance of the channel, Warbah and Bubayan, the better to protect Umm Qasr and its offshore facilities. The two islands would give Iraq direct access to the Gulf. Kuwait's adamant refusal to hand over the islands was one of the causes of the Iraqi invasion. Possession and fortification of these islands would also enhance Iraq's capacity to build a bluewater navy, and allow it to bring into the Gulf several vessels, built for Iraq by European companies and berthed outside the Gulf. If the outcome of the Kuwait crisis fails to resolve Iraq's problem of access to the Gulf, relations with a restored Kuwait and the rest of the GCC will remain very contentious. Iraq's desire to possess the two islands is an issue that will also poison relations with Iran, which is adamantly opposed to Iraq's territorial expansion into the Gulf and to any development of an Iraqi navy at the head of the Gulf.

Iraq is also likely to have contentious relations with the Arab Gulf states over oil production and pricing. To a large extent, Iraq's invasion of Kuwait was a struggle over control of the Gulf's rich oil resources, and this struggle is likely to be even more intense in the aftermath of the conflict. Under any conceivable outcome to the crisis, Iraq's economic needs will be greater than those preceding it. As a result, it will probably want to force both higher oil prices and a greater market share. If, in the aftermath of the crisis, Western troops remain in the Arabian peninsula, consuming countries may well be accused by Iraq and other Arabs of manipulating oil production and prices for their own benefit; indeed, this was precisely Iraq's chief accusation against Kuwait and the UAE before its occupation of Kuwait. Iraq claimed that they were clients of the United States and the West, overproducing to satisfy Western consumers and to weaken Iraq's economy. How much influence Iraq retains in OPEC will depend on how well it comes out of the crisis. In a peaceful solution that enables Iraq eventually to increase its oil production capacity to 5 million barrels a day, it could end up with considerable ability to use its oil capacity to its advantage. In a war scenario, Iraq may need a decade to rebuild its capacity. And in any case, it will meet stiff competition from its competitors and its previous adversaries, Iran, Saudi Arabia, and a reconstituted Kuwait.

Iraq and Iran

Iran will remain a primary concern of Baghdad despite its apparent willingness to settle the Iran-Iraq war, mainly on Iran's terms. Iraq still greatly fears Iran's potential hegemony over the Gulf and a rebuilding of its military capacity, although this still seems at least a decade away. Indeed, it was against this possibility that Iraq developed its military arsenal—the chemical weapons and missiles and its experimentation with biological and nuclear weapons. Curbing Iraq's ability to undertake these programs and forcing a reduction in the size of its military, whether through war or through arms control measures, will be viewed with alarm in Baghdad. Iraq is unlikely to willingly accede to such measures without a regionwide security arrangement that includes Israel.

Baghdad will also be suspicious of attempts by the GCC states, the United States, and the Soviet Union to develop closer ties with Iran. Baghdad's exchange of ambassadors with Iran in 1990 was more than an attempt to patch up a quarrel; it was also a means to check the growing rapprochement between Iran and the Arab Gulf states.

At the same time, Iraq and Iran will be able to make common cause on two issues of concern to both—removal of the Western (mainly US) military presence from the Gulf, and higher oil prices. But commonality on these two issues will not be sufficient to overcome mutual animosity and rivalry between the two contenders for dominance of the Gulf, which can be expected to persist through the decade.

The Fertile Crescent

Iraq's occupation of Kuwait has sundered the Arab Cooperation Council (consisting of Iraq, Egypt, Jordan, and Yemen) and set back attempts by pro-Western countries, like Jordan, to bring Iraq into a pro-Western Arab constellation. Indeed, Iraq has turned two of these three countries, Jordan and Yemen, in a more anti-American direction. Polarization of the Fertile Crescent countries is more likely than coalescence in the wake of the crisis. Egypt is now locked in bitter rivalry with Iraq for leadership of the Arab world, a rivalry likely to be infused, on the Iraqi side, with anti-Western tensions as a result of the crisis. Indeed, Saddam has used the crisis to generate considerable popular support among Arab populations in other countries for his confrontation with the United States and with Israel. His ties with Jordan and the Palestinians, some of whom have settled in Kuwait, will probably outlast the crisis; indeed, given Jordan's support for Iraq and King Hussein's attempts to mediate the crisis, these links will probably be strengthened, if Saddam remains. So, too, will rivalry with Egypt and with Syria for leadership in the region. In this rivalry, Iraq under Saddam may assert itself as the leader of a more radical, anti-US, anti-Israeli movement building on some of the sources of support it has received from the populations of Jordan, Syria, Yemen, and North Africa. If Saddam remains, he is likely to continue his pose as a champion of Arab nationalist forces standing against Israel and the imperialists. If Saddam's position is weakened by the crisis, his potential for mobilization of this element may be reduced. But this is one area where he may lash out at the West, if he should be tightly constrained by economic forces in the aftermath of the crisis.

Iraq and Israel

As a result of the Kuwait crisis, Iraq has emerged as a champion of Palestinian rights and has already received credit in the Arab world for having pushed this issue to the front of the international agenda. Saddam skillfully used the issue in an attempt to drive wedges in the Western alliance and the Arab coalition allied with the West. There is little doubt that he has succeeded, in the minds of Arabs and possibly of Westerners, in linking his withdrawal from Kuwait to Israeli withdrawal from the West Bank and Gaza and Syrian withdrawal from Lebanon.

In the course of the Iran-Iraq war, Iraq made substantial public shifts in its position on the Arab-Israeli issue. In a celebrated interview with US Representative Stephen Solarz in 1982 (published in 1983), Saddam Hussein stated that Iraq would accept any solution to the problem acceptable to the frontline states and to the PLO.[23] As the decade opens, Iraqis as a whole genuinely seem to want to put the Palestinian problem behind them, although on terms satisfactory to the PLO. Anti-Israeli rhetoric and intensity of feeling, however, have always been stronger in Baghdad than in most other Arab states, in part because of Iraq's greater distance from Israel and in part because it has never had to face an Israeli army on its territory. However, it is unclear whether this moderate position will remain in the aftermath of the crisis, particularly in the event of war.

A far more serious Iraqi-Israeli conflict looms on the horizon as a result of the arms race in the area. Iraq's development of the Third World's largest stock of chemical weapons, its possible development of biological weapons, its technological breakthrough on missile development, and, most recently, increased evidence that it may be in the preliminary stages of a nuclear weapons program have all become extremely worrisome to Israel, the United States, and the European community. While Iraq has denied the nuclear allegations, its purchase of dual-use technology and other material (such as the detonators it was caught shipping illegally from the United States in March 1990) suggests that it may be taking steps in this direction. How far it can go without outside technical help and without clandestine sources of weapons-grade nuclear material, and how fast it can acquire the technical proficiencies to develop a nuclear weapon, particularly in an international environment hostile to such activities, are questions that cannot be answered here.[24] There is little doubt, however, that should Iraq cross the threshold of a viable nuclear weapons program, it would dramatically alter the balance of power in the Middle East, especially against Israel. It is highly likely that Israel would seek to disrupt the program either by covert action or by another air strike. The latter may now be more difficult, as Iraqi facilities are better protected. Moreover, such an event would probably generate an Iraqi response—as the previous strike did not. Given Iraq's recent statements that it would respond to an Israeli attack and its capacity to reach Israeli territory with missiles and possibly with CW warheads, this eventuality must be taken seriously. Despite Arab unease at Baghdad's military breakthroughs, there is widespread resentment of the military asymmetry in the Middle East and the fact that Israel's nuclear arsenal is accepted by the West whereas similar Arab developments are regarded as proscribed, thus prohibiting the development of genuine parity. In any event, the brinkmanship of this scenario would generate severe tensions in the area, damaging US-Iraqi and probably US-Arab relations.

Iraq's chemical weapons and its developing missile capacity are also disturbing to Israel. Israel's main fear is of a chemical weapons attack on its civilian population. Iraq has forcefully stated that it would retaliate if attacked by Israel with chemical weapons. Iraq's missile program is potentially more threatening to Israel largely because of the warheads it can accommodate. Iraq may develop the capacity to put a rocket into space before the end of the decade (although these programs will be set back because of Iraq's economic difficulties). Among other outcomes, this would give it the potential to orbit a communications satellite for intelligence purposes and to carry warheads for distances of over 1,000 kilometers.[25] If it is allowed unfettered development and it can generate the resources from oil revenues, Iraq can be expected to increase the accuracy of its missiles, to decrease its dependence on outside suppliers of technology, and to wed its missiles to chemical agents and possibly nuclear warheads.

The Kuwait crisis and the possibility of war with Iraq has intensified the stakes in this arms race. Israel has let it be known that it regards Iraq's nuclear potential and its missiles and weapons of mass destruction as a greater threat to regional security than Iraq's occupation of Kuwait. Israel favors the removal of Saddam Hussein and his arsenal as a solution to the crisis. If both Saddam and the arsenal survive the crisis, this issue is likely to dominate Israeli thinking and to affect Israeli-Iraqi relations and Israeli-US relations. Indeed, the issue may well bring an Israeli-Iraqi military confrontation closer. The United States seems certain to favor measures that constrain Iraq's capacity to develop these weapons in the aftermath of the crisis, but unless these measures are coupled with a regionwide security system that includes Israel's nuclear arsenal, Iraq may be unwilling to cooperate. Moreover, there will be widespread resentment in the region over unilateral measures to curb Iraq's development of such weapons. With Iraq's oil resources and a European recession looming on the horizon, it may be difficult to enforce such an agreement. Thus, this issue promises to be one of the most controversial of all in any scenario that involves Iraq's peaceful withdrawal from Kuwait.

Iraq's Relations with the United States and the Soviet Union

In any postcrisis environment, US-Iraqi relations are likely to remain strained at best and may become decidedly hostile. Much will depend on how the crisis is settled and on whether Saddam remains in power or is replaced by a regime more moderate in tone. US leadership in opposing Iraqi occupation of Kuwait is likely to leave a bitter legacy, which will only worsen in the event of war.

Gorbachev's more ambiguous stand toward Iraq in the crisis may result in an Iraqi "tilt" toward the Soviet Union, particularly since a weakened Soviet

Union can constitute no threat to Iraq. Iraq is also likely to strengthen ties with select European countries, especially France and Germany. Unless there is a profound upheaval in Baghdad, closer ties with the United States are difficult to imagine. Meanwhile, Iraq, like other Arab countries, will continue to develop independent links and ties with Europe and Japan and among the new Eastern bloc countries in need of the oil that Iraq may be in a position to supply, in return for breaking out of its isolation.

Notes

The views and findings in this chapter are those of the author and should not be construed as representing the policy or position of the National Defense University, the Department of Defense, or the US government.

1. For an analysis of Iraq's situation prior to the crisis, see Phebe Marr, "Iraq: A Brutal Invasion and an Uncertain Future," in *Current History*, January 1991.

2. Fereidun Fesharaki et al., "OPEC and Lower Oil Prices: Impacts on Production Capacity, Export Refining and Trade Balances," in E. Stanley Tucker, "Oil Exporting Countries: The Impact of Lower Prices," *Petroleum Economist*, vol. 56, no. 3 (March 1989): 79. These figures, substantiated by other sources, put Iraqi production second to Saudi Arabia.

3. *Middle East Economic Survey* (MEES) vol. 32, no. 32 (May 15, 1989): A2.

4. Charles T. Maxwell, "The Price of Crude Oil Is Bound to Come Down," C. J. Lawrence, *Energy Projections* no. 1255 (New York: C. J. Lawrence, Morgen Grenfeld, Inc. November 14, 1990).

5. Vahan Zanoyan, "Oil Markets and Financial Conditions in Iraq," paper presented at the United States–Iraq Business Forum, Washington, DC, November 14, 1989, p. 11. These and other figures cited here must be treated with caution; all are only approximations, as Iraq has rejected complete financial disclosure.

6. In March 1990, four Iraqis and the export manager of a London-based front company were indicted in San Diego for conspiring to smuggle forty detonation capacitors, made to specifications that would enable them to be used for nuclear weapons, to Iraq *(Washington Post*, March 30, 1990, p. A6). The Iraqis denied their intent to use the capacitors for nuclear weapons, but this episode and other evidence that Iraq was attempting to purchase technology for such a future use left strong suspicions that Iraq did, in fact, aim at a nuclear weapons program.

7. In November 1989, reports surfaced in Baghdad and Cairo that thousands—perhaps tens of thousands—of Egyptian workers were leaving Baghdad, and a large number (102, according to the November 8 issue of the Cairo daily *al-Akhbar*) were killed in Baghdad under circumstances yet to be explained. At least one riot involving Iraqis and Egyptians was reported in Baghdad, but much of the pressure to leave came from harassment, especially as Baghdad tightened up on remittances Egyptians could take out of the country. *Al-Akhbar*, November 8, 1989; *Al-Ahram* (international edition), November 7, 1989; George Moffett III, "Strains Appear in Egyptian Ties," *Christian Science Monitor*, January 17, 1990, p. 4.

8. Phebe Marr, *The Modern History of Iraq* (Boulder, CO: Westview, 1985), p. 259. In 1988, US credits for the export of agricultural products to Iraq approximated $1 billion. US Department of Commerce, "Foreign Economic Trends and Their Implications for the United States," (Washington: GPO, January 1989), p. 12.

9. Philip Robins, "Tug-of-War over the Euphrates," *Christian Science Monitor*, March 12, 1990, p. 18; J. A. Allan, "Water Resources in the Middle East" (London: Arab Research Centre, October 1989), p. 3. The maximum decline will come in the mid-

1990s when the dam is filling.

10. Keith McLachlan maintains that Iraq "contains only small proportions of rich, stable and productive land and very high proportions of varieties of marginal, degraded and uncultivated cultivable land. What is more, the surface area of productive land is diminishing as a result of over optimistic attempts at irrigation on the extensive margin." Keith McLachlan, "Iraq, Problems of Regional Development," in *The Integration of Modern Iraq*, ed. Abbas Kellidar (New York: St. Martin's Press, 1979), p. 188.

11. J. A. Allan, "The Agricultural Sector in Iraq," paper presented at the RIIA Conference, "Iraq in the 1990s," London, March 8, 1990, p. 1.

12. Ibid.

13. Marr, *Modern History of Iraq*, pp. 264–267.

14. MEES 32, 32: A3–4: Jonathon Crusoe, "The Prospects for Industry," paper presented at the RIIA Conference, "Iraq in the 1990s," London, March 8, 1990.

15. Marr, *Modern History of Iraq*.

16. Simon Henderson, "Iraq: New Directions in Economic Policy," paper presented at the RIIA Conference, "Iraq in the 1990s," London, March 8, 1990, p. 6.

17. Between 1958 and 1968 there were four different changes of regime and many more attempted but unsuccessful coups. The last coup brought the Ba'thists to power in July 1968.

18. Amazia Baram, "The Ruling Political Elite in Ba'thist Iraq, 1968–1986," *International Journal of Middle East Studies* (IJMES) vol. 121, no. 4 (November 1989): 472–475.

19. Phebe Marr, "Iraq," in *Ideology and Power in the Middle East*, eds. Peter J. Chelkowski and Robert J. Pranger (Durham, NC: Duke University Press, 1988), pp. 207–208.

20. Chibli Mallat, "The Shias," paper presented at the RIIA Conference, "Iraq in the 1990s," London, March 8, 1990. See also Chibli Mallat, "Iraq," in *The Politics of Islamic Revivalism*, ed. Shireen Hunter (Bloomington: Indiana University Press, 1988).

21. These figures, taken from the State Department's *Human Rights Report, 1989*, are cited in Caryle Murphy, "Iraqi Leader Presses Drive for Regional Dominance," *Washington Post*, March 23, 1990, p. A-16.

22. MEES, 32, 32: A1–2.

23. Frederick W. Axelgard, *U.S.-Arab Relations: The Iraqi Dimension* (Jacksonville, IL: National Council of US-Arab Relations, 1985), pp. 8–9.

24. Most estimates place Iraq's capability to obtain a nuclear weapon in a range of the middle to late 1990s.

25. In December 1989 Iraq conducted an experimental test of what it claimed to be the first stage of a rocket capable of lifting a satellite into orbit, but it is still some way from achieving that aim. According to published reports, Iraq has enhanced the range of its Scud B missiles from 300 to 600 and now 900 kilometers. Upgrading has been achieved by "adding fuel, extending the missile fuselage, reducing warhead size and strapping on booster rockets." Michael Nacht, "Cold War: The Arms Race Isn't Over Yet," *Washington Post*, April 15, 1990, p. D-4.

5
Arms and the Gulf: The Gulf Regional Arms Race to the Turn of the Century

Michael Collins Dunn

All wars end, and generals set about preparing for the next war usually by planning to refight the last one. But the cease-fire in the Gulf war was followed quickly by a general turning of Western attention away from the Persian Gulf. Only months after US naval forces were directly engaged with the Iranian navy, the United States and its allies began to draw down their forces in the Gulf; policymakers seemed to assume that the war was over, the threat had been removed, and now everyone could safely go home. To some extent this reflected an eagerness by the smaller Gulf Arab states to see foreign forces removed quickly. But it also reflected a sort of wishful thinking, that the nightmare of war in the oil fields had finally passed and that now attention could be redirected elsewhere and the Gulf essentially ignored.

The degree to which such assumptions were merely wishful thinking became forcefully apparent on August 2, 1990, with Iraq's invasion of Kuwait. It was suddenly obvious to all that the Gulf remained a key Western interest, that the security of the oil-producing states was far from assured, and that real threats existed. The unprecedented deployment of a quarter of a million US and allied (including Arab) forces to the Gulf underscored the centrality of Gulf security to any "post-postwar" international order.

As this book was being prepared for press, the ultimate resolution of the Kuwait crisis was uncertain. However, almost any scenario one could imagine leads to the same conclusion: The security of the Gulf will be a critical issue for the world for the rest of the decade, and that security will most probably be assured (or lost) through the balance of military forces and armaments.

The crisis is a reminder that deterrence can fail. It also provided the West with a much needed "reality check" amid the euphoria of the end of the cold war and the dissolution of the Eastern bloc. And it raised the disturbing possibility that while the end of superpower rivalry has meant a reduction in the danger of global war, it has also removed some traditional constraints on regional aggressors and local military powers. Once, the Iraqi dependence on the Soviets as a source of arms would have made the Soviets a restraining influence. In 1990, there was no restraining influence.

The crisis also demonstrated that the new, nonconventional weaponry developed by Iraq during the war with Iran could even threaten a superpower such as the United States, or at least provide a certain deterrence. The use of missiles against Iran marked a return to missile warfare on a scale unseen since the V-2 barrages of World War II. The low accuracy of Middle Eastern missiles makes them weapons of terror. (Missiles of greater accuracy might decrease the terror factor, since they would be more likely to be dedicated to military targets.) The United States and other allies had to prepare for possible missile and chemical attacks, and this proved a constraining factor. Whatever the fate of the Iraqi government, other potential aggressors will remember that, when missiles and chemical weapons are in the arsenal, even a superpower can be made to take you seriously.

Changes in the Strategic Environment for the 1990s

Recent history has shown that declining oil revenues have far less effect on arms acquisitions than on other budget categories. The already visible trend toward unconventional weapons, particularly chemical weapons and surface-to-surface missiles, might accelerate. First, they work: The Gulf war proved that, although prior to 1988 this did not seem so, and without major new technological breakthroughs in terms of accuracy and size of payload they may not profoundly alter warfare in the region. Second, they are cheap: A missile may cost much more than a bomb, but not more than a frontline bomber combined with the cost of training one or two pilots for several years. If chemical, biological, or nuclear weapons are used, accuracy is not so important.

Iraq's invasion of Kuwait has reshuffled the deck in the Gulf. However the crisis ultimately is resolved, old alliances have crumbled and new ones have been formed. By opening the Pandora's box of redrawing colonial borders, Iraq has introduced a fundamentally destabilizing concept into regional politics. Many old and more recent conflicts—Iran-Iraq, Iraq-Syria, Turkey-Iraq, Saudi Arabia-Yemen, and more—may seek resolution in the context of a broad regional conflict.

Iran has not by any means reconciled itself to peace with Iraq, but it, too, faces other challenges. It could easily find itself drawn at least as an arms supplier into a lingering Afghan war, and its post-cease-fire diplomacy already shows evidence of a new eastward-looking strategy, so that the future of Pakistan could engage it. The disagreements already apparent between Iran's support of several Afghan Shiite groups and Pakistan's backing of the Sunni-dominated Peshawar coalition could prove the seed of greater competition in the future. Iraq's massive superiority in hardware might be destroyed in a general war with the West. But if the Iraqi military can survive the confrontation over Kuwait more or less intact (regardless of what regime is in power in Baghdad), then continued rivalry with Iran seems inevitable. Although Iraq is likely to remain, militarily, the more advanced in the short term, Iran's other challenges and interests could lead to shifts in its military capabilities that might, over the longer term, transform the situation. Thus neither of the recent belligerents will merely be racing with the other but seeking to achieve a deterrent balance against all possible competitors. Each must still watch the other closely but be aware of new challenges on its other flanks.

Syria's efforts to achieve military parity with Israel may provoke an effort by Iraq to achieve parity with Syria (which it would arguably have if Iran were not there).

Saudi Arabia already maintains a two-sea naval strategy. While it cannot realistically hope to be a considerable ground-force power, even with unlimited Pakistani or other foreign brigades, it is already moving rapidly toward becoming a significant regional naval power, and its air force, despite some training problems, has the equipment to become a major force.

There are other potential considerations just over the horizon. India has already shown its interest in projecting power in the Indian Ocean basin. Its interventions in Sri Lanka and the Maldives may seem unimportant to Gulf state interests, but India already has two aircraft carriers (France has only one), long-range reconnaissance and in-flight refueling capabilities, and a naval infantry force that make it a regional power of the first order. Since Pakistan is already very much a Gulf power, the Indo-Pakistani rivalry could cause ripples in the shallow waters of the Gulf.

And the pace of change in the Soviet Union has been so rapid that even the most optimistic (or pessimistic?) forecasters seem to have been overtaken by events. The rise of ethnic nationalism in Azerbaijan, Armenia, Uzbekistan, and potentially other Soviet Asian republics opens up entirely new questions of future interactions in the region. The flux of feeling between Soviet and Afghan Tajiks, Kirghiz, and Uzbeks has already had an apparent result, though evidence is still not fully available. Although the year 2000 may be a bit soon to project some major upheaval in the steppes of central Asia, events already occurring in that region and Soviet Azerbaijan guarantee Iranian engagement and thus reverberate in the rest of the Gulf. Iran, whatever its political stance, may of all the regional countries find itself having to evolve the most multidirectional foreign policy.

Some General Assumptions

For the purposes of this chapter, I have made the following basic assumptions:

1. Geography never changes. Strategic choke points such as the Strait of Bab al-Mandab will forever control access to the Indian Ocean. And because the Indian Ocean is the major link not only between Europe and Japan but also between the eastern and western ports of the USSR, it will remain significant. The growing power of India as a naval force, soon to be a three-carrier navy, will enhance this importance.

2. Access to Gulf oil will remain a fundamental US and Western interest

over the period concerned. This is somehow independent of the price of oil. The Gulf region is still the site of the world's largest proven reserves, and as other oil fields dwindle it will become more important than ever, barring some unexpected new discovery. There may be a brief Western temptation to underrate the importance of Gulf oil because of the availability of oil elsewhere, but any strategist who does not think forward far enough to see the importance of the Gulf as an oil source in the next century is not doing a good job. (In other words, it will remain a fundamental US interest: The question is only whether the United States realizes this.)

3. The Iran-Iraq war of 1980–1988 and the confrontation resulting from the Iraqi invasion of Kuwait in 1990 have assured that all states of the region will seek to accelerate military buildup against any future aggression. Even if Iraq were to have its military capabilities destroyed by Western attack, Iran would remain as a potential aggressor. States such as Saudi Arabia have now seen clearly that dependence on a few prestige systems is no substitute for the building up of significant ground forces.

4. Because the Kuwaiti incident has reminded the Gulf states that their very survival may be at stake, the price of oil will not be a major impediment to arms acquisition. In the late 1980s, low oil prices did not significantly impede arms acquisitions, so the higher prices already evident in the 1990s are unlikely to prove much of an obstacle.

5. The major unpredictable element as of the autumn of 1990 was the outcome of the confrontation between Iraq and the rest of the world over the occupation of Kuwait. Potential scenarios range from the destruction of Iraq as a regional power to the collapse of the monarchies of the Gulf. For the purposes of this chapter, it has been assumed that there will be no fundamental revolutionary change in Saudi Arabia, that Iraq will at least survive as a nation-state with significant military capabilities, and that while there may be a change of regime in Iran, there will be no fundamental collapse of the Iranian polity. But in a broad-based, regional war with external participation, all these assumptions could be swept away.

Iran is almost certain to remain a destabilizing force in the region, even if its course is relatively peaceful, if only because the rapidity of demographic growth makes Iran a *potential* threat to its neighbors. Ironically, Iraq's much smaller population would not, on paper, make it appear to be as great a threat to its neighbors as Iran. The nature of Saddam Hussein's regime and the conviction that Iraq won the war with Iran were major factors, one presumes, in his decision to attack Kuwait.

Again, Iran's population, strategic location, and the likelihood that it will remain a political question mark for some time will guarantee that neighboring states build up their defenses against a possible Iranian expansionist move, regardless of the outcome of the confrontation with Iraq.

6. Regional forces will again be more important than external superpower influences in determining the international policies, including those relating to

arms purchases of the regional players after the end of the Iraq-Kuwait crisis. Regional forces will include the ethnic nationalisms of the Soviet Union as well as all those already mentioned. While East-West tensions are changing, strategic assessment is slower to respond because of fear that the changes may not be permanent.[1]

Future Trends in the Regional Arms Race

We now examine the perspectives of various countries regarding likely trends in arms acquisition and the military situation in the region over the next decade.

Iraq

The outcome of the Iraq-Kuwait crisis will have much to do with the future role of Iraq and its arms procurement patterns. The Middle East is a region notoriously unkind to its own prophets—forecasts made in the autumn of 1990 could be dangerous when a major regional war may very well alter some basic assumptions.

The least radical change that would appear to be possible as an outcome of the crisis is the continued existence of either the present Iraqi regime or a successor regime with similar nationalist goals, following a forced withdrawal from Kuwait. The most extreme change, should major regional war erupt, could be as extensive as the partition of Iraq among its neighbors.

For the purposes of this analysis, it is assumed that Iraq survives as a polity, and that whatever regime rules in Baghdad, that regime has Iraqi nationalist credentials.

Saddam Hussein, following his "victory" over Iran, aspired to become not merely a major regional power—which Iraq naturally was—but *the* major regional power. Such aspirations are always dangerous, particularly if a miscalculation occurs. Saddam miscalculated the response of Saudi Arabia and the United States to his invasion of Kuwait, expecting neither the degree of US response or the willingness of the Saudis to provide bases.

Clearly, Saddam misunderstood the lessons of the Iran-Iraq war, a very different sort of conflict from the sort he would face in a full-scale confrontation with the United States and the Western powers.

Iraq's successful military offensives, beginning with the reconquest of Faw and continuing with operations east of Basra and in the Majnun Islands area, demonstrated considerable improvement in Iraqi coordination of offensive assaults. This better organization came at a time of increasing demoralization on the Iranian side. It also came at a time when Iraq maintained an overwhelming control of the air (Iran's air force being almost impotent) as well as a great superiority in armor, artillery, and mobility. These superiorities offset the demographic advantages of Iran's much larger population. But Iraq's success included a strong psychological warfare dimension. In the "war of the cities," Iraq's greater arsenal of missiles allowed it to pound Tehran and other Iranian cities with far greater frequency than Iran could respond to. Baghdad was hit mostly by missiles falling in its outer suburbs and around an oil refinery, whereas Tehran suffered badly enough to see a major exodus of population. The fear of chemical weapons may have done more to demoralize Iranian forces than the actual use of those weapons, and this terror was reinforced by the horrifying pictures Iran continually released for propaganda effect. Ironically, Tehran's drum beating about Iraqi chemical use may have helped persuade Iranian troops of the horrors awaiting them on the battlefield.

These results certainly confirmed for Iraqi planners the advantages of sophisticated, modern means of warfare. Missiles and chemical weapons are now, as already mentioned, probably to be considered part of the basic military landscape in the Middle East, however much this may be deplored. After years of grinding, immobile war with hundreds of thousands dead, the casualties incurred in the last offensives of the war probably seem few enough in proportion to the results achieved.

Perhaps more important for forecasting future trends is Iraq's recognition that, in the war, it had to depend on its superiority in training and equipment, as well as greater mass mobilizations, to overcome Iran's manpower advantages. There are only some 16 million Iraqis versus some 52 million Iranians. Yet according to some estimates, Iraq may have actually had more men under arms in the latter part of the war than Iran, despite Iran's having more than triple the population.[2] To overcome the problem of its smaller population, Iraq is encouraging population growth, seeking a figure of 25 million by the year 2000. (President Saddam Hussein's decision to take a second wife is reportedly being used in this campaign.)[3]

While seeking to spur population growth, Iraq must also try to maintain the technological superiority it enjoyed when the war ended. It has clearly committed itself to a major expansion of its domestic arms production capability, particularly in the areas of aircraft and armor. These were areas in which both Iran and Iraq suffered severely from resupply difficulties in the early years of the war. After about 1983, Iraq began receiving arms from France and the Soviet Union, and these problems were much reduced; Iran, though, continued to find it difficult to obtain spare parts throughout the war. To focus attention on its planes, a major international air show was held on Saddam Hussein's birthday in April 1989.[4]

Iraq's Military Production Authority is under the direction of Hussein Kamil Hassan, minister of industry and military industrialization and a relative of Saddam. In several press conferences and interviews, he stressed that Iraq hopes to assemble domestically sophisticated fighter aircraft and trainers, with the ultimate goal of local production. He also stated that Iraq is well advanced in plans to produce a version of the Soviet T-72 tank locally.[5]

Iraq's rearmament program after the war with Iran seemed likely to proceed rapidly. It had created a close working relationship with the Egyptian defense industry, on which it was partially modeled,[6] and was aligned with Egypt in the four-nation Arab Cooperation Council (ACC). At the Baghdad Air Show in 1989, Western manufacturers, particularly the British, French, and other Europeans, were eager to market their wares. Although Western pressure reportedly led Egypt and Argentina to suspend their participation in the Badr 2000 (Condor II) missile project, there was every reason to believe that Iraq would be able to turn to Western or Soviet suppliers for its requirements for frontline combat aircraft, an advanced jet trainer, and new main battle tanks.

Although the Soviet Union did provide Iraq with MiG-29 fighters and Sukhoi Su-24 bombers, Iraq's search for new weapons from abroad was suddenly aborted by the attack on Kuwait. That attack also ended the relationship with Egypt, with the other ACC members (Jordan and Yemen) siding with Iraq.

If the Iraqi arms industry survives the crisis over Kuwait, it may be expected to concentrate more heavily on locally produced equipment, having clearly seen the unpredictability of foreign suppliers if their products are used for expansionist purposes.

As Iraq seeks to strengthen its conventional forces, guaranteeing spare parts through local manufacture, it is also likely to continue to pursue unconventional technologies. The missile projects have already been mentioned. In early April 1989 there was a flurry of press reports alleging that Iraq was developing a nuclear warhead for the Condor II/Badr 2000 missile, and in the wake of these reports (and Iraqi denials) came an exchange of threats between Israel and Iraq. The Iraqis clearly fear another Israeli attack on their nuclear facilities comparable to that of 1981. In the absence of a source of nuclear materials, however, it is questionable just how far Iraq has been able to advance since the bombing of the Osirak plant. Leonard Spector, the acknowledged expert on nuclear proliferation, characterized Iraq's program in his most recent report as "dormant" as of mid-1988.[7] Nevertheless, Iraq remains likely to be the first Arab state to cross the threshold into a nuclear weapons capability at some time in the next decade or two.

Iraq's use of chemical warfare in the Iran-Iraq war, and allegations by Israel that it also has achieved a biological warfare capability, makes the chemical/biological warfare field the area of unconventional weaponry most likely to bear new fruit in the shorter term. While Iraq did not use any such warheads on its missiles during the war, it would not be difficult to adapt its existing missiles for some sort of primitive chemical warhead. These would not be of the sophistication of US binary chemical submunitions to be sure, being likely to be more on the order of a chemical artillery shell adapted for missile launch. There would be considerable dangers in such a primitive system, the greatest being the possibility that the missile could fall short and contaminate the user's own territory. Safer binary chemical warheads require more sophisticated technology than Iraq is likely to have at the moment, and, whereas the technologies involved are not fully public, many experts question whether any Middle Eastern power is likely to achieve such a capability in this century. A chemical warhead that goes wrong can be very embarrassing politically, for obvious reasons—provided some constituency remains.

The outcome of the Gulf crisis for Iraq cannot be favorable, though if the West limits its objectives to those that may be obtainable diplomatically or through limited use of force—namely the restoration of Kuwait—they need not be disastrous. But Israeli and some Western analysts have called for the destruction of Iraq's warmaking ability, including elimination of its nuclear, chemical, biological, and missile capabilities.

This is easier said than done. Today Iraq's nuclear program is not centered in one place, as was the case in 1981; it is a broad technology base that could only be destroyed by removing virtually the entire industrial base of the country. Destruction of the chemical weapons capability or of the biological research factory at Salman Pak could lead to massive civilian casualties. To eliminate entirely the ability to produce missiles might require destruction of every machine tool plant in the country. Mass strategic bombing, thousands of sorties reminiscent of the destruction of the German industrial base in World War II, and not some "surgical strike," would be necessary.

If Iraq's industrial base is *not* destroyed, then the Iraqi government, whether the Saddam Hussein regime or a successor, is likely to retain at least some of the nonconventional warfare capabilities developed by Saddam. Some sort of regional disarmament pact could be a result of a major war. But the results of a major war are so unpredictable that it would be irresponsible to speculate in great detail. The results of the Iraq-Kuwait crisis are as unpredictable at this writing as the results of World War I were in July of 1914: major changes may result throughout the Arab world. What can be said with certainty is that the arms race in the Gulf will more intense after the crisis than before.

Iran

It is far more difficult to discern Iran's directions than Iraq's, given the dramatic shifts that have occurred inside the country since the cease-fire. Longer-term geopolitical realities will, however, remain unchanged regardless of specific policy decisions. Certain trends can be extrapolated confidently, but the precise course to be followed in the military arena is as uncertain as the political. The speed and relative smoothness with which Ali Khamene'i was chosen to succeed Khomeini and the apparent working alliance between Khamene'i and Majlis Speaker (now President) Hashemi-Rafsanjani suggested that the clerical regime has a certain basic stability. This does not necessarily translate into Iran's being a stabilizing factor in the region, however. Even if the Iranian leadership does not continue to pursue a policy aimed at exporting the Islamic revolution, the likelihood of continued political competition and the experience of the Salman Rushdie affair suggest that such a policy could be resumed at any time. Even without such active interventionism, however, Iran is something of a destabilizing force because of its sheer size and location and the bitter legacy of the war with Iraq.

Militarily, Iran left the war in disastrous disarray. Whole sectors of the front were reportedly collapsing under the final Iraqi blows. The fear of chemical weapons, so ironically reinforced by Iranian propaganda, broke Iranian formations to pieces. After the Iraqi recapture of Faw in the spring of 1988, intense recriminations seem to have ensued between the regular armed forces and the Pasdaran (Islamic Revolutionary Guards). Khomeini's appointment of Rafsanjani as acting commander in chief of all the fighting forces was a tacit admission of this collapse of confidence between the two main bodies, returning the situation to one of rivalry such as had prevailed in the earliest years of the war.

The internal political disputes that erupted in the first half of 1989 and then the death of Khomeini and the imminence of presidential elections forced postponement of any major changes in organizational structure, despite a theoretical commitment to eventually merge the armed forces and the Pasdaran into a single body. In April 1989, Rafsanjani announced the arrest of a "CIA spy ring" that included a number of senior military officers, including a brigadier general and a naval commodore. This may have been another indication of continuing confusion or even outright dissent within the armed forces. After Rafsanjani's election as president, a new ministry of defense and logistics was created to more closely coordinate both the armed forces and the Pasdaran.

It is relatively certain that in the first months after the war, though the military forces seemed to have welcomed the cease-fire, there continued to be political elements who rejected it and whom Iran was eagerly seeking to rearm. Early reports spoke of major new deals with China (President Khamene'i made an important visit to China and North Korea, the two most dependable wartime arms sources, in May 1989), and new deals with the East bloc. Specific deals were claimed with Poland, Romania, and Czechoslovakia, and during his visit to Moscow in June 1989, Rafsanjani reached agreements with the Soviets on unspecified aid for Iranian defense that would be imminently forthcoming.

Leaving the question of political leadership aside, a few general projections can be made with some confidence for at least the major part of this decade:

1. Iran, even in order to assure basic self-defense capability, must rebuild its shattered air force in some form. This military imperative would be incumbent upon even the most pacifist regime, for the air force had virtually no serious air defense or ground attack capabilities remaining at the end of the war. Reports that Iran was seeking Chinese aircraft and possibly the Brazilian-Italian AMX fighter-trainer in the months after the war reflect this urgent need. But none of these aircraft would be able to match Iraq's MiG-29s and Mirage F-1s (with the Mirage 2000 expected soon). Thus Iran needs to break from dependence on second-string suppliers and acquire a major frontline aircraft, as its F-14s are mostly useless now. The Soviet MiG-29 might be one acquisition that could emerge from the Soviet arms deal, and this could make the Iranian air force a real competitor again. It has always had a reputation of being better trained than Iraq's,

but in recent years it has simply lacked equipment.

2. The Iranian navy, shattered by confrontations with the United States in 1988, is in scarcely better shape.

3. The United States and the major Western European powers are unlikely to sell major weapons systems to Iran for several years.

4. Iran has claimed a fairly sophisticated domestic production capability, but this is not generally conceded by Western observers.

5. Because of its demographic power, its strategic location, and the continuing uncertain relationship between its large armed forces (both regular and Pasdaran) and the political leadership, Iran is likely to remain a destabilizing factor for years to come, certainly to the end of the century.

There is no question that *eventually* Iran's superior size and capabilities should give it an edge over Iraq. But given its lack of revenues for purchasing arms, the year 2000 is probably too soon for it to overtake and surpass its rival. Potential challenges on its other borders further complicate the task, as does the potential for continued insurgency in Kurdestan or other ethnic regions. But beyond the year 2000—and a decade is not a long time in geopolitical terms—Iran's inherent strengths will begin to restore to it the natural superiority it lost in a decade of revolution and war. A study focusing on projections to the year 2020, for example, might draw rather different conclusions.

Saudi Arabia

If there is one word that springs to mind when it comes to the policies of Saudi Arabia, at least until the invasion of Kuwait, it is "cautious." The tanker war and other developments alarmed the kingdom enormously. Saudi Arabia, since the 1930s at least, has not sought adventures beyond its present borders and often gives the impression of simply wishing the world would leave it alone. But the Gulf is not a quiet place, and the Saudis have had to react to the dangers confronting them.

Recent years have seen a significant evolution in the arms policies of Saudi Arabia. Not only has it continued to acquire world-class fighter and air defense capabilities (though its ability to use the equipment remains only partially proven), but it has shown considerable strategic insight in concentrating on such key areas as development of modern command, control, and communications networks and—given the challenges posed by the war—a modern, two-sea navy. These projects have been singularly immune to cutbacks owing to budgetary restraints. The Saudi acquisition of DF-3A ballistic missiles from China does suggest a willingness to escalate arms acquisitions into new categories of weaponry.

The major characteristic of the late 1980s was an increasing dependence of Saudi Arabia on arms supplied by Western Europe and a marked decrease in dependence on the United States. This has primarily come about as a result of political opposition in the US Congress to major arms sales to the Saudis, first strongly evident in the narrow victory of the AWACS sale in 1981 and reinforced by the Reagan administration's willingness to withdraw or modify proposed arms sales to avoid congressional defeat on several successive issues from 1985 to 1988. Saudi Arabia has continued to express a preference for US weaponry but, when denied, has proven willing to turn to Europe.

When it was unable to acquire additional F-15 aircraft from the United States, Saudi Arabia turned to the United Kingdom for a major order of Tornado fighters and ground attack aircraft, Hawk and Pilatus trainers, and other equipment. This large Yamamah deal was followed in 1988 by a second (still not firmly concluded) set of orders for additional aircraft, air base construction, and naval vessels. Besides these British purchases, Saudi Arabia turned to France for Crotale/Shahine air defense missiles and for a variety of major naval systems. US firms are building the Peace Shield air defense command and control system, but most of the rest of Saudi air defenses will be French or British. Saudi Arabia is also seeking submarines, and the United States is not even competing here.

Saudi Arabia's purchase of CSS-2 (DF-3A) intermediate-range ballistic missiles from China marked a major departure from past Saudi acquisitions patterns. This was the first purchase from a communist country, a country with which Saudi Arabia did not have diplomatic relations. The deal, orchestrated by Prince Bandar bin Sultan, ambassador to Washington, was part of a rather innovative new Saudi arms policy toward countries such as China. The DF-3As represent a qualitative leap forward for Saudi Arabia, though their accuracy with conventional warheads leaves something to be desired. The Saudis agreed to sign the Nuclear Nonproliferation Treaty (NPT) and to give assurances that they would not fit chemical warheads to the missiles, but they rejected US efforts to inspect the missiles and launch sites. Positioned where they are, south of Riyadh, the missiles would appear to be intended as a deterrent against Iranian and perhaps Iraqi missile threats rather than as a threat to Israel.

The DF-3A purchase showed, however, that the Saudis are determined to maintain a deterrent capability toward any new weapons system introduced in the region (they were installed at the height of the war of the cities), and that US censure was not a major consideration. The missiles were bought without consulting the United States. If Prince Bandar were increasingly the primary Saudi secret negotiator abroad, this action might be regarded as sending a particular message to the United States.

From a Saudi point of view, the relatively black-and-white confrontation of the Gulf war has been replaced by a more complex world in which potential threats to the kingdom could come from several directions. The invasion of Kuwait confirmed this view. Saudi Arabia used the period of the war to strengthen its own defenses and to build up the GCC. But it has certainly not forgotten the relatively aggressive efforts of Iraq in the late 1970s to assert leadership of the Gulf Arab states. When the Arab Cooperation Council was formed in February 1989, linking Iraq, Egypt, Jordan, and Yemen, Saudi Arabia did not appear to have been overly pleased. King Fahd made highly publicized visits to Iraq and Egypt and in Iraq signed a "nonaggression pact," the exact need for which remains something of a mystery given the countries' close ties during the war. An even less publicized security pact was also signed. Clearly, the Saudis want to protect *all* their flanks, not merely those with Iraq and Iran.

This concern with potential threats from several directions was partly responsible for the Saudi invitation to the United States to send military forces at the time of the Iraqi invasion of Kuwait. In the spring of 1990, the two Yemens had precipitately united—six months ahead of schedule—and the Saudis were at best lukewarm about the new country, which has 13 million people and is the most populous on the Arabian peninsula.

Jordan's King Hussein, though long friendly with the Saudis, provoked some surprise in Saudi Arabia when, in the tense moments leading up to the invasion of Kuwait, he told Parliament that he would be honored to be addressed as "Sharif"—the title his ancestors held as rulers of Mecca before being driven out by the Saudis in the 1920s.

When Saddam Hussein invaded Kuwait and the Kuwaiti royal family arrived in Riyadh, the Saudis were faced with a major crisis. Iraqi troops could conceivably have taken the Saudi oil fields in three days' time. Reports the Saudis believed said that two to three squadrons of Iraqi aircraft had been deployed to Yemen. Jordan supported Iraq. The possibility that not merely the oil fields but the kingdom itself was in jeopardy seemed real.

There is no external evidence of any "plot" among Jordan, Yemen, and Iraq to partition Saudi Arabia, but many Saudis believed that such a plot existed. They invited the US forces in.

The realities of the small population and rich resources of Saudi Arabia remain a serious temptation to any potential aggressor. Saudi Arabia's missiles and relatively well-equipped air force, though perhaps inadequately trained on its equipment, provide a deterrent, a trip wire, and a holding force, but they could not prevent the kingdom from being overrun by a serious land-force attack, whether Iranian, Iraqi, or (within the limited northwestern sector at least) even Israeli.

Saudi Arabia's traditional approach to its self-defense will likely change in the wake of the Gulf crisis. It has already indicated its desire for a larger number of M-1 Abrams tanks and F-15 fighters. It will almost certainly have to recognize that its traditional concern about a large army must be subordinated to the real need to have a capable force for ground defense and deterrence. Conscription is a very real possibility; a much larger ground force is essential. These will be combined with a strengthening of the national guard and a continued buildup of the air force and air defense forces.

The Saudis are increasingly cultivating their new links with Beijing and Moscow, establishing relations with both in 1990. The Saudis, once virtual US clients, have diversified not only their sources of arms but their international ties as well. That has given them a new independence of diplomatic initiative, but in the final analysis they cannot survive a direct attack from a major foreign land force without the support of external powers. The United States is likely to remain the external power most willing to support Saudi Arabia and provide a deterrent umbrella against such an attack.

Saudi Arabia's defense buildup in the wake of the Gulf crisis will of course depend to some extent on the resolution of that crisis. One result may be a return to heavier dependence on US equipment, if, as seems possible, the US Congress begins to recognize that there are real threats to the survival of the kingdom and that these weapons are not likely to be turned against Israel.

The Other Gulf States

The smaller Arab states of the Gulf were in some ways the front line of the noncombatants during the Iran-Iraq war. Kuwait, in particular, found itself under fire repeatedly: "accidental" Iranian bombings of Kuwaiti targets early in the war, followed by Iranian attacks on Kuwaiti shipping, followed by Silkworm missile attacks on Kuwaiti loading docks and ships in the latter period of the war. Oman found its role as protector of the Straits of Hormuz seriously challenged by Iranian interceptions; the UAE suffered air attacks by Iraq on its oil platforms (an apparent mistake) and otherwise found itself caught between the combatants.

Kuwait in 1988 ordered US F-18 aircraft and other sophisticated equipment, and in 1989 was seeking US M-1 tanks even while ordering Yugoslav versions of the Soviet T-72. The Kuwaitis have also ordered heavily from Egyptian, Western European, and East bloc sources. Yet in the end the lack of major gound forces guaranteed that Kuwait collapsed almost immediately when Iraq attacked. Its air force, however, escaped mostly intact to Saudi Arabia.

Assuming that Kuwaiti independence is restored, either under the emir or some other form of government, there is likely to be some sort of guarantor force—Arab or Western—in place for the immediate term. But the Kuwaiti government can be expected to seek to continue its arms buildup.

Kuwait's arms acquisition patterns are not easily characterized but are unlikely to change much: Suppliers are a mix of US, European (including non-NATO European, such as Swedish and Swiss), and some Soviet sources. The Soviet connection may well expand beyond the largely symbolic level it previously had, and the Soviets may well aggressively market the MiG-29 to the Gulf states. Over the longer haul, though, there seems little reason to expect that Kuwait will abandon a long-standing policy of not depending overly much on a single source of arms.

The United States and the West

The Western interest in the Gulf is easily stated: The Gulf remains the source of a significant portion of the energy supply for the West and Japan. In addition, the Gulf represents the southwestern flank of the Soviet Union and, long before oil,

Iran and the Indo-Persian Corridor were defined as strategic regions because they blocked the Russian (later Soviet) drive to the south. Mikhail Gorbachev notwithstanding, the historical Soviet impulse toward warm-water ports cannot be considered dead, though it may for now be somewhat dormant.

The entire traditional pattern of "over the horizon" presence by the United States, already weakened during the US naval intervention in 1987–1988, collapsed completely with the massive US and allied intervention in Saudi Arabia in the late summer of 1990.

The future of that presence depends, at least in part, upon the resolution of the Gulf conflict, still unclear at this writing. But US talk of a future security system in the region after the crisis has already provoked negative reactions in the region. Clearly the states of the region themselves want foreign forces out, once the immediate crisis is past; yet they want those forces once again "over the horizon."

The issue of permanent bases will be raised. It will be resisted (except perhaps by the Kuwaitis, now much chastened in their longtime neutrality).

The relationship between the peninsular states and the United States, and their attitude toward the US military, may evolve into something completely different from the old "over the horizon" dependence. But US pressure to create a sort of Middle Eastern NATO, or a revived Baghdad Pact, would be unwise and counterproductive until the crisis itself is resolved and the new political landscape that results is fully understood

Future Patterns: Some Conclusions

The end of the Iraq-Kuwait crisis will not end the arms race in the Gulf; in fact, the crisis itself will be a major determinant in procurement decisions. The one lesson all the regional states have learned from the war is that chemical warfare and surface-to-surface missiles work.

As far as patterns of acquisition go, Soviet sales will increase, including sales to countries not previously considered likely clients; the Chinese will continue to be everywhere. New suppliers, such as China, Argentina, and Brazil will find a major market for missile technologies and perhaps other unconventional systems that the United States, the USSR, and Europe will refuse to sell.

It is also clear that the postcrisis world in the Gulf will be more complicated than either the precrisis or the crisis world. Iraq's choice of aggression may prove its downfall—in any event its power will be limited and probably rolled back. Saudi Arabia and the GCC will increasingly seek to form a third bloc in the region, though their military clout will be limited to air and naval forces. Iran will remain regionally isolated and in search of arms supplies for some time.

Notes

1. See General H. Norman Schwarzkopf, commander in chief, US Central Command, Witness Statement before the Senate Armed Services Committee, April 20,

1989.

2. International Institute for Strategic Studies, *The Military Balance 1988–1989* (London: IISS, 1988), estimated total active Iranian armed forces at 604,500 and total Iraqi active armed forces at 1 million. This estimate listed the 650,000 members of the People's Army as "reserves," though at the time many People's Army units were stationed at the front. A Western military source in Baghdad estimated Iraqi ground forces as approximately 1.1 million men some months after the cease-fire.

3. Based on a conversation with a Western diplomat in Baghdad, April 1989.

4. See, for example, Thalif Deen, "Rebuilding Iraq's Armed Forces," *Jane's Defense Weekly,* April 22, 1989, pp. 697–698; "Baghdad Show Reveals Modified MiGs, Missiles," *Defense News,* May 8, 1989, p. 6.

5. "Baghdad Exhibit Shows Increased Egyptian-Iraqi Cooperation," *Defense News,* May 8, 1989, p. 6; "Minister Denies Missile Industry Cooperation" (Hussein Kamil press conference), Baghdad, Iraq News Agency, April 27, 1989, quoted in Foreign Broadcast Information Service (FBIS), *Near East & South Asia Daily Report,* April 28, 1989, p. 18; "Industry Minister Discusses Military Production" (interview with Hussein Kamil), Cairo, *Al-Akhbar,* May 7, 1989, p. 7, translated in FBIS, *Near East & South Asia Daily Report,* May 9, 1989, pp. 18–21.

6. On Egypt's defense industries and society, see Michael C. Dunn, "Egypt: From Domestic Needs to Export Market," in *The Implications of Third World Military Industrialization: Sowing the Serpents' Teeth,* ed. James Everett Katz (Lexington, MA: Lexington Books, 1986), and Michael C. Dunn, "Arming for Peacetime: Egypt's Defense Industry Today," *Defense & Foreign Affairs* (October–November 1988).

7. Leonard Spector, *The Undeclared Bomb* (Cambridge, MA: Carnegie Endowment, 1988): 207–214.

6
Saudi Arabia in the 1990s: Plus ça Change . . .

David E. Long

This study is an attempt not only to forecast what Saudi Arabia might look like in the 1990s but also to seek a more conceptual means to analyze factors that will influence future Saudi policy responses to issues of major importance to the United States and other key Western powers. Evocative but imprecise terms such as "political stability," "moderation," "pro-Western," and "pro-Soviet" will be used sparingly.

My basic premise is that state policies are responses to objective realities, tempered by perceptions. For example, Saudi Arabia's position as a major oil producer and exporter is and will likely remain an objective reality well into the twenty-first century no matter how stable (or unstable) its political regime, and future Saudi oil policies will reflect that reality. On the other hand, the degree to which Saudi Arabia will be willing through its oil policies to accommodate the United States and other major oil-consuming states will be greatly influenced by its perception of the degree to which such accommodation is in its total national interests, political and military as well as economic.

The term "accommodation" might need some clarification. Clearly, Saudi Arabia, like every other country, bases its policies on its own self-interest and not just out of friendship or humanitarianism. There is latitude, however, in how the Saudis compute the costs and benefits of given policies. How accommodating to the West and the United States they are likely to be within the parameters of their own interests will depend on how much they value the closer relations the accommodation is intended to encourage.

A second premise is that politics tends to drive economic policies in the short run but economics tends to drive political policies in the longer run. In looking at Saudi Arabia over a ten-year period, economics becomes a key determinant of policy. For a country that is so dependent for its political and economic welfare on a single resource, oil, this is particularly so. The oil market realities in the coming decade will be absolutely crucial to determining Saudi political policies as well as its relations with the United States and the West.

Beginning with these premises, the following analysis will attempt to forecast the most likely perceptions of these realities by the Saudi political leadership. Discussion will focus on Saudi policies relating to oil, economics, politics, and national defense. A concluding section will be devoted to the possible impact of resulting Saudi policy responses on US and other major Western interests.

Saudi Oil Policies in the 1990s

The most crucial factors in forecasting Saudi political as well as economic policies over the next ten years are the state of the international oil market and the Saudi role as a major producer and exporter. As the world's largest holder of oil reserves and with a large productive capacity and small domestic consumption, Saudi Arabia has emerged as an international oil power and a regional political power.

The International Oil Market

Gulf oil is discussed in more detail elsewhere in this book. To summarize, the international oil market, like most commodity markets, has been cyclical, with alternating periods of shortage and glut. Following a severe oil shortage in the 1970s, the 1980s saw a return to a period of oil glut. Prices bottomed out in 1986 and remained more or less stagnant until events following the Iraqi invasion of Kuwait forced up prices in the second half of 1990. Assuming the international economy cannot long sustain these prices, there is a good chance that the Kuwait situation, once the crisis phase is over, will have created recessionary trends that will maintain the glut to late in the decade.

Saudi Perceptions and Oil Policy

The Saudis are acutely aware that, despite their huge reserves, oil is a wasting asset. With few other natural resources, they fear that when the oil is gone they will find it difficult to maintain their standard of living. Their anxieties are exacerbated by the Saudi public perceptions of economics, which are still more mercantilist than capitalistic, and the difficulty of getting used to the idea of living off the productivity of their capital. As a result, Saudi Arabia long ago adopted an oil policy of maintaining prices and production at rates low enough to ensure a long-term export market for its oil.

This policy is in sharp contrast to the approach of OPEC price hawks, who seek to maximize their revenues with higher prices for near-term profits. The Saudis have also differed with many of their OPEC colleagues about price stability. OPEC's main function has never really been price stability but rather to serve as a mechanism for dividing market shares and setting overall production quotas among its members. The Saudis have always been concerned that precipitous price fluctuations would create free-world economic dislocations that would lead to negative political effects.

To maintain what it thought were reasonable (i.e., higher than the consumers wished but lower than the price hawks wanted) and stable prices, Saudi Arabia assumed the role of "swing producer." The Saudis raised production to keep a cap on prices during the energy crisis, reaching 9.9 million barrels per day by 1980; and to keep prices from collapsing during the glut they lowered production to 3.4 million barrels per day in 1985.

Since then, the Saudi role as swing producer has been problematic. Frustrated by growing cash flow problems and OPEC members cheating on production quotas, they increased production, in 1986, collapsing the price for a brief period to under $10 per barrel. OPEC discipline still could not be maintained, and in 1988 the Saudis again increased production and collapsed prices. Following the Iraqi invasion of Kuwait in August 1990, the Saudis announced that they would increase production to keep prices at about $28 per barrel, but prices spiraled, nevertheless. Despite their inability to maintain price stability, however, the Saudis apparently want to retain their role as swing producer.

Forecast for the 1990s

Given the rather benign projection for the oil market in the 1990s, Saudi Arabia, with its huge reserves, high productive capacity, and relatively low domestic consumption, seems assured of remaining in its position as the most significant oil-exporting country well into the twenty-first century. Moreover, the kingdom's policy of maintaining prices and production rates that would ensure a long-term market for its oil is likely to stay the same in the 1990s no matter what internal political changes take place.

In the long run, Saudi Arabia will probably not be able to dominate the oil market to the extent it did in the 1970s. Iraq, for example, has large reserves, and regardless of what regime is in Baghdad, it may eventually challenge Saudi predominance in OPEC. As a result of the Kuwait crisis, however, this is less likely to happen in the 1990s. The domestic revenue needs generated by years of conflict—the Iran-Iraq war followed by the Kuwait crisis—would seriously hamper any Iraqi attempts to become the swing producer. Moreover, with an oil glut likely to extend into the next century, the scope for an Iraqi challenge to Saudi Arabia as swing producer is substantially diminished.

Short-term crises such as the Kuwait invasion or another monumental oil spill could again temporarily run up prices, but the resulting market disruptions would probably extend the glut even further. Just as the Kuwait crisis took the entire world by surprise, there is no way to predict a future crisis or its impact on the long-term oil market.

In the event of another Arab-Israeli conflict, rendered even less likely by the end of the cold war and the split in the Arab world over the Kuwait invasion, with most countries condemning Iraq, the chances of a successful Arab oil boycott in the 1990s are considerably less than in the 1970s. Moreover, consuming countries are much more energy-efficient, governments have created strategic reserves, and consumer-country policies to deflect an embargo would, it is hoped, be more enlightened.

Saudi Economic Policies in the 1990s

It is an obvious though no less basic reality that fluctuations in oil revenues have been a major determinant of Saudi economic policies and prospects. It is hard to believe that Saudi Arabia was one of the poorest countries in the world in the 1930s, and the US Lend-Lease Act, extended to the kingdom in the 1940s, was to stave off economic, not military, collapse. Less obvious is that the senior Saudi leaders experienced real economic poverty during their formative years, indelibly affecting their perceptions of wealth and the relationship between social welfare and economic well-being. The younger generation has never been poor and takes economic prosperity far more for granted.

Revenues and Cash Flow

With the great increase in oil revenues in the 1970s, Saudi development spending took on an air of unreality. Revenues rose even faster than expenditures, however, and by the end of the decade Saudi Arabia had amassed reserves of somewhere in the neighborhood of $150 billion.[1]

The 1980s were a different story entirely. Both falling oil prices and falling production drastically cut Saudi revenues, from $102.2 billion in 1980 to $28.5 billion in 1986.[2] No one thought the oil glut would cut prices so deeply or last so long. As a result, the Saudis experienced a negative cash flow for most of the 1980s and were forced to make up the shortfall by drawing down reserves. By 1989, their reserves had declined to about $50 billion, or by over two-thirds.

In response to falling revenues, the Saudis tried to cut spending. Some programs were abandoned and others were stretched out; new proposals were deferred and debts were rescheduled or payment simply tardy. It is difficult to see a pattern in how the austerity program was administered, however. All ministries and agencies were affected, but many cuts appear to have been done on a random basis, probably reflecting the negotiating skill (or lack thereof) of the various ministers. It was, of course, harder to deal with programs involving longer-term financial commitments and those in advanced stages of completion. Defense and security programs were among the least affected, owing in great part to the continuing threat of the Iran-Iraq war, but also because so many of them were long-term projects that could not easily be curtailed. Nevertheless, even many defense contracts were stretched out or canceled.

In addition, early in the decade the Saudis diversified their foreign exchange holdings, which previously had been predominantly in dollars, so that when the dollar began to decline later in the decade, the Saudis were not so badly hurt as they could have been.

Despite the negative cash flow problems, there was a general consensus among the Saudi political leadership that too stringent an austerity program could cause serous political strains, since government contracts were a major means for the government to distribute the national wealth to the people. In effect, the Saudis were betting that the oil market would turn around before they drew down their reserves to dangerously low levels. It appears that they have won their bet. Revenues already seem to be picking up. Even though increased Saudi production in 1988 lowered prices, for example, increased Saudi production more than made up for it in terms of revenues.

The increase in prices as a result of the kuwait crisis provided windfall revenues for the Saudis, but much of this was eaten up in defense expenses in the face of the Iraqi threat to the kingdom itself. It is doubtful that higher oil prices created by the crisis will be sustained, or that they will benefit the Saudi economy to an extent even close to the higher prices in the 1970s.

Saudi Perceptions and Economic Policies

Part of the problem in assessing Saudi economic policies is the difference in Saudi and Western perceptions and priorities.

Domestic economic perceptions. Because the public oil sector totally dominates the Saudi economy, government contracting has become the principal source of private domestic revenue earning in the kingdom. At the same time, Saudi government contracting is one of the most chaotic and influence-ridden systems of public funding in the world. Even the most rudimentary Western standards of public ethics regarding nepotism, conflict of interest, and so on are largely ignored.

As a result, there has long been concern in the West that excessive greed and corruption in the public sector, particularly in the royal family, might eventually undermine the political stability of the regime. If that ever does become the case, it will not happen because of failure to observe Western ethical standards. Judged by their own standards, Saudis are no more corrupt than any other public servants.

To assess Saudi ethical standards in public spending, one should begin with their perceptions of the economic responsibilities of the government to the people. These views are changing, but traditional attitudes still prevail. Throughout Islamic history, loyalty was given to the leader, not the government. Governments traditionally only levied taxes and drafted sons into the army. The less one had to do with them the better. To this day, the role of the ruler in Saudi Arabia is seen more as a paramount chief than a chief of state, and there is still a profound distrust of government institutions and a dogged reliance on personal relationships. Moreover, it is not necessarily immoral to pay for personal services rendered, no matter how corrupt the practice might appear to Westerners.

Saudis also differ in their perceptions of public welfare. In Western democracies, the concept of the welfare state has become predominant in the last century. It is considered the responsibility of the state to provide for the public welfare mainly through tax revenues. The prevailing Saudi view is that individual welfare is primarily the responsibility of the extended family and providing for the poor is a religious obligation.[3]

Finally, Saudis do not make a clear distinction between public and private resources. All material blessings come from God and belong to all of His people. It behooves everyone, therefore, to acquire as much of the national wealth as possible. In this context, Saudi Arabia's vast oil wealth is seen as belonging to the people, not the government, and it is not necessarily corrupt to get what rightfully belongs to one in the first place.

Traditionally, the duty of distributing the national wealth to the people fell to the leader, and in Saudi Arabia it is still ultimately the obligation of the king. Senior military and civilian leaders share the responsibility for the personal welfare of their subordinates. Moreover, with so many opportunities outside government to become wealthy, such expenditures are necessary to keep good people. A large part of the monies accumulated by senior leaders, therefore, is not for personal enrichment but to pay for the huge informal overhead costs that a traditional system like the Saudi government incurs.

Nevertheless, with the enormous rise in government revenues and resulting growth in operations, responsibility for distributing the national wealth has been increasingly delegated to public administrators. As perceived by the people, therefore, the main responsibility of the Saudi government is not to create a welfare state but to devise a means for equitably distributing the national wealth to the people. The system by which this is done is not important, only the result. Indeed, if the opportunities for private gain were cut off by stringent administration of contracting procedures, there would probably be greater public disaffection than there is with the present system.

A chronic misconception of Saudi economic policies has to do with the annual Saudi budget. It is a monumental document, requiring much of the resources of the entire government for weeks in order to produce it. The budget is not, however, a statistically meaningful document except in the broadest terms. It could more aptly be described as a negotiated, composite wish list. Each ministry and agency in the government competes for resources in what amounts to a grand political-bureaucratic free-for-all. The upper limits are determined more by political consensus and expediency than by economic constraints, but seldom do expenditures reach budget allocations at any rate. Also, the budget does not reflect the extrabudgetary expenses of senior leaders mentioned above. Thus, the most important value of the budget is to serve as a detailed order of priorities for Saudi government expenditures, not as a source of authoritative statistics for determining the state of Saudi economy.

Foreign economic perceptions. As the Saudis amassed increasing foreign currency reserves in the 1970s, there were great fears that they might adopt punitive economic policies against both political adversaries and foreign monetary and fiscal policies, and that they would have the resources to back them up. Quite the contrary, Saudi fiscal policies were so conservative at the time that relatively safe returns on longer-term investments were turned down in favor of lower-yielding but more liquid short-term holdings.

The Saudis have become far more sophisticated since then, but they have not become less conservative. Reinforcing their policies is the firm conviction that a strong Muslim world depends on a strong free-world economy. A weakened free-world economy, to their way of thinking, would undermine the West's ability to withstand communism, which, because it is an atheist doctrine, the Saudis view as a major threat to their Islamic foreign policy.

The Islamic influence on Saudi economic foreign policy perceptions can be graphically seen in their foreign aid priorities: first to Arab states, second to non-Arab Islamic states, and third to non-Arab, non-Islamic states facing communist threat. Saudi aid priorities thus differ significantly from the more usual ones based on more secular political interests and economic need.

The close linkage of politics and economics has also been demonstrated in Saudi willingness to accommodate Western economic interests in order to foster closer political ties. For example, in the 1970s, Saudi Arabia, in response to US urging, often held out for even lower price rises than it thought necessary. It also placed a great proportion of its foreign exchange holdings in US securities, as this was the largest market and best able to absorb its huge balances. At US urging, however, the Saudis held even more US securities than they probably needed for strictly economic reasons. It was a time when the Saudis were seeking a "special relationship" with the United States in political, economic, and defense matters. The Saudi desire for a special relationship was both manifested in and reinforced by the kingdom's acceptance of US military protection in the Kuwait crisis. It is hard to say, however, what lasting effect this cooperation will have in sustaining the Saudi political motivation to accommodate the United States economically in the 1990s—for example, in placing reserves in US securities—beyond what is clearly in Saudi economic interests.

Saudi Political Policies in the 1990s

Since the kingdom emerged as a major oil power in the 1970s, a great deal of concern has been expressed in the West about the continued survival of its monarchical system. Western observers consider nonrepresentative monarchies to be anachronisms in the late twentieth century and thus "unstable." The Saudi regime is no more impervious to overthrow than any other nonrepresentative regime, but the likelihood of its survivability or demise cannot be based on Western standards. In order to assess Saudi stability, we must know something about the Saudi political process.

The Saudi Political Process

Saudi Arabia is a traditional Islamic monarchy, and its constitutional system is based on Islamic law. It is not an absolute monarchy in the predemocratic European sense, and an Islamic monarch is not analogous to a Christian monarch ruling by divine right. The king is subject to Islamic law the same as any other Muslim and rules by consensus.

Islamic political ideology. The Saudi political process is based on a systematic, comprehensive Islamic political ideology developed by an eighteenth-century Arabian religious scholar, Mohammad Ibn Abd al-Wahhab. His Islamic fundamentalist revival movement, generally called Wahhabism,[4] was adopted by the Al- Sauds as its political ideology and has remained so ever since.

One must use a bit of caution in looking at Wahhabism as a political ideology. It has no independent doctrine other than Islam. Wahhabism is based on the ultraconservative Hanbali school of (Sunni) Islamic jurisprudence[5] and the teachings of an early Hanbali political theorist, Taqi al-Din Ahmad Ibn Taymiyya (d. A.D. 1328).[6] It was Ibn Taymiyya's call to reject the innovative practices of his day and go back to the original doctrines of Islam that appealed to Ibn Abd al-Wahhab. At the same time, Ibn Taymiyya's teachings make up one of the most revolutionary political ideologies in Islamic history, rivaling in purely intellectual terms the Shiite Islamic fundamentalist teachings of Ayatollah Khomeini.

Ibn Taymiyya lived at a time when the caliphate was in decline and many petty Muslim rulers were seeking legitimacy from local religious leaders. He denounced this practice and claimed that the only legitimacy came from strict adherence to the fundamental teachings of the *shari'a* (Islamic law). He also claimed that any ruler who did not follow God's law, Muslim or not, was not legitimate and that the Muslim community was obliged to rise against him in *jihad* (usually interpreted "holy war" but literally meaning the struggle for good and against evil).

The Saudi regime was initially quite militant, waging war against its neighbors in the pursuit of good against evil. Over the years, it has lost some of its revolutionary fervor, but not its fundamentalist principles. Ironically, they are the same principles espoused by contemporary Sunni Muslim fundamentalist revolutionaries seeking to justify violent opposition to secular governments of Muslim and non-Muslim states alike. For the latter, the act of political violence and terrorism is raised to a religious obligation, *jihad.*

The Wahhabi revival movement has provided the Saudi regime with an egalitarian, universal, and moral ideology that has served to bind ruled and rulers together through many crises and troubles. Hanbali Islamic jurisprudence is the basis of the constitutional and legal system of Saudi Arabia. All Saudi students are given instruction in Islam, whose teachings are deeply embedded in the psyche and culture of the people. Indeed, one could argue that the Wahhabi Islamic revival is the ideological glue that has kept the Saudi state from collapsing throughout the nearly 250 years of its history.

Political legitimacy. In Western democracies, political legitimacy is granted by the consent of the governed, who exercise their consent through regularly elected representatives. There is also an assumption that if the rulers are not regularly elected, the government is not really legitimate.

In Saudi Arabia, there are no elections and no elected representatives. There is a process of conferring legitimacy, however, by the traditional institution of *ijma'*, or consensus. *Ijma'* has even been incorporated into Islamic law on the assumption that the consensus of the entire Muslim community is divinely inspired.

As are most informal institutions, *ijma'* is very intricate and complex. Yet virtually all collective decisions, public and private, are based on consensus. Decisions of the state that most affect its citizens are keeping public order, providing for national defense, and distributing the national wealth. The urgency with which most Saudis view these decisions is based mainly on how they perceive themselves (or their families) to be personally affected.

Consensus is not established by formal vote but through another traditional, informal institution, *shura* (consultation). Those consulted can vary widely, depending on the nature and urgency of the problem addressed, and can include all those most critically involved—royal family members, technocrats, personal associates, trusted businessmen, and so forth. If there is no consensus, the decision will usually be deferred and no action taken. To act outside the consensus is to become a pariah. Thus, no one, including the king, can with impunity ignore consensus in taking a decision any more than he can ignore Islamic law. The key to consensus is including a representative body of opinion.

Participation by the technocrats. The Saudi royal family does have a privileged position in the Saudi political and social system. It has not, however, barred upward mobility in the government bureaucracy for anyone with the talent and ambition to serve. The regime has been very careful to insist on qualified persons to fill positions of technically demanding responsibility, in some cases replacing royal family members with more qualified technocrats.

In the 1960s, one could count college-educated Saudis on the fingers of one hand. Many of the educated, such as former petroleum minister Zaki Yamani and planning minister Hisham Nazer, rose quickly to high positions. As the number of college graduates expanded, there was concern that there would be disaffection among those who could no longer get to the top so quickly, but this concern has proven to be groundless. Government operations have increased rapidly, so that lesser positions now are as demanding as senior positions were thirty years ago. Professional burnout and the lure of the more lucrative private sector have also eased the pressure. As the bureaucracy continues to become more efficient, the need for managerial talent has grown, not shrunk.

There is still frustration at the sometimes slow and inefficient bureaucratic operations, but this has not translated, at least at present, into political disaffection, much less dissidence. Thus, the Saudis' commitment to maintain a broadly based technocracy has served as an important safety valve within the political process.

Political Threats to the Regime

Internal political threats. Despite its often stormy history since it was founded in the mid-1700s, the Saudi regime has never been ousted through denial of legitimacy by its subjects. In the late nineteenth century, however, warring among rival Al Saud princes so weakened the regime that it toppled mainly because of conflicts. The possibility that rival factions in the royal family could again undermine the legitimacy of the regime has been a constant cause of concern to outside observers, but if the Al Sauds have learned anything in 250 years, it is the necessity of presenting a united front.

The legitimacy of the regime was indeed put to the test during the chaotic reign of King Saud (r. 1953–1964). Saud's arbitrary and capricious policies had brought the prestige of the regime to an all-time low, at home and abroad. Yet it was the royal family working within the political process, not the public at large, that forced a change. In 1964 a body called Ahl al-Aqd w'al-Hall (People Who Bind and Loose), made up of members of the royal family, senior government leaders, and leading religious figures, declared King Saud no longer fit to rule. It was an affirmation of consensus, legitimized by a *fatwa*, a binding Islamic legal opinion.

Since then, there have been two peaceful royal successions, and there is a consensus within the royal family on the next two successors, the heir apparent, Prince Abdallah, followed by Prince Sultan. Rumors appear in the Western media from time to time of rivalry between these two, and, indeed, rivalries have always existed in the royal family. But for the order of succession to change, a consensus within the royal family would have to be created, and that is neither contemplated nor likely to succeed.

There have also been domestic plots against the regime. In the late 1960s, a plot was uncovered among the Saudi military. In the 1960s and 1970s, dissident left-wing Saudi groups operated out of Iraq, where they were given safe haven. Despite these activities, however, there has never been the large ground swell of public opposition that, for example, marked the downfall of the shah. Barring a major externally caused crisis, therefore, it is difficult to imagine an internal threat to the regime in the 1990s with more than a remote chance of success.

If a credible internal threat to the regime did arise, it is even less likely that it would come from the left. Communism and socialism are anathema to Muslims; Saudis are deeply attached to their faith, and they equate communism with atheism. Antipathy to Marxism is not necessarily a guarantee against a tactical relationship by antiregime individuals or even of those mouthing the slogans of socialism. With a lessening of East-West tensions, however, and the possibility of the regime's establishing diplomatic relationships with the Soviets sometime in the 1990s, the possibility of politically disaffected elements seeking and receiving support from the Soviets for socialist revolution in the 1990s appears remote.

A far more likely credible threat to the regime would come from the right. Using the regime's own Wahhabi ideology against it, it is conceivable that Muslim fanatics might seek the overthrow of the regime, not for what it stands for but for not living up to what it stands for. As was noted above, Wahhabi ideology is potentially revolutionary. It espouses the same teachings of Ibn Taymiyya that were used by Egyptian Muslim fanatics to justify the murder of

President Anwar Sadat. Opposition to the regime's ties with the secular United States and, by association, with Zionist Israel, could much more easily be justified by revolutionary Islamic ideology than communist ideology.

One should not assume that all segments of the population accord the regime the same degree of legitimacy. The kingdom was united by the sword, and regional feelings are still strong. Saudi Arabia is basically a Najdi (central Arabian) monopoly. Hijazis on the Red Sea, who boast the holy cities of Mecca and Medina and whose country was far more advanced than Najd, have never gotten over being second-class citizens. Still, were they to seek independence, they would deprive themselves of Saudi oil revenues, which are all located in the eastern provinces along the Gulf. If for no other reason than that, Hijazi separatism has not been a factor for years.

There is one group that is almost totally outside the political process, the Shiite minority, located mainly in the eastern province. Although it could not engineer a coup against any Sunni government, it could pose a sufficient threat to internal security to seriously threaten the regime.

The Shia have historically been uninterested in Arab world politics and in the 1950s and 1960s were given sensitive, skilled jobs in Aramco oil installations, among other reasons because they were not responsive to the antiregime rhetoric of Arab radicals. After the fall of the shah, however, there was serious concern that the Shiite minority, identifying with the Iranian Islamic revolution, might become a major security threat, particularly to the oil installations. The median age of the community is around seventeen years, and it was thought that younger people, more easily persuaded by Iranian urging, might rise up against the regime.

Despite a few incidents, such as the Shiite riots of 1979 and 1980, the Saudi Shiite community has remained basically loyal to the regime. The reasons are not entirely clear. In part, the Shia see their future linked to the Sunni majority and appear to have resented unprovoked Iranian incidents against the Saudi regime, such as the uprisings at the 1987 Mecca pilgrimage. They are also generally horrified at human conditions inside Iran. It is also possible that Shia are less Persian-oriented than was commonly believed. After all, Shiite Islam originated in Iraq, and most of the Saudi Shiite clergy are trained there, not in Iran. At any rate, the Shiite community does not appear to pose the internal security threat that was feared in the early 1980s.

External political threats. External political threats have waxed and waned. For years, the principal external threat was from secular, socialist Arab nationalism, supported by the USSR. In the 1960s, the greatest of these was Nasserism, whose brand of Arab nationalism divided the Arab world into radicals and conservatives. It is difficult to imagine, a quarter century later, the intense political emotions President Nasser could arouse. And for him, Saudi Arabia was the most prominent conservative Arab adversary.

By the end of the 1980s, the political threat of Arab radicalism had greatly receded. Of the remaining radical Arab states, Algeria is increasingly liberalizing its political system and its economy and is seeking closer ties with the West; Syria is politically isolated for siding with Iran in the Iran-Iraq war; Yemen is too poor and too isolated to be a major threat; and Libya is virtually a pariah, even in the Arab world. The other leading radical of the 1960s, Egypt, has signed a treaty with Israel. On balance, therefore, Arab socialism and other leftwing doctrines should not pose a significant external political threat to the Saudis in the 1990s.

The threat from Iraq presents a special problem. With the Kuwait crisis continuing as I write, it is impossible to determine what the ultimate outcome of the crisis will do to the political alignment of the Gulf states, including Saudi Arabia, or to the political coloration of Iraq. Assuming that President Saddam is successfully thwarted in his attempt to annex Kuwait, he will probably not have the political power Iraq needs to constitute a major threat to Saudi Arabia for the next few years. Moreover, the serious domestic economic dislocations resulting from years of fighting have left Iraq's finances in chaos, and it would be more likely to turn inward to solve its problems than outward, as Saddam did in August 1990. A change of regime would make an inward focus of the regime even more likely.

The Arab-Israeli problem has also long been considered a major external political threat. However, the Saudis do not consider it as much a threat to the survival of the regime as they once did. When Arab radicalism was at its height in the 1960s, Saudi Arabia's strong anticommunism and close relations with the United States were viewed by its radical Arab adversaries as tacit support for Israel and all the more reason for them to support efforts to undermine the Saudi regime.

The Saudis were not, in fact, so totally preoccupied with the Arab-Israeli problem as some of the radicals were: In their view, the godless ideologies of the Arab radicals and the support they received from the USSR posed an equal threat to the Muslim and Arab worlds. In the late 1960s, these perceptions began to change.

The loss of East Jerusalem in the 1967 war placed al-Aqsa, the third holiest site in Sunni Islam after Mecca and Medina, in Israeli hands. This was as intolerable to the Saudis as having the Western Wall in the hands of the Arabs was to the Israelis. Whatever else the radicals think of Saudi Arabian leaders, they do not accuse them of being soft on the issue of Jerusalem.

By the 1970s, Arab radicalism was in decline, Islamic fundamentalism was on the rise, and the energy crisis had made Saudi Arabia a major Arab political power. The Saudis were no longer apologetic about their position on seeking a political settlement to the Arab-Israeli problem. At the same time, they were less inclined to follow a US lead when they perceived that it was not going anywhere. For example, they were horrified with the Camp David Accords, which they saw as a successful Israeli effort to lure Egypt into a separate peace while not really coming to grips with the Palestinian right of self-determination. Nevertheless, they reserved judgment until the Egyptian-Israeli treaty of 1979, which, to Saudi eyes, confirmed their worst fears.

Convinced that the Camp David Accords could not obtain a just settlement, King Fahd came up with his own proposal in 1982, the Fahd Plan. In the absence of any real forward motion on the peace process since, the Fahd Plan is still the extant statement of Arab consensus on terms for a settlement.

Saudi Perceptions of Political Policy

Saudi political views are indelibly linked to Islamic political theory. More than a religion, Islam is a universal way of life. The Saudi belief in its special guardianship for the Muslim world, noted above, guides foreign and domestic policies alike.

Despite the assault of wealth, technology, and new ideas; despite the indifferent record of often incompetent government; and despite the monopoly of political power in a hereditary royal family, family-based Saudi society is as strong and resilient as any society in the world. That is to say that Saudi political stability is in large measure the product of Saudi social stability.

The debilitating influences of modernity might ultimately take their toll and undermine the society enough to threaten internal security, but so far the cohesion of the traditional family-based society has remained basically intact. In the 1990s, therefore, it would take a monumental political or economic disaster to seriously harm the society.

Foreign policy perceptions. The Saudis, as guardians of Islam's two holiest sites, Mecca and Medina, have long felt a special responsibility as guardians of the Islamic way of life and the well-being of the Islamic world. This sense of guardianship is a basic factor in setting foreign policy priorities. Underlying it is a very distinct Islamic world view. It is not solely based on the Wahhabi revival but is also due in part to Saudi history.

The Saudis were never colonialized by a Western power and thus did not develop the deep-seated psychological phobias against "colonialism" and "imperialism" of other Third World states. Moreover, unlike that of most of their Arab neighbors, their highly developed sense of Arab nationalism did not originate as a reaction to Western nationalism. The Saudis' sense of Arabness is based mainly on lineage. Arabians are the original and, in the Saudi view, only "pure" Arabs.

As a result, the Saudi world view conforms closely to that of the bipolar world of classical Islam. In that world, there is *Dar al-Islam* (the realm of submission [to God]) and *Dar al-Harb* (the realm of war). The former is the abode of monotheists, which, in addition to Muslims, includes Christians, Jews, and Zoroastrians, and the latter is the abode of atheists. Saudi acceptance of other monotheist religions (called *Ahl al-Kitab*, or "People of the Book") is an important point, since it distinguishes them from Islamic fundamentalist revolutionaries who consign all non-Muslims, as well as Muslims not accepting their interpretation of Islam, to *Dar al-Harb*.

It is easy to see how the modern bipolarity of the free world and the communist world conforms to the bipolar world of classical Islam. Considerations of the Third World and North-South dialogue have always been of secondary importance to the Saudis. In the long run, atheistic Marxism and secular Arab socialist doctrines have been considered a greater threat to the kingdom and to the Muslim world at large, for which the Saudis feel a special responsibility.

It is also easy to see some discrepancies in this world view. Judaism is accepted as a revealed religion, but Israel is a major threat. To cope with this dichotomy, the Saudis view secular Zionism rather than Judaism as the source of the threat. The United States is secular, but it is also the final defense against communist world domination. Thus, it is viewed by the Saudis as a Christian rather than a secular nation. Of course, long-term frustration with US pro-Israeli policies could at some point change this perception to that of the godless, depraved, and violent society often portrayed in the US media and motion picture industry.

Though firmly opposed to Zionism as a secular political doctrine, the Saudis continue urgently to desire a peace settlement. They see the Arab-Israeli problem as a cancer in the Muslim Middle East, radicalizing young people and turning them away from the true tenets of the faith.

In recent years, the Saudis have had to wrestle a new threat: the rise of revolutionary Islamic fundamentalism. The Saudis are comfortable opposing godless, left-wing doctrines, but the rise of militant political Islamic fundamentalism is very disturbing, particularly since the Islamic interpretations used to justify the use of violence are similar if not identical to the Saudis' own political ideology.

In this context, Iran is viewed less as a political threat than a security threat. Shiite fundamentalism has virtually no appeal to the Sunni majority in Saudi Arabia and little appeal to the Saudi Shiite minority. The Iranian threat is seen mainly in terms of attempts to undermine the Saudi regime through subversion, terrorism, and threat of military force. Iranian military and subversive activities are a greater danger than Iran's revolutionary doctrine.

On the other hand, Iran is definitely seen as challenging Saudi Arabia for the role of guardian of the Islamic way of life. Thus far, Iran's appeal in the Muslim world has been limited to xenophobic elements who get vicarious pleasure from Iran's disregard for international rules of conduct, particularly in dealing with the West. Nevertheless, Iran does constitute a challenge that the Saudis take seriously and that in the 1990s might well result in a somewhat less tolerant and more rigidly religious foreign policy orientation. This could be manifested in stricter living conditions for foreign nationals working in the kingdom, in more vocal criticism of civil or human rights issues seen in violation of Islam, and so on.

Forecast for the 1990s

The collapse of the Saudi regime has often been predicted, and in time may come to pass. It could even happen in the near future. Indeed, a political-military crisis of the magnitude of the Kuwait situation could cause the regime to fall. Other than through a crisis, however, there is currently no compelling evidence to conclude that the Al Saud will not remain in power in the 1990s. There is even less likelihood that the regime will fall to a radical Arab socialist revolution.

If it does fall, it will most likely be because it has cut itself off from the people by ceasing to strive for a representative consensus on which to base its policies, thereby losing its legitimacy. Its most likely successor would be militant fundamentalists, justifying their rise to power on the same Wahhabi doctrine espoused by the current regime.

An Islamic revolutionary regime would probably be strongly anticommunist but even more anti-Western, seeing the West as decadent and secular. It would also be more stridently anti-Zionist, and willing and probably able to use its oil resources as an effective policy tool in seeking the creation of a Palestinian state. Relations with Iran, assuming that Iran still espouses its Islamic revolution, will be more strained, not less so, as the two regimes compete more openly for leadership of the Muslim world.

Such a new regime would probably not basically change oil and economic policies but would not accommodate the West or the world economy over more narrowly defined economic interests. It would still buy arms from Europe rather than from the USSR and, were the United States to allow it, would even wish to purchase US arms, which are clearly the best.

There is more likelihood of a change in leadership than a change in regime. Many of the senior Saudi leaders will be in their seventies in the 1990s. A younger generation in power would differ more in tone than in general policy direction. It would probably be more self-assured and more independent of Western and even other Arab views than the current leadership, although it would still proceed carefully and from consensus.

Even with no changes, the Saudis are likely to act more independently on a number of key political issues in the 1990s.

The Arab-Israeli problem. For any peace proposal to succeed, the Saudis must agree to it. Not only is Saudi Arabia the leading moderate Arab state and a key part of the Arab consensus that would make it possible, but the Arab financing required to put a Palestinian entity on a sound economic footing must come mainly from the Saudis. The need for Saudi financing is generally conceded by everyone, including the Saudis themselves.

Regarding terms, the Saudis are not likely to agree to anything short of full self-determination for the Palestinians, as stated in the Fahd Plan. They are also not likely to agree to peace without reestablishing their sovereignty over Tiran and Sanafir Islands at the mouth of the Gulf of Aqabah. Most people have forgotten these two Saudi islands occupied by Israel in the 1967 war, but the Saudis have not. For them, Israel has never given *up* land for peace; it has only given *back* land for peace. The Saudis totally dismiss Israeli claims of sacrifice in giving up Arab lands for peace and mean to get theirs back also.

The Northern Gulf. Aside from the threat from Iraq in the Kuwait crisis, Iran's activist revolutionary Islamic foreign policy is likely to remain the major political threat to Saudi Arabia in the northern Gulf in the 1990s, particularly if the current leadership remains in power in Iran and Saudi Arabia. An ouster of the clerical regime in Iran could lessen tensions significantly, but deep-seated Arab-Persian rivalry ensures that Saudi-Iranian competition will not disappear, no matter what political changes are in store.

Saudi National Defense Policies in the 1990s

The Saudi state was mainly created by the sword. In the eighteenth, nineteenth, and early twentieth centuries, Bedouin warriors loyal to the Al Saud waged continuous campaigns against their adversaries, winning some and losing others. The last major military confrontation was with the Yemen in 1934. Since then, the Saudis have been engaged in skirmishes and battles, but no major wars.[7] Nevertheless, external military threats, most recently from Iraq, continue to be a major Saudi concern.

External Military Threats

The Saudis have faced many external threats over the years. Following the ouster of the Hashemites in the mid 1920s, the two Hashemite regimes of Iraq and (Trans) Jordan were considered major threats. In the late 1950s, the monarchy was overthrown in Iraq, and Saudi Arabia and Jordan have become close if not warm allies.

Israel is the longest continuous military threat to Saudi Arabia, dating back to 1948. While it is doubtful that the Israelis would even think of physical occupation of the kingdom, the northwestern corner of the kingdom has long been considered within their strategic interests. The Israelis have continuously violated Saudi air space as a form of psychological warfare to deter the Saudis from considering participation in Arab military operations against Israel.

Prior to the end of the cold war, one could make a case that the USSR was the greatest military threat to Saudi Arabia. The Saudis would probably not have disagreed. Even though the direct Soviet threat may have lessened, the Saudis continue to see radical left-wing states as a major threat. Over the years, they have perceived threats from a number of such countries, including Egypt, North Yemen and South Yemen (united in 1990), Somalia, Ethiopia, and Iraq. At the height of the Yemeni civil war in the 1960s, more than 50,000 Egyptian troops were engaged in the Yemen, and in the years following its independence in 1967, South Yemen has had two brief military skirmishes with the Saudis.

Throughout the 1960s and 1970s, the greatest military threat from the northern Gulf came from Iraq. During the 1980s, the Iran-Iraq war and the Gulf "tanker war" made Iran Saudi Arabia's primary military threat, and even though fighting ceased in 1987, Saudi-Iranian tensions have remained high.

Forecast for the 1990s

As the 1990s begin, the most dangerous threat to the kingdom is posed by a hostile and militarily very powerful Iraq. With the Kuwait crisis, the military balance was tipped in favor of Saudi Arabia by the deployment of troops from many nations—the Arab world, Europe, Asia, but principally from the United States. Depending on how the Kuwait crisis plays out, the threat from Iraq could decrease dramatically. On the other hand, an anti-Western Arab backlash is also possible, which could gravely threaten the regime by associating it with Western and particularly US troops stationed on Arab soil. At any rate, in the first years of the 1990s, Iraq will be the most visible and immediate military threat to Saudi Arabia.

By contrast, Saudi-Iranian relations improved measurably once the Iran-Iraq war wound down. It would be wishful thinking, however, to assume that relations between the two countries will become cordial in the the 1990s. Historic Arab-Persian rivalries, exacerbated by religious, ideological, and other rivalries, will remain a constraint on friendly relations even in the best of times.

The military threat of radical states greatly declined in the 1980s as Iraq moderated its policies as a result of the Iran-Iraq war, South Yemen moderated its policies because of domestic political rivalries and mounting economic problems and then united with North Yemen, and the Soviet Union's attentions were turned to Afghanistan and its foreign policies were moderated by *glasnost*. Nevertheless, the rise of a new radical threat in the 1990s is not totally to be ruled out, as the Iraqi invasion of Kuwait has so clearly demonstrated.

The changing nature of the military threat is not likely to alter Saudi strategic planning. Basic Saudi threat perceptions, the encirclement syndrome in particular, have developed over centuries; the current military development programs have developed over decades, mainly based on advice from the United States. There are likely to be few changes in overall Saudi armed forces, with emphasis on hardware over manpower and a high priority for its air force. Specific development will be mainly influenced by political, and to a lesser extent, economic constraints on weapons acquisitions. As of the time of writing, nearly all Saudi military assets are deployed to meet the Iraqi threat.

Implications for the United States and the West

Assuming a favorable conclusion to the Kuwait crisis, the basic realities affecting Saudi domestic and foreign policy interests are not likely to change drasticallly in the 1990s. Moreover, Saudi perceptions, short of a change in regime, are not likely to alter greatly either. Even in the event of a new regime, firmly held perceptions such as an Islamic world view, an encirclement syndrome, and collective action taken on the basis of consensus are not likely to loosen.

At the same time, the political and strategic environment in the region will probably be transformed, no matter how the Kuwait crisis is ended. A basic question thus arises: How much will change and how much will stay the same from the standpoint of the United States and the West (including Japan)?

Oil Interests

It has long been standard litany in the US government to say that a major policy interest in the Gulf is "secure access to oil at reasonable prices." To the degree that phrase means anything, the Saudis share it also, not out of pure humanitarian friendship with the West, but because it conforms to their own interests in guaranteeing a long-term market for their oil and in avoiding severe world economic dislocations that overpricing would produce. Even the 1973–1974 Arab oil embargo does not belie Saudi oil priorities. The embargo was a political policy and, in fact, undermined the Saudis' own oil policy preference for more gradual price rises.

The mutuality of US and Saudi interests in reasonable oil prices and in price stability is not likely to change drastically in the 1990s. Moreover, differences over oil price levels are not likely to be sharp, assuming that the oil price rise resulting from the Kuwait invasion produces recessionary trends that maintain an international glut throughout much of the decade.

This does not mean, however, that the United States will be entirely pleased with Saudi oil policies. After all, the Saudis are sellers and the United States and the West are buyers, and that alone will always produce a degree of tension in oil relations. Moreover, the United States, in particular, has never been serious about the term "reasonable prices" and is not likely to be so in the 1990s. What the United States wants are cheap prices, regardless of the long-term economic costs to itself, much less the Saudis, and once the tight oil market of 1990–1991 recedes, conservation efforts are likely to suffer the same fate they did in the oil glut of the 1980s. Until the average US voter is convinced that personal mobility provided by the automobile is not a basic right, neither the executive nor, more especially, the legislative branch, is likely to have the intestinal fortitude to limit demand through taxes, as has virtually every other major industrial country.

In the short run, Saudi Arabia will probably be anxious to accommodate the United States and other major consumers in attempting to moderate oil prices, run up by the Kuwait crisis. The Saudis are also sincerely appreciative of the manner in which the United States came to its support during the crisis. In the longer run, however, a younger, more self-assured Saudi leadership is not likely to be quite so responsive to the desires of the United States and other major Western consumers in their oil policies as today's leadership was in the 1970s. As the glut stretches out, Saudi and US oil interests will diverge. As the glut ends, most likely toward the end of the decade, the Saudi leadership will no doubt oppose precipitous price rises due to their own interests, but not so strongly as the West would like them to. When that day comes, more independent Saudi oil policies, to the degree that they force the United States to be more energy-efficient, might not be all to the bad, even though the extra revenues will accrue to the Saudis rather than to the United States, as they would with a surtax.

Economic and Commercial Policies

Saudi economic policies will obviously be closely tied to oil revenues. As with oil policies, Saudi economic policies in the 1990s are likely to remain basically unchanged in overall direction but will be much more independent. For example, in the 1970s, the Saudis invested large sums in US Treasury notes, to some degree to accommodate the United States. When the glut is finally over and their foreign currency holdings increase in the 1990s, they will no doubt reinvest in Treasury notes, but not with the same degree of accommodation.

As their revenues increase, commercial opportunities will also increase. US goods and services have a competitive advantage in that they are highly regarded in the kingdom and US businesspeople have the reputation of delivering on their obligations. Other countries also have advantages, such as the Koreans in heavy construction, but the Saudis are generally willing to pay for the best regardless of price. Moreover, because the Saudis separate business and political affairs, US goods would probably continue to be competitive even if there were an anti-Western regime.

Probably the greatest potential market in Saudi Arabia for US goods and services is in arms sales, yet the United States has forced the Saudis to go elsewhere. During the mid-1980s, the United States forfeited tens of billions of dollars in arms sales and tens of thousands of US jobs by refusing Saudi arms requests. The decision is basically political, dictated by the desire to avoid offending Israel and its partisan US supporters. In the aftermath of the Kuwait crisis, the United States appears once again ready to increase arms sales to Saudi Arabia, always subject, of course, to political constraints exercised by the Senate. Additional revenues could help the deteriorating US trade balance with the Gulf as the United States becomes increasingly dependent on imported oil.

Political Policies

The United States has long believed that Saudi Arabia should continue to push the other Arab states into being more forthcoming on what they will accept in peace settlement and to get the PLO and the leaders of the *intifada* to moderate their activities in the interests of peace. In the late 1980s, the Saudis were encouraged by what they saw as signs (e.g., in US public statements and its dialogue with the PLO) that the Bush administration was seriously trying to get the peace process back on track.

The picture changed markedly in 1989 and 1990. First, the thawing of the cold war greatly reduced the ability of the radical Arabs to play East against West in the Arab-Israeli conflict. Indeed, the prospect of the United States and the Soviet Union cooperating on a Middle East peace might give real hope for a comprehensive peace for the first time since the creation of Israel in 1948.

The Iraqi invasion of Kuwait in 1990 further undermined Arab unity when the Palestinians and Jordan openly expressed support for Iraq, the only Arabs to do so other than the Yemen. This behavior will greatly restrain Saudi support for a heavy PLO involvement in the peace process; the Saudis are particularly bitter at what they believe is treacherous behavior by Jordan.

What this might do to the peace process is hard to say. If a just and secure peace is possible without giving the PLO a major role, then these developments could actually encourage peace. On the other hand, the Saudis will still be watching closely to see how far, in their perception, the United States is willing to press Israel into accepting a Palestinian state.

Saudi relations with the communist world are likely to expand in the 1990s. Not only has the end of the cold war made this more palatable to the more conservative voices in the Saudi leadership, but as the communist states move toward capitalism, commercial opportunities may also increase. Full diplomatic relations with most of the communist countries are likely by the end of the decade.

Military Policies

In the unlikely event that an Islamic revolutionary regime emerges in Saudi Arabia in the 1990s, the military relations with the West will change as drastically as they did in Iran in the 1980s. Far more likely, however, is a continuation of current relationships. The Saudis will continue to look to the United States and the West for ultimate protection against external foes they are unable to defeat. They will also look to the West as their primary arms suppliers and source of training.

Saudi Arabia: Plus ça Change

For years Saudi Arabia has been taken more or less for granted by Western policymakers. Whatever changes occurred, even including the energy crisis of the 1970s, basic political, economic, and defense policy patterns always seemed to remain relatively constant. Barring dire consequences from the Kuwait crisis to Saudi stability, there is reason to believe that these patterns will continue to remain fairly constant in the 1990s.

Nevertheless, changes are taking place, most notably the maturing of a desert kingdom into a major regional political actor and an international oil power, and the growing sophistication of its people through advantages of modern communications, transportation, and Western education. These do not appear to have changed basic conservative Saudi social values, but they have greatly expanded the horizons of Saudi personal as well as governmental interests.

Once the immediacy of the Kuwait crisis recedes, and assuming the Saudi political system escapes unscathed, these changes are likely to be most reflected not in major policy shifts but in an incremental decrease in Saudi willingness to accommodate US oil, economic, political, and defense interests. Less willingness to accommodate could also be reinforced by changing political and strategic conditions. A reduction of the threat from Iraq as it looks inward, continued easing of East-West tensions, and the possibility of real progress on the Arab-Israeli peace could serve to undermine the sense of urgency with which Saudi Arabia has looked to the United States for support and protection. Thus, while the Saudis will continue to see their own interests closely linked to those of the United States, they will probably be much more independent in pursuing their interests, with the United States when possible but without it if necessary.

When changes in relationships with a country are gradual and incremental, there is always a threat that formerly valid conventional wisdom can become outdated before anyone realizes it. With Saudi Arabia in particular, one needs constantly to test the basic assumption upon which oil, economic, political, and defense relations are based. In order to avoid the possibility of unnecessary and painful friction, perhaps the old adage should be turned around: "Plus c'est la même chose, plus ça change."

Notes

1. Exact figures conflict. There is even doubt whether the Saudis themselves knew precisely what their total reserves were.
2. Anthony H. Cordesman, *Western Strategic Interests in the Southern Gulf: Strategic Relations and Military Realities* (Boulder, CO: Westview Press, and London: Mansell Publishing), Table 2.1, p. 17.
3. One of the five pillars of the Muslim faith is to give alms (*zakat*) to the poor.
4. Strict adherents avoid the term "Wahhabism," which emphasizes a mortal. Strict monotheists, they prefer the term *Muwahhidin*, or "Unitarians."
5. The Hanbali school is quite liberal on economic and commercial matters so that it is no anomaly that Saudi Arabian business practices are so wide open.
6. For a discussion of Ibn Taymiyya's views, see John Alden Williams, ed., *Islâm* (New York: George Braziller, 1961), pp. 205–210.
7. The Saudis sent troops to Jordan during the 1967 Arab-Israeli war, but they did not arrive in time; Saudi units in Jordan did engage during the 1973 Arab-Israeli war.

7

The Gulf Cooperation Council: The Smaller Gulf States and Interstate Relations

Joseph Wright Twinam

The GCC—Always Exclusive, Now Fashionable

In terms of membership, the Gulf Cooperation Council, formed in May 1981 among Saudi Arabia, Kuwait, Bahrain, Qatar, the United Arab Emirates, and Oman, is right where it wants to be and probably intends to stay. It is a grouping of the like-minded. The members are monarchies based in tribal and traditional societies in a notably revolutionary environment. They enjoy affluent, oil-related economies in a wider neighborhood of considerable want. History, economics, and security considerations tend to face them toward the West in a part of the world where such orientation is not always in fashion.

In February 1989 the Gulf Cooperation Council passed a milestone. Four Arab states neighboring the Gulf Council countries—Iraq, Jordan, Egypt, and North Yemen—announced the formation of the Arab Cooperation Council. Three are states that had indicated some sensitivity to being excluded from Gulf Council membership when Saudi Arabia, Kuwait, Bahrain, Qatar, the United Arab Emirates, and Oman formed the GCC in 1981. The fourth, Egypt, is the Arab country of greatest geopolitical importance to Gulf Council members. Almost simultaneously the five Arab states of North Africa proclaimed a Maghreb Union.

Astute observers of the Middle East were quick to point out both the bleak prospects for significant economic integration among the four ACC members and that the political ramifications of the new bloc might give some pause to Gulf Council states, especially Saudi Arabia, and particularly with respect to the closer Iraqi–North Yemeni tie.[1]

In our present context, however, surely the main significance of the four ACC members deciding to go their own way is that it further proves, if further proof were needed, that the Gulf Council is here to stay. At the council's inception leaders of the member states seemed anxious to establish that such an exclusive regional grouping of six Gulf Arab monarchies was not inconsistent with the Arab League Charter or the broader concept of one Arab nation. Now, clearly, the Arab world has conceded the point. From Baghdad to the Maghreb, regional groupings are not only acceptable but fashionable, and the Gulf Council led the way.

The formation of the ACC also seems acknowledgment that its member states have no near-term prospects fo joining the affluent Gulf Council club, the "inner six" of the eastern Arab world. Iraq reportedly urged Kuwait to join the ACC, which is proclaimed as open to all Arab countries.[2] Some Gulf Council leaders have gone to pains to explain that other Arab states, such as Iraq and North Yemen, might in time be invited to join the GCC.[3] Yet it remains clear that the Gulf Council is comfortable in its own membership, and there will be for the foreseeable future strong motivation for the six Gulf Council members to hang together and to remain exclusive. A concern about the recent history of revolution, turmoil, and aggressiveness in places such as Iraq, Egypt, and the Yemen—to say nothing of Iran—is to some degree what the Gulf Council is all about.

As the Gulf Council enters the 1990s, it has demonstrated a dynamic and momentum that might well have surprised even the observer optimistic at its birth. In part its success reflects the cautious and sensible way in which member states eased toward cooperation, carefully establishing a consensus and putting some important building blocks of joint economic ventures in place before the council's creation. In part it reflects the reaction to pressures of the Iranian revolution and the related Iran-Iraq war that propelled council members along the path of internal security and defense cooperation far faster than they would have surmised at the founding.

Since May 1981 there has been an impressive number of meetings of senior officials of the council states. In addition to the annual meetings of chiefs of state (Supreme Council) and quarterly meetings of foreign ministers (Ministerial Council) stipulated in the charter, there have been several emergency meetings of the foreign ministers and rather frequent meetings of ministers of interior, defense, oil, finance, trade, labor, information, and so forth. Military chiefs of staff gather together, as do subcabinet-level officials. The council secretary general and his senior staff are frequently in contact with leaders in the individual member states. There is, moreover, a significant level of exchange of bilateral visits among senior leaders of member states.[4] In short, there is today a level of contact, a pattern of familiarity and working relationships among policymakers in the GCC states that would have been hard to imagine twenty years ago, when the British protecting power was the normal means of official communication among most of the Gulf Arab monarchies, and even the rulers were barely acquainted.

This is a development warranting some emphasis. Gulf Arab leaders, even before the council was created, had begun to develop a momentum of coming together to pursue mutual interests. The council charter and the subsequent evolution of the institution have formalized and accelerated this trend. Council meetings have established challenging goals of cooperation in various areas. Member state leaders have asserted that cooperation, perhaps even eventual unity, among GCC states fulfills the aspirations of their citizens.

The Gulf Council has created a psychology of cooperation and a structure for achieving it. Member governments, no more immune from the shortcoming of drift and inertia than governments elsewhere, are locked into a discipline. GCC rulers and their various ministers are expected to come together frequently, and there is pressure on them to agree to further steps toward cooperation. The institution has become a forcing mechanism. It cannot force the unforceable, but it does put the burden on member-state leaders of explaining why they failed to agree rather than why they cooperated.

At the founding of the council, leaders involved were careful to stress that its focus would be on economic integration. In part this reflected the sensitivity of concentration on security cooperation, an issue on which Oman at the time was far more ardent than other members, particularly Kuwait. An important consideration here was that Oman, having recently concluded an agreement giving US military forces access to certain of its air and sea facilities, was much more willing at the time to be seen in the Arab world as linked to the West in a strategic sense than were other members, even Saudi Arabia and Bahrain.

The council was quick off the mark on the economic front, adopting by June 1981 its ambitious Unified Economic Agreement and moving off energetically toward implementing its goals. Then the Iran-Iraq war, somewhat stalemated at the moment of the council's founding, turned much more threatening to the security—both external and internal—of the council states. Consequently, the drive toward union took a new tack, in which efforts toward internal security and defense cooperation and diplomatic initiatives to end the war became more prominent than the steady if less dramatic march toward economic integration.

Economic Cooperation

Gulf Council countries have come a long way toward economic integration since 1981, although they understandably have chosen to tread the easier parts of the path first. The itinerary is laid out by the Unified Economic Agreement. Its ultimate goal is a bold one. As Secretary General Bishara has described it, "By the end of the 1980s the Gulf will be one common market, with all the obligations and privileges which that step entails."[5]

The council has already made strides to facilitate commerce and communication among member countries and simplify outside contact with them. There has been substantial progress in standardizing technical regulations or practices, such as the Transit System Regulations approved by the Financial and Economic Committee in 1982. Professionals in GCC countries are now more or less free to pursue their vocations throughout the region—something of unexpected importance to many Kuwaitis in exile in August 1990. There has been some progress toward collective GCC buying of commodities from abroad, a particular benefit to consumers in the smaller states with relative lack of bulk buying power.

There is a significantly implemented agreement on facilitating the free movement of citizens among council countries, an important step that has been given added weight by the development of good roads from Oman to Kuwait, plus the Saudi-Bahrain Causeway. There is a Gulf University in Bahrain, as well as access of GCC nationals to educational and training institutions throughout the region. Much is going on to imbue the next generation with a sense of GCC identity.

The tough obstacles. More taxing has been the effort to permit freedom of investment, in either real estate or commerce and industry, by citizens of one Gulf Council country in another. The boldness of the initiative can be measured against the general policy of each Gulf state, since the discovery of oil, of more or less restricting ownership of each economy to its citizens. Within the Gulf Council community the basic concern remains that high rollers from the rich members, notably Saudi Arabia and Kuwait, will be able to buy and bid up real estate and take advantage of commercial and industrial opportunities in relatively less affluent states. In such small communities the local business interests concerned are likely to be close to the political leadership, if not identical to it. Therefore we might expect ongoing efforts to restrict the absolutely free flow of capital within the council countries in the years ahead.

The council states have virtually implemented a negligible internal tariff in an historically low-tariff region. The GCC pushed to have a common external tariff of from 4 percent to 20 percent by 1990. There was pressure for exceptions, particularly from Oman, which for reasons of the relative timing of its economic development has a special claim to protecting infant industries. The loophole is in Article 24 in the seventh chapter of the Unified Economic Agreement: "Consideration shall be given to differences in the levels of development between the member states and the local development priorities of each."[6] In some degree the need for Gulf Council countries to present a common front to the world beyond, particularly in dealing with the European Community on access of GCC petrochemicals to the European market, will provide a motive toward a common external tariff, although particular interests may resist this goal.

In the decade of the 1990s there is likely to be a perception that the drive of the Gulf Council countries toward economic cooperation is slowing down, and that the goal of total integration might never be achieved. That possibility was foreshadowed well before the creation of the council, when Kuwait's initiative for a Gulf Currency Union foundered in the mid-1970s. In the years ahead the council's accomplishments may not fulfill the promises of rhetoric.

But who cares? From a strictly economic standpoint, integration of the GCC economies is hardly a vital issue. There is little complementarity among Gulf Council economies. A variety of factors—climate, location, lack of raw material and indigenous skilled labor—work against significant development of non-petroleum-related industry in the Gulf Council states. The primary problem is the smallness of the market. The GCC countries boast no more than 15 million residents, and the number is not likely to grow significantly by the year 2000 if governments are successful in the goal of replacing the strikingly large number of foreign workers with their own citizens. Much of the market is in Saudi Arabia, which has three distinct major population areas spread over a minicontinent, one of them far indeed from the other GCC countries.

Industrial or other trade with one another is not going to be the economic salvation of the GCC countries. They simply lack the characteristics driving the European Community toward integration. GCC economies rise and fall with the oil market. When oil runs out, as in Bahrain, the first line of defense will be a service economy fueled by the oil economies in friendly neighboring countries. The ultimate salvation is the rentier economy, living off investment abroad, toward which Kuwait, long the prototype GCC economy, had already pointed the way before the Iraqi invasion.

What does matter. Fascinated by the success of the European Community in taking the economic path to union and keenly aware of the failure of several politically oriented unity attempts in the Arab world, Gulf leaders developed a general strategy en route to forming the Gulf Council. The primary goal was to be political cooperation that would permit the member states to sustain one another and present a more or less united front to the outside world. Economic cooperation was to be the means of getting to that end, a way of achieving enough measurable progress toward cooperation to keep the flame of political cooperation burning.

The elusive grand symbol. In the Gulf Council's formative years, proponents searched for some dramatic but sensible common economic venture that would symbolize and reinforce the benefits of union. They are still looking.

The problem is not getting some member states to join with others in a venture. Saudi-Kuwaiti-Bahraini partnership in the aluminum, petrochemical, and cement industries demonstrates that this is feasible. The joining of Bahrain, Qatar, the UAE, and Oman as owners of Gulf Air is even greater proof that some of the GCC governments can successfully go into business together some of the time.

The difficulty has been finding the project that would attract all of the GCC members and, in one way or another, usefully serve all of the GCC territory. A major setback was the decisions of Kuwait Airlines and Saudia to keep winging it alone rather than merging with Gulf Air. Another sound possibility, a major Gulf dry dock, had already been preempted by a wider grouping, the Organization of Arab Petroleum Exporting Countries (OAPEC), in which the GCC states are but a portion of the membership. Several other undertakings, in areas such as shipping and banking, have included Iraq as well as the GCC states.

The Gulf Investment Corporation. A partial solution to the problem of cooperation was the creation of what is now called the Gulf Investment Corporation (GIC), launched in 1984, with each member state pledging an equal share of the $2.1 billion capital. Finding difficulty in identifying major projects warranting collective ownership, members of the GCC joined together to help finance a variety of private and public undertakings in the member countries, ventures on a scale that realistic marketing prospects could sustain. By 1988 the GCC had reportedly committed $775 million to help finance nine projects within the member states and had some sixty others under study.[7] This type of activity, the multilateral development-financing institution with which all Gulf Council states have some experience, can have a significant impact on spurring non-petroleum-sector economic growth in member states, can help to rationalize industrial development among the GCC economies, and can bring the benefits of union home to important segments of society throughout the council's territories.

Cooperation in oil policy. While the extent of Gulf Council economic integration may not have critical impact on even the GCC economies, what certain Gulf Council countries do in oil policy will be of increasing importance to the world. The council mechanism provides a forum in which the five members that are significant crude oil exporters and the four (excluding Oman) that are OPEC members can, if they choose, coordinate their production and price policies. The four council members in OPEC account for roughly half of OPEC's production capacity, roughly two-thirds of its currently excess capacity, and over two-thirds of OPEC proven reserves—indeed, half of proven world reserves. Thus when the GCC bloc presents a firmly united front in OPEC deliberations, it carries a very big stick.

Saudi Arabia is, of course, by far the major player among the council's "OPEC four," as it is within OPEC as a whole. In the pre-GCC days, when Saudi Arabia was working for price restraint in a rising market, as well as in OPEC's troubled times since 1981, Saudi Arabia has usually been able to count on the support of at least two if not all three of GCC oil producers during various stages in efforts to influence OPEC. Meetings of or contacts among GCC oil ministers have been important in setting the stage for key OPEC agreements on price, such as the March 1983 reduction of the bench mark, and on production quotas. The recent refusal of the UAE to adhere to its OPEC quota, partly because of Dubai's unwillingness to heed any outside authority on oil matters, illustrates, however, that there is not a perfect GCC solidarity on oil policy issues. The members are still struggling with their commitment in Article 11 of the Unified Economic Agreement to "endeavor to coordinate their policies with regard to all aspects of the oil industry." Indeed, the June 1989 OPEC ministerial meeting, which featured a Saudi-Kuwaiti confrontation on quotas, vividly illustrates that even when GCC members are in accord on long-term oil policy strategy they can disagree sharply on tactics.

This disarray within GCC ranks continued into 1990, with Saudi Arabia unable to persuade Kuwait and the UAE to keep production within their OPEC quotas. This resulted in a dangerous correlation of forces by summer of 1990, with Saudi Arabia on the side of Iraq and Iran in pressuring the two smaller Gulf producers to toe the OPEC line. Saddam Hussein then seized this issue to pursue a different agenda—and precipitated an international crisis. By mid-August, in the wake of Iraq's invasion of Kuwait and the UN embargo of oil exports from

Iraq and occupied Kuwait, the GCC members of OPEC were once again united in pressing for Saudi and UAE production increases to make up for oil exports lost by the embargo. But at that stage the larger issues were whether OPEC was still relevant—and whether Kuwait would be restored.

It seems likely that sometime before the year 2000 growing demand for Gulf oil will absorb the present excess capacity in the GCC states, as well as in Iran and Iraq. At this point a significant and expensive effort to expand GCC production capacity might be necessary if sharp upward pressure on world oil prices is to be avoided. This would require a more complicated type of coordination among Saudi Arabia, Kuwait, and the UAE. Will the Saudis bear the main burden of meeting rising demand? Is there a prospect for a system in which the GCC determines its overall production level and then parcels out quotas among member states?[8]

How the GCC coordinates production and pricing policies is likely to become increasingly critical to world economic health and broad US interests as the year 2000 approaches.

Security Cooperation

The threats of the Iranian revolution and the Iran-Iraq war pushed the Gulf Council countries rather far down the path of security cooperation.

Internal Security

In response to threats—indeed some acts—of subversion, terrorism, or sabotage, the council developed frequent exchanges and close coordination among interior ministers and their senior subordinates. When the draft GCC Security Agreement of 1982 initially failed to obtain necessary Kuwaiti acceptance, Saudi Arabia moved on to conclude substantively similar bilateral agreements with other council states. Kuwait, most subject to terrorist acts during the Iran-Iraq war, cooperated closely in this area with other GCC countries and at the December 1987 GCC summit joined them in ratifying the agreement.

Activities of certain Shiite dissidents in Kuwait since the Iran-Iraq cease-fire and the recent attacks on Saudi diplomats in Bangkok, Karachi, and Turkey suggest that there is scant chance that Gulf Council governments will soon regard threats to internal security as a thing of the past.[9] Iraqi threats since August 1990 vividly reinforce the point. The pressure for close cooperation in internal security measures remains, a considerable momentum has developed, and the GCC is likely to keep taking useful steps in this area.

Defense Coordination

In their first regular meeting in September 1981, the GCC foreign ministers refused to approve an Omani paper urging close cooperation in defense matters. The Iran-Iraq war began to move out of stalemate in the fall of 1981. By January

25, 1982, the Gulf Council defense minsters convened their first meeting in Riyadh to discuss military cooperation. In response to Iranian criticism of the meeting, the GCC asserted its legitimate right of self-defense.[10]

Thereafter, the GCC states engaged in numerous collective or bilateral meetings of senior defense officials. There was serious common defense planning. Wealthier members pledged some $2 billion to bolster Oman's defense capability. By middecade the GCC members were responsible for roughly half of all defense equipment spending in the Arab developing world.

The Saudi air defense shield came to envelop Bahrain and Qatar. Saudi Arabia began to share some AWACS intelligence with Kuwait. A GCC defense command was formed. The joint "Peninsula Shield" exercises were but the most dramatic of a growing number of land, air, and sea exercises, most of them bilateral or trilateral. Eventually the GCC developed a joint strike force, the Saudi-led Peninsula Shield command stationed at Hafr al-Batin in Saudi Arabia near the Kuwait border. Even the GCC secretary general has acknowledged that this 7,000-man force is essentially symbolic, but the symbolism is significant.[11]

An area in which Gulf Council countries have made little progress is in standardizing equipment. The individual governments have long found a certain political comfort in seeking a variety of Western sources of supply, and the Kuwaitis have from time to time found it convenient to acquire some Soviet weapons as well. Over time the smaller states, formerly protected by the United Kingdom, have added US or French weapons systems to their once largely British arsenals. In the late 1980s the Saudis, long heavily but far from exclusively reliant on US systems, made a major shift toward British arms, while procuring Chinese missiles in a way and of a sort that troubled US policymakers. In August 1990, however, Saudi Arabia turned back to the United States as main supplier in a massive way.

The major aircraft systems most clearly tell the tale. The Saudis, long heavily invested in US F-5s and F-15s, have also made a strong commitment to the British Tornado. Oman still relies on British aircraft, while the development of Qatari and the UAE air forces has depended largely on French supply. Kuwait, currently with US A-4s and French Mirages in its arsenal, has made a big commitment to US F-18s. Bahrain, on the threshold of developing a modern aircraft arsenal, has acquired modest amounts of US equipment, first the F-5 and now the F-16. With such a melange there is little serious prospect that GCC governments will soon reduce the heavy cost of maintaining and repairing six separate air forces by significantly sharing support facilities.

The Now and Future Peninsula Shield

The GCC is no NATO and cannot be. Because fuzzy thoughts often have a tendency to predominate, it is necessary to state that GCC military capability never had even a potential role in what used to be considered the East-West military balance—and in reality has no significant role in the Arab-Israel equation under foreseeable situations. The military potential of the GCC is limited to deterring threats around the Gulf and peninsula. In the absence of some sort of massive leadership failure, the GCC can deter any conceivable challenge posed by the sometimes erratic behavior in the Yemen.

As the GCC moved toward defense cooperation, however, it was not the Yemen but the Iran-Iraq factor that motivated action. Gulf Council governments recognized that Iraq had been a threat before the Iranian revolution and that Iran had been a danger since. They feared the spread of the Iran-Iraq war and knew not what risks might lurk in its aftermath.

Obviously the GCC states could not muster sufficient land forces to be credible deterrent to the massive armies of either Iran or Iraq. Until the summer of 1990, however, a ground-force threat from either neighbor seemed remote. Several international and regional geopolitical pressures—including Iran and Iraq's military preoccupation with one another—were presumed to keep an invasion attempt by either against a GCC state beyond the realm of realistic contingencies.

On the other hand, GCC states had hard evidence that Iran could mount air and sea threats and no real certainty that Iraq might not do so in the future. The combined air and naval strength of the GCC states is respectable in comparison to Iraq or Iran.

On August 2, 1990, Iraq shattered all the assumptions. As massive Iraqi ground forces quickly crushed Kuwait, the GCC was not relevant militarily. Moreover, it was immediately apparent that the armed forces of Saudi Arabia and the other council members were not adequate deterrent to further Iraqi aggression. The United States, supported by an impressive array of Western and Arab countries, had to come to the rescue. GCC forces responded as well as they could, but they were not the critical factor. Thus the GCC states face difficult questions, once Kuwait is restored, about what sort of outside military support they will need to assure the future survival of all.

Diplomatic Coordination

The Gulf Council has been impressive in forming common positions on, and taking energetic diplomatic action to resolve, a variety of conflicts in the region. The council served as a useful forum for deliberation of the Fahd Plan, which with modification became the agreed Arab position on Middle East peace at the 1982 Fez Summit. Council members were persistent and adroit in easing the long-standing tension between South Yemen and Oman and bringing those neighboring states into a modus vivendi that has held since late 1982.

The most impressive performance of the council in the diplomatic arena was the tireless and generally skillful effort to end the hostilities between Iran and Iraq, including obtaining UN Security Council action to urge limitations on the hostilities. Over the years these initiatives experienced frustrations familiar to other would-be mediators—including the Islamic Conference, the Nonaligned Movement, Algeria, and the UN secretary general. When Iran finally accepted UN Resolution 598 in July 1988, no one party could claim all the credit for ending the conflict, but certainly the Gulf Council played a constructive role.

As the Iran-Iraq cease-fire held, council states had to develop strategies for coming to terms with Iran while maintaining good relations with Iraq. Some difference in approach was apparent. Indeed, in the last years of the conflict there was evidence that Oman and the UAE pursued more conciliatory approaches toward Iran than did Saudi Arabia and Kuwait, yet Kuwait was the first off the mark in seeking reconciliation with Iran once the shooting ceased. This does not reflect a fundamental weakness in the capacity of the Gulf Council to pursue a common diplomatic strategy. In fact it may represent a subtle point of strength in such a cooperative arrangement. The Gulf Council framework gives flexibility for each state to pursue its individual tactical approaches within a broad common strategy. There is scope for both "good cop" and "bad cop" roles.

Having spent a fortune and endured Iranian retribution supporting Iraq during the war, Kuwait hoped to settle marginal territorial disputes with Iraq amicably after the cease-fire. Iraq took a hard position, which became threatening by 1990.[12] The GCC as institution did not become engaged in this dispute. The Saudi-Iraqi security agreement of 1989 troubled Kuwait as a sign of a break in the GCC front at a critical moment in its dealings with Iraq. When Saddam Hussein's threats against Kuwait became ominous in July 1990, Saudi Arabia was vigorous, but unsuccessful, in diplomatic efforts to avoid conflict. After the Iraqi invasion the Gulf Council made the appropriate moves toward condemnation and presented a united front in support of Kuwait in the Arab League. But by then the crisis had reached the international level and UN action overshadowed GCC efforts.

If and when the Arab-Israeli peace process regains real momentum, the Gulf Council may face another critical test of its ability to coordinate member-state foreign policy and play a useful role in resolving regional conflict. There is ample past evidence, from the US perspective, that Gulf Council governments, while desirous of a lasting peace, are prone to run for cover when the going gets tough in the Middle East peace process. How the process unfolds will largely determine what, if any, constructive role Gulf Council states might play in supporting it. The issue could well prove too burdensome for the council. In any event Saudi Arabia remains the key player among council states when the United States looks for "moderate Arab" support in its efforts to move Arabs and Israelis toward peace. It is quite uncertain what role Saudi Arabia might play. It is more certain, however, that other Gulf Council members, whether or not they join as a group with any Saudi initiative toward peace, are not likely to try actively to undermine it.

Circling the Wagons

The Gulf Council is an experiment in survival through unity. The acid test is the institution's effectiveness in discouraging or managing two sorts of threats to stability within its territories that might otherwise invite outside intervention.

One is dispute between member states. There are unresolved territorial claims that are potential sources of tension. The problem of defining the Saudi–Abu Dhabi–Omani dispute (known as the "Buraimi Oasis issue") seems to have been put to rest as a result of an agreement between King Fahd and Sultan Qaboos immediately after the 1990 GCC Supreme Council meeting in Oman. A more malignant dispute, between Bahrain and Qatar, is over Hawar and other islands, notably Fasht al-Dibal, near the Qatari coast. When this issue flared to the point of confrontation in 1986, the Gulf Council, which had dealt with the Hawar dispute in 1982, moved quickly to reduce tensions and undertake a Saudi-led mediation effort. Recently, however, there have been renewed rumblings.[13] Left unresolved, this dispute is a serious threat to the general atmosphere of cooperation among council members. So, potentially, are other unresolved territorial issues. There is a challenge to the council to resolve these problems, relics of a bygone era, before the next century.

The other sort of threat, political instability within a member state, has occurred only once since the council was established. In June 1987 the brother of the ruler of Sharjah attempted to seize power. The federal government of the UAE and the other Gulf Council members responded quickly and were notably successful in exerting pressure for maintenance of order and peaceful reconciliation. There was no opportunity for outside forces to intervene in this dispute in ways that might have threatened the stability of the region.

The outside world took little heed of the Sharjah incident, as the GCC did what had come to be expected of it. Yet handling of this event goes to the heart of what the Gulf Council is all about. When the British protective treaty relationships were terminated in 1971, it was not preordained that the six Arab monarchies of the Gulf would develop strong bonds of cooperation and mutual support. Indeed, there were some reasons in history to fear the contrary. Fortunately, these states were diligent in pursuing policies that led to the founding of the Gulf Council in 1981 and its subsequent success. Had they not done so, a coup attempt in Sharjah in 1987 while a major war raged between Iran and Iraq could have been a temptation for a variety of outside powers to get involved in ways that might have created serious additional instability in a very strategic part of the world.

The Five Smaller States and Interstate Relations

The Critical Relationships

With the British withdrawal over a quarter century ago, the Kuwaitis started to preach the necessity of solidarity among the five. The lesson has been learned well. There is some room for cultural rivalry and commercial boosterism among them, even some limited tolerance for Dubai's rogue elephant tendencies, but in essence these states have no safe alternative to getting along and working together. There is very little scope for the sort of frictions evidenced in the Bahrain-

Qatar territorial disputes.

Togetherness is essential, but it is not an unmixed blessing. In the years ahead, each of the five governments will face a variety of pressures for economic, social, and political change—in areas ranging from welfare benefits to women's rights to popular participation in governance. The abilities and willingness of the ruling groups in each state to respond will vary. Yet concessions in one country will surely increase pressure for similar change in the others.[14] The council is likely to become a forum for considerable mutual prodding and restraining on sensitive issues that rulers once regarded as essentially their own domestic affairs.

In today's world, the smaller states have no good alternative to bonding with Saudi Arabia in a union of unequals, although they must swallow the sometimes bitter pill of Saudi influence in their lives. Given this reality, the smaller states are well served by having a Gulf Council context in which to work with their powerful partner. There is no evidence of a tendency for the five Lilliputians to gang up on the Saudi Gulliver, and little likelihood of it.

Some of the smaller GCC states, especially Kuwait, spent considerable treasure and incurred notable risks in helping Iraq survive Saddam Hussein's ill-fated 1980 decision to save the Arab world from the menace of Khomeini by invading Iran. Such sacrifice should have justified expectations that postwar Iraq would remain as "moderate" as King Hussein of Jordan, manfully suppressing memories of demise of Hashemite relatives in the 1958 revolution, throughout the 1980s proclaimed it to have become.

But all the leaders of the five smaller states were already experienced in high office in those prewar days when Iraq, that "mad house run by gangsters," was viewed as a serious threat to stability down the Gulf, checked to some degree by Iran under the shah. They were furthermore aware that Iraq had never definitively relinquished certain claims on Kuwait's territory. They appreciated that Iraq in the war had been through an experience comparable to the trauma of France in World War I. Thus they must have been apprehensive about where Iraq would head in the postwar era, recognizing their miniscule capacity for influencing political trends within Iraq.

In helping to assure proper Iraqi conduct toward them they thought they had some impressive assets: foremost their Saudi connection and the capacity of the Gulf Council states collectively to help ease the financial stress of Iraqi reconstruction. Beyond that, the smaller states, with Saudi Arabia, could with some confidence reach out for the support of other Arab states, which had reason for concern about their continued welfare, notably Egypt. In the crunch they could turn to some Ba'thists every bit as tough as Saddam Hussein's crowd, the Hafiz Asad gang in Damascus. But Saddam Hussein's recklessness and ambition took them by surprise.

Until the summer of 1990, the potential Iraqi threat was largely ignored as the smaller Gulf Council states considered the quality of life in a neighborhood with revolutionary Iran. What goes on within Iran is fundamentally out of their control. So long as the revolution still seeks expression, so long as what goes on in Iran seems often out of even Iran's control, the neighborhood must look ominous to the small Gulf monarchies. Future Iranian conduct is clearly the wild card in their future, as it is in the destiny of the Gulf region generally.

The Health of the Five

A quarter century ago, with the British gone from Kuwait and the handwriting of withdrawal on the wall down the Gulf, with Aden reeling toward chaos and the Arab world generally swept by revolution, few Western observers would have bet their wads on the survival of the monarchies that now compose the Gulf Council. By the beginning of the 1990s, these small states were generally off the lists of those who worry about where tumult will come next. But Western observers should have learned a bitter lesson from their misplaced confidence in the survival of the shah of Iran. In August 1990, Saddam reminded the world that it is prudent to keep worrying about such small and valuable countries in such a tough neighborhood.

The Points of Strength

The five states, however, face a threatening world with some impressive assets.

Legitimacy of ruling families. By Middle East or world standards, the eleven dynasties, including the seven of the UAE, have good credentials with respect to their legitimacy as rulers. Their positions are based on tribal support and in all cases go back a century or two. Building on this tribal base, these dynasties had little difficulty co-opting those who immigrated to their domains in the years before and early into the oil bonanza. Newcomers, particularly those not of Arab peninsula origin, have traditionally clung to the ruler as closely as possible. There are, of course, some important exceptions to the general rule of citizen acceptance of the ruling dynasties. Clearly not all of the native Shiite Baharnah of Bahrain are yet comfortably reconciled to the legitimacy of the Sunni Al Khalifah's "Norman conquest" of that island over two hundred years ago. The persistence of the Imam Ghalib's uprising in inner Oman and then the Dhofar rebellion raises questions, even after two decades of effective nation-building under Sultan Qaboos, of the depth of loyalty to the Al Bu Said throughout Oman.

Ruling family solidarity. Except for the squabbling among the aristocratic Qasimi of Sharjah, it has been a long time since intrafamily power struggles seriously threatened the stability of regimes in the five smaller GCC states. A long and rather bloody history of sheikhly aspirants for power killing one another off seemed to come to an end when the ruling families realized that oil wealth had pushed their fiefdoms from obscurity into the full glare of a covetous world. By historical standards the power seizures—by Sheikh Zayid in Abu Dhabi in 1966, Sultan Qaboos in Oman in 1970, and Emir Khalifah in Qatar in 1972—were pretty tame affairs, in all cases carried off with broad support in the ruling families.

Questions of succession have been resolved from Kuwait down through the UAE member states. The disturbing exception is Oman, where after almost two decades of the reign of Sultan Qaboos, there still is no heir apparent.

The federation in the UAE is, of course, a special case. It is hard to contemplate the UAE after Sheikh Zayid, who is approaching his twentieth year as president. By early American federal standards, this makes Zayid the UAE's equivalent of Washington, Adams, and Jefferson. Zayid has made the UAE work with a unique blend of generosity and permissiveness. It is hardly a Prussian experiment in federation, but it far exceeds the initial minimum expectation of simply finding a hook on which to hang the law-and-order function of the Trucial Oman Scouts. When Zayid passes from the scene there is a strong precedent for his heir as ruler of Abu Dhabi to assume the presidency of the UAE, with Sheikh Rashid's heir in Dubai in the vice-presidency. A tradition has been set that Abu Dhabi, so long as it continues to pay the piper, can call at least that much of the federal tune. The gut question for the UAE is how effectively the second-generation team will work together and what leaders from the other states will emerge to give the federation strength and direction. It is to be hoped that some guidelines have been established in the instructive interaction between Zayid and Rashid in the formative years, a minuet between a federalist and a states' righter. It is important that the UAE faces the future surrounded by a Gulf Council framework that will help keep its building blocks in place.

Experienced government. Longevity of leadership does not assure stability, but it can lend an element of legitimacy and public acceptance. In tenure in office, the leadership of the smaller GCC states is remarkable by world standards and, except for the still vigorous Zayid in the UAE, still barely into middle age. The longest-reigning monarch, Emir Isa of Bahrain, has ruled for a quarter century, aided by a cadre of contemporaries, both royal and commoner, who have served in key cabinet posts with considerable distinction. The newest chief of state, Emir Jabir al-Ahmad of Kuwait, has been in key positions of governance for over twenty-five years, as have his Al Sabah relatives Crown Prince–Prime Minister Sheikh Saad and Deputy Prime Minister Sheikh Sabah al-Ahmad. The latter is also the world's longest-serving foreign minister. Such experience and survival augur well for coping with problems ahead.[15]

The curse reversed. The basic flaw of these states in coping with the outside world—their tiny populations—is ironically a source of strength in the effort to build stable societies, as large ruling families in societies of small citizen population can, if they are attentive, rather easily keep in touch with public opinion. There are two noteworthy aspects of the benefits of a small population:

A cup still rather full. The Gulf states have faced sharp economic declines since the oil market began to sag early in the 1980s. The sharp drop in oil prices in 1986 in particular put budgets accustomed to surplus deep into the red, applied some hard brakes on government spending in economies addicted to that source of locomotion, and thus created considerable hardship in commercial markets, particularly the construction industry.

Yet during the toughest of the hard times, most of the five smaller states were still running balance of trade surpluses and had little, if any, foreign debt—indeed, in some cases they retained substantial reserve funds abroad. In all cases budget deficits were manageable in relation to likely future oil revenues, and the development of a "national debt" was at worst only in the experimental stage.[16] There is no doubt that the oil market will improve. There is no question that all five governments are in very sound financial shape—even the government-in-exile of Kuwait. Citizens, still enjoying substantial welfare state benefits, pay no significant taxes to these distributive governments. In short, times may be relatively lean, but they are still remarkably good by world standards.

Moreover, the harder blows of the recession have been taken by foreign workers rather than citizens. Even before Iraq's move in August 1990 there was significant reduction in the foreign work force in places such as Kuwait and Abu Dhabi, creating hardship not just to the individuals concerned but to the home economies dependent on their remittances. It is perhaps possible to trace political unrest to economic sluggishness in the Gulf states, but the places to look for it are Egypt and Jordan.

A generation of bonding. Even the sharpest critics of the Gulf societies must acknowledge that over the years the leadership in each state has seen that the oil wealth was rather widely spread among its citizens. Some citizens are certainly much more equal than others, and this must remain a cause for concern about continued social harmony. But it is hard to find a citizen thirty years of age or more who has not participated in an extraordinary epoch of prosperity and nation-building.

The Points of Stress

Oman, where almost a quarter of the residents in the five states live, is such a special case that it warrants separate consideration. The population is overwhelmingly native and Ibadhi. The question, starkly put, is whether the natives consider the now and future Oman to be their country or still someone else's. Sultan Qaboos, over almost two decades, has made great strides in co-opting the thin ranks of the first generation of Omani "nationalists," in pacifying rebellion, in spreading the benefits of a new and perhaps short-term oil wealth. He has sent younger generations of Omanis away to school. Now they are coming home to a land still notable for the influence of the foreign adviser and the dominance of non-Arabs in the commercial sector. There is a heritage of privilege and cronyism in a society still making hard guns-or-butter decisions. There are perceptions that the British soldiers dawdle in departing whereas the US military "visitors" keep pouring in.

The jury is simply still out in terms of prospects for future political tranquility in Oman. Much will depend on the evolving state of mind of an "Omanized" officer corps and on how firmly the sultan can hold the support of traditional leaders in the interior. But the critical test may be finding satisfying roles for the new generation of Omanis educated abroad.

In the remaining four smaller states of the GCC, the citizens over thirty make up scarcely a quarter of the population. Two-thirds of them may feel they have bones to pick since fate has made them either Shiite or female or both. This leaves rulers a pretty narrow slice of the population, under 10 percent, as a political base with no reasonable grounds for complaint.[17]

The Shiite factor. For years most Western observers tended to ignore the Sunni-Shiite division in the emirates as a relic of the past. After all, the "Iranian bloc" in the early Kuwaiti parliaments was composed of loyal Tories—it was the aristocratic Sunni Arab families, constitutionalists in Arab nationalist clothing, who raised the challenge to the "divine right of sheikhs." Shia, both Baharnah and those of Persian origin, were highly visible in the merchant elites throughout the emirates. Baharnah came to hold significant government posts in Bahrain.

Then the election of a generally antigovernment and conservative Shiite faction to Bahrain's short-lived parliament indicated that even as the last quarter of this century began, the "Shiite question" was far from dead.[18] The Iranian revolution a few years hence forced that lesson home with a vengeance. But it is an unclear lesson because it tends to confuse Shiite disaffection and Islamic fundamentalism, two somewhat different things in the Gulf Arab context.

It is hard to get a handle on the Shiite question; that is the nature of the Shia. In fact there is even some significant disagreement about how many Shia there are in Qatar and the UAE.[19] But a decade of trauma in the context of the Iranian revolution and the Iran-Iraq war—including a coup attempt in Bahrain, terrorist acts (among them an assassination attempt on the emir in Kuwait), and the tragic riots at the 1987 *hajj*—give some framework for calculating the seriousness of the Shiite problem to the stability of the Gulf Arab monarchies.

The situations and degrees of contentment within Shiite communities obviously vary considerably among and within the emirates. Presumably many Shia feel strong bonds to the established order. The large majority of the Shiite populations are not demonstrably moved by exhortation from Iran to rise up against Sunni overlords. There is not likely to be a Shiite rebellion, at least not a successful one, anywhere in the GCC states, not even in Bahrain. The Sunni regimes have the power and the will to reinforce one another to make this scenario an unattractive proposition to most Shia in these countries.

But at least some Shia in some of these states have demonstrated their alienation. Thus there is an undeniable "Shiite threat" to public order—a risk of sabotage, demonstration, subversive exhortation, and political assassination. The future state of GCC relations with Iran will obviously have major bearing on the extent of this threat, but there is already ample evidence that for the immediate future revolutionary Iran, in the best of circumstances, may not speak with one voice in this regard.[20] Moreover, Shiite militancy in the Gulf states need not have a clear and direct order from Tehran. The Shiite terrorist can be just as deadly if his inspiration comes from the Shia down the road or from some ayatollah in Iran.

Thus, at least some of the states, especially Kuwait and Bahrain, must take essential precautions against this threat. In the process they must check, perhaps even reverse, a once remarkable trend toward becoming "kinder and gentler nations."[21] In any event, old animosities between Sunni and Shia are being rekindled in these lands. In the long run, beyond the year 2000, these factors may weaken the social fabric more than the potential temporary shock of an assassin's bullet.

Youth and women. The role of women is likely to become more controversial in the years ahead. In a rather short time, much has been accomplished, particularly in Kuwait and Bahrain, in opening professions and other useful roles in society to women, but the Gulf states still lag behind most Arab and Islamic societies in this regard.

Roughly half of the citizens in these five states are under thirty years of age. As a group they are far more schooled than their elders. Few have vivid recollections of the impoverished times before the oil bonanza. They may well be collectively the most "spoiled" groups of children in the history of mankind. They now face harder times than many were brought up to expect.

This problem also needs to be put in the peculiar perspective of the Gulf societies. These youth live in societies with strong family structures in which the time-tested perceptions of the elders still rival the influence of fresh insights of the young. Although their sights may need some lowering, these young people are entering notably prosperous and dynamic societies. The problem of absorbing the rising educated generation is not brand new in the Gulf states. Bahrain and Kuwait have been working at it for quite some time with considerable success. The lesson learned is that a great deal of room at the top is not essential if there are satisfying ways to contribute in the middle. There remains significant scope for the younger generation in the Gulf states to pull its weight. There are, for instance, still hordes of foreign experts to replace.

But the possibility of alienation among the younger generation on the way to maturity in the twenty-first century must be noted. In this respect, the apparent attraction of Islamic fundamentalism to youth in these countries is special cause for concern, if only because it suggests a disaffection from what has gone before.[22]

How to have a say. Western observers have long worried about the lack of democratic institutions in the five smaller GCC states. Except for Bahrain's brief experiment in 1974–1975, only Kuwait has dared to establish a popularly elected parliament. The Kuwait National Assembly was suspended, for the second time, in 1986; a "halfway house" National Council was established in mid-1990. The appointed consultative councils in Qatar, the UAE, and Oman are fairly tame bodies. Should pressures build in these societies, there is no channel of the sort familiar to the democratic West for the people to voice their concerns, debate their destiny, and determine the popular will.

This is proper cause for concern, but the problem needs to be viewed in the context of the peculiar nature of these countries. There is, as we have seen, a certain silver lining in the disadvantages of being a tiny nation. The emirs of Bahrain and Qatar as well as the president of the UAE are not, of course, elected by their people, but each "represents" far fewer citizens than does a member of the US Congress. The small numbers are much the same in Kuwait and Oman. Each ruler is surrounded by ministers who represent important elements of the society. In addition, the tradition of the *majlis* gives leaders some feel for the popular pulse and citizens a channel for venting their concern.[23] As a result of these factors, the yearning for representative democratic institutions may not be so strong in these societies as Western observers are conditioned to believe.[24]

In addition, leaders in these states have reason for concern that parliaments are inclined to debate not just the condition of streets and sewers but sensitive foreign policy issues as well. The foreign policies of these tiny states are mainly guided by the principle of survival, of trying not to offend any neighbor.[25] Rulers have some cause for concern about national parliaments that might invite the hostilities of a dangerous neighborhood in for public examination.

Notwithstanding these considerations, the lack of movement toward more representative government in the five smaller GCC states is troubling. The initial shock to the rulers of Kuwait and Bahrain, long faithful in their dedication to the *majlis* system, at the harshness of the criticism hurled at them in their new parliaments illustrates the problem. The citizen who petitions in the sheikh's palace simply does not speak his mind as frankly as in his own assembly hall. The ruling groups in the smaller states of the GCC are demonstrably going to move cautiously in finding ways to let the people voice their will, but in the absence of truly democratic institutions, they risk losing touch with public opinion in their remarkably dynamic societies.[26]

The lingering guests. Leaders in the emirates have long been uneasy about the number of foreigners in their midst. Each state is dedicated to reducing the percentage of foreigners in the work force. Yet even after a substantial departure of foreign workers as a result of economic contractions, the populations of Kuwait, Qatar, and the UAE were roughly two-thirds foreign at the moment Iraq invaded Kuwait. Since most of these noncitizens are men without families in-country, the percentage of foreigners in the adult male population is strikingly larger.

The situation has obviously been one of mutual advantage. The foreigners have made an enormous contribution to the economic development of these countries while faring better economically than they would have back home. The significant numbers of British and other Europeans and the quite large group from the Far East are genuine "guest workers." They tend to leave when the job is done.

But the hard core of these foreign work forces, those from other Arab countries, Iran, and South Asia, are by and large a different matter. They tend to stay and, when possible, build families in the Gulf. The large Palestinian population is, of course, a special and poignant case since at present they have nowhere else to go.

There are now many second-generation foreigners in these states, and the third generation is on the way. Yet, with the rarest of exceptions, this society within a society languishes without benefit of citizenship, is generally restricted from property ownership and denied many of the generous benefits these states bestow on their own citizens. Complex questions of security, cultural preservation, and justice are involved.

There are no easy answers to this problem. Each government has demonstrated the skill to keep it under control for the near future. But as far as the stability of the five smaller states is concerned, it is a time bomb that will tick into the twenty-first century.

Implications for US Interests

The United States has developed mature and significant relations with all the GCC states. The basic US interest in this strategic region is a level of peace and tranquility that will assure world access to the Gulf's vital oil resources. The vigorous US response to Iraq's aggression has firmly cemented ties with all the GCC governments. The future, however, is hostage to the outcome of the Gulf crisis of 1990.

US commerce with Kuwait and the UAE, and to a lesser degree with Bahrain, is not unimportant, although these export markets are small in contrast to trade with Saudi Arabia. As Gulf oil revenues begin to recover, there are prospects for increased US trade with all the GCC states and for a resurgence of services and financial transactions.[27] Competition with Western allies and Japan will remain keen. To the extent that the GCC becomes more of a "common market," the interest of US business in the smaller states might grow. Most important, the nature of the economies of these states will keep them oriented toward the West.

The years immediately ahead are likely to witness increasing efforts by both the Soviet Union and China and to develop ties to GCC governments. The Sino-Saudi missile deal demonstrates how this can complicate US diplomacy. In the future, inspired by Kuwait's skillful playing off of Washington against Moscow in the reflagging of ships in 1987, Gulf governments may be tempted to play the Soviet card when annoyed with the United States. But the new acceptability of the Soviet Union in the Gulf states reflects to some degree the realization that for forty years the West successfully held the line against Soviet pressures on the region. Looking ahead, it is difficult to build a credible scenario of Soviet gains in the GCC that would significantly damage US interests. There are limited opportunities for GCC states to pursue trade, arms purchase, and even investment with both the Soviet Union and China. There is at least a superficial argument that all GCC states should have relations with both of these great powers as evidence of their membership in the community of nations. Moreover, most GCC states seem to have concluded that if the United States and the West cannot make revolutionary Iran behave, then it is prudent to take out a supplementary insurance policy with the Soviet Union that might some day in some way be able to influence Iran not to threaten them. But it is hard indeed to see any of the GCC countries becoming profoundly attracted to either the Soviet Union or China in terms of what they have to offer in the way of goods, markets, technology, or political support, to say nothing of ideology.[28]

In the years ahead, as in the past, two regional problems will complicate US relations with all the GCC states. One is how to cope with revolutionary Iran. The GCC states sorely need to find ways to live in some tranquility with Iran. For the near future, until the revolution finds some equilibrium, US-Iranian tension seems inevitable. Thus the GCC states cannot escape the dilemma of balancing their need for a tie with the United States and their desire to get along with Iran.

The Arab-Israeli conflict has been the perennial problem complicating otherwise relatively trouble-free US relations with the Gulf Council states. Ironically, the perception of US ability to bring about peace has been the greatest single source of US influence with these governments, while dissatisfaction with the US performance in this regard has been the main cause of tension in the relationships. Based on past experience, a future US effort to move vigorously in the Middle East peace process will need, and deserve, more Gulf Council support than it is likely to get. Moreover, whatever the United States realistically might do to push for peace is likely to be regarded by the Gulf Council states as too soft on Israel. Thus this key issue contains much potential for causing hard feelings all around. But in the long run the quest for Arab-Israeli peace is the acid test for US relations with the Gulf Council states. For over forty years the Arabs of the Gulf have been caught up in the centrality of the Palestine cause to the concept of Arab nationalism. Gulf leaders have long viewed the persistence of the Arab-Israeli conflict as a major long-term threat to the survival of their regimes. Thus the frustrations about the US approach to this key concern eat at the foundations of relationships otherwise firmly based in economic and security ties. Absent the perception that the United States is seriously and constructively working on this problem, all other efforts to secure US interests in the Gulf are simply pushing against the current.

The dramatic US response to Iraq's invasion of Kuwait signaled a new era in the US relationship with the Gulf Council states. The earlier US naval buildup in the Gulf in 1987–1988 had paved the way—proving the constancy of US support for GCC security and that GCC states could cooperate quietly with US military presence in confidence that it was a temporary phenomenon sufficient to the threat of the hour. By the fall of 1990, however, the United States was close to being in alliance with six governments that, *in extremis*, had shed long-standing inhibitions about the US connection. However the Gulf crisis of 1990 is resolved, it serves both US and GCC interests to work skillfully to sustain the promise of this new relationship. In the process, US policymakers would do well to bear in mind the positive potential of the Gulf Cooperation Council as an institution capable of making some contribution to the "new world order."[29]

Notes

1. See Fred Axelgard, "Saudi Arabia Looks Ahead," *Middle East International*, no. 346 (March 17, 1989), and Godfrey Jansen, "The Pressures on King Fahd," *Middle East International*, no. 347 (March 31, 1989).

2. Seif bin Ali, al-Azmina al-Arabia, March 16, 1989, as reproduced in *Middle East International*, no. 346 (March 17, 1989).

3. In his "History and Development of the Gulf Cooperation Council: A Brief Overview," *The Gulf Cooperation Council: Moderation and Stability in an Interdependent World*, ed. John A. Sandwick (Boulder, CO: Westview Press/American-Arab Affairs Council, 1987), p. 7, John Christie notes that Bahrain's Development Minister Yousuf Shirawi made this point in a London speech a few years after the council's creation.

4. R. K. Ramazani's *The Gulf Cooperation Council: Record and Analysis* (Charlottesville, VA: University Press of Virginia, 1988), presents in Appendix B an impressive chronology of the gatherings of GCC leaders from 1981 to 1986.

5. Abdulla Yacoub Bishara, "The Gulf Cooperation Council: Achievements and Challenges," *American-Arab Affairs*, no. 7 (Winter 1983–1984).

6. Unified Economic Agreement of the Cooperation Council for the Arab States of the Gulf, June 8, 1981.

7. OPEC News Agency, Riyadh, September 9, 1987.

8. This possibility is discussed by Hossein Askari and Babak Dastmaltischi in "Evolution of A GCC Oil Policy," chapter 5, Sandwick, *Gulf Cooperation Council*.

9. *Middle East Journal*, vol. 43, no. 2 (Spring 1989), Chronology, p. 284.

10. Ramazani, *Gulf Cooperation Council*, Appendix B chronology.

11. J. E. Peterson, "The GCC and Regional Security," chapter 8, Sandwick, *Gulf Cooperation Council*, p. 197.

12. Axelgard, "Saudi Arabia Looks Ahead."

13. See Ramazani, *Gulf Cooperation Council*, chapter 5, for a brief discussion of GCC handling of the Bahrain-Qatar disputes.

14. An early portent of this sort of problem occurred in the labor relations area as early as 1975, well before the creation of the council. The government of Bahrain managed to defuse a quite explosive wave of labor unrest centered at the ALBA plant by, among other more forceful measures, a wage increase that looked generous by modest Bahraini standards. Within weeks, the government of Kuwait resolved a troublesome labor dispute there with a wage settlement easily sustainable in the rich state but well beyond the reach of a Bahraini government relatively strapped for funds. The Bahraini leaders were understandably distressed by the renewed pressure this put on labor relations in their country.

15. For a useful discussion of aspects of the legitimacy of Gulf dynasties, see Emile A. Nakhleh, "Political Stability in the Gulf Cooperation Council States: Challenge and Prospects," *Middle East Insight*, vol. 6, no. 4 (Winter 1989).

16. See US Department of Commerce, *Foreign Trends and Their Implications for the United States*, UAE, November 1987; Kuwait, June 1986; Qatar, May 1988; Oman, March 1988; and Bahrain, January 1988.

17. Ramazani, *Gulf Cooperation Council*, Appendix A, has useful statistical breakdowns of Gulf country populations in terms of percentages of youth, foreigners,

and Shia.

18. In early summer 1974, reporting from Bahrain, I warned Washington of a problem of fundamentalist Shiite opposition to the modernizing of Gulf societies. As I recall, the US intelligence community, long focused on Sunni Arab nationalists as the "troublemakers," was shocked into urging our little embassy to go out and get to know some Shiite fundamentalists. We never did in any useful way. We of course had significant contact with modernist Shia, but they are perhaps the worst possible source for explaining to Westerners what fundamentalist Shia are all about. The problem this still poses for the West trying to meet the East was perhaps most pithily expressed by a senior US diplomat who had been deeply involved in US efforts to cope with the Iranian revolution. After the event, he told me in so many words: "I guess we should have been talking with Khomeini all along. But what would we have talked to him about?"

19. Ramazani, *Gulf Cooperation Council*, Appendix A, notes that two respectable sources differ significantly in their estimates of the percentage of the population that is Shiite in Qatar and the UAE.

20. See R. K. Ramazani, "Iran's Foreign Policy: Contending Orientations," *Middle East Journal*, vol. 43, no. 2 (Spring 1989), pp. 206–217, for a discussion of the "idealist" and "realist" tendencies within Iran's revolutionary power structure. But note Speaker Rafsanjani's extraordinary May 5, 1989, speech (reported inter alia in *New York Times*, May 6, 1989) urging assassinations of US, French, and British citizens. This is the leading Iranian "realist," considered by some as a force for "moderation" in dealing with the outside world.

21. See *The Economist*, April 18, 1987, p. 39, for a perceptive discussion of how Kuwait's reaction to terrorist threats has checked the trend toward liberalism in that state. See also Nadim Jaber, *Middle East International*, no. 302 (June 12, 1987), for discussion of the Shiite problem in Kuwait.

22. As early as 1987 a Gulf ambassador asserted to me that all of the student unions of his country, at home and abroad, had fallen under the control of fundamentalist factions. By early 1989, however, this official indicated that his concern on this score had much abated.

23. See Youssef M. Ibrahim, *New York Times*, April 29, 1989, for a rather sanguine view of the effectiveness of the *majlis* system in Saudi Arabia. The impact of the system is roughly similar in the five smaller states of the GCC.

24. When Bahrain suspended its popularly elected parliament in 1975, I found no hard evidence that most citizens of that country were as dismayed as I as US ambassador was. Indeed the people seemed less distressed by this failure in establishing democratic institutions than the emir and certain of his key ministers professed themselves to me to be.

25. To illustrate the sensitivity of public discussion of foreign and national security policy issues, a senior minister in one of the Lower Gulf states once joked to a visiting high-level US official: "If you want to know about our foreign policy, go talk to the Kuwaitis. If you want to know what our defense policy is, go ask the Saudis."

26. Saudi sensitivity to the march of democracy in the GCC region cannot but weigh heavily on the minds of leaders in the smaller states. The Saudi situation is truly remarkable. Twenty years ago the present King Fahd, long before he was even crown prince, publicly called for a constitution and some kind of popular conservative assembly in the kingdom. As crown prince some years later he reiterated this call. Fahd has now reigned almost a decade. The world still waits for the constitution and the representative body. But there is no evidence of Saudi citizens' taking to the streets to push this cause.

27. At the recent second regional meeting of Arabian peninsula Amchams there was a consensus that prospects for US business activity in the GCC states would grow, but only moderately, in the years immediately ahead. American Business Council of

Dubai, *The Council Caucus*, vol. 12, 1989.

    28. I have discussed the limitations of Soviet prospects with GCC states at some length in "Soviet Policy for the Gulf Arab States," a paper presented at a seminar at Villanova University, October 1988, and published in *Domestic Determinants of Soviet Foreign Policy Toward South Asia and the Middle East* (London: Macmillan, and New York: St. Martin's Press, 1989).

    29. For discussion of how the growing importance of the council as an institution might strengthen the fabric of US relations with the smaller member states, see Twinam, "Reflections on Gulf Cooperation, with Focus on Bahrain, Qatar and Oman," chapter 2, Sandwick, *Gulf Cooperation Council*.

8
A New Soviet Role in the Gulf?
Shahram Chubin

The Background and Outlook

In projecting probable Soviet policies toward the Persian Gulf in the next decade and beyond, it is important to assess the nature of past policies in that region. The past four decades may not be the best yardstick for such an assessment because of changes within the USSR and in US-USSR relations. Nevertheless, the nature of regional instabilities, and the problems and opportunities they have posed for the USSR, remain characteristic of the range of issues likely to arise periodically. The primary determinant of Soviet policies in the region will remain the nature of its central relationship and competition with the United States.

The post–World War II period that appears to be ending has been characterized by a superpower rivalry that has been as much geopolitical as it has been ideological. In this respect, at least, there are grounds for caution in assuming radical discontinuities between the past and the future in Soviet-US relations. Soviet definitions of security led to the extension of claims made on its immediate (and numerous) neighbors that made them inconsistent with a balance of power in Eurasia. Essentially, the USSR insisted upon the right to dominant influence—if not control—on the Eurasian continent, the right to be militarily equal to any combination of putative foe (equal security), and the right to demand of its neighbors "friendly" relations, which in Moscow were equated with a right to hegemony. The upshot was that Soviet definitions of security were incompatible with the continued sovereignty of its neighbors and amounted to a claim to effective dominance of Eurasia.

Such excessive claims were bound to be resisted by the principal maritime power, which could hardly afford not to contest them. The result has been a competition in which Soviet attempts to achieve paramount power and influence on the Eurasian periphery have been stymied by US—and US-led—efforts to offset the Soviets' proximate and overwhelming power. What for the United States (and the West) was the construction of alliances for containment was seen by the Soviets as a continuation of encirclement. The USSR continued to define its security and interests as the achievement of dominance in the wide arc covering its far-flung borders from the Barents Sea to the Sea of Okhotsk. The corollary was to seek to exclude, weaken, or counter US power on or from the Eurasian periphery and to weaken the local bases of support for the extension of this alien power.[1]

The USSR in the postwar period has thus not had a Gulf so much as a northern tier or southern flank policy. This policy—more an outlook and a set of aspirations than a coherent integration of means and ends—has had as a dominant theme a concern for security seen in military and geographic terms, focused on the states immediately adjacent to it. Policy toward these states naturally varied, reflecting their own differentiation, weight, and strategic importance (for instance, Turkey as a member of NATO had to be treated differently from nonaligned Afghanistan). On the other hand, Soviet interest in bordering states was hardly a product of ideological claims or hubris but an extension of the historical and tsarist preoccupation, generally supported, which saw its immediate borders as potential areas of both vulnerability and opportunity. This instilled in the Soviets a predisposition to see in developments on its borders potential security threats and to deal with them, where its power was adequate, with a sense of brusque and overbearing menace.

In World War II, the USSR had been supplied US lend-lease overland through Iran, and Iran had acted as a bridge to the USSR that could as easily become another invasion route. To the Soviets' very geographical perspective of security was added concern about nuclear weapons. In the 1950s the United States sought forward-defense posts on the Soviet periphery, and bases for Strategic Air Command bombers—and later Jupiter missiles—were found in at least one neighboring country. The risks the Soviets ran in the Cuban missile crisis were at least in part explicable by the sense of equity and symmetry involved in the analogies between Cuba and Turkey.[2]

Competition in the region, specifically local issues, regional conflicts and alignments, and ideological rivalries were all perceived in the service of the broader strategic competition of the superpowers.

This policy drove Turkey and Iran into alliances with the United States in the Baghdad Pact and later CENTO, confirming for the Soviets the United States' ill intentions and the need to break the links between these states and Washington.[3]

In the Gulf proper, security was assured by the small, almost symbolic presence of Britain. Until the decision was announced (in January 1968) to leave the area by December 1971, Britain's presence (of some 7,000 troops in Sharjah) and occasional naval deployments not only assured the security of the smaller, not yet fully independent sheikhdoms, but effectively shielded the area from the cold war. In recognition of the new era symbolized by Britain's withdrawal, the Soviet fleet made its first significant visit to the Gulf in May 1968. At the beginning of the 1970s, the USSR remained a marginal actor, maintaining diplomatic relations only with Iran, Iraq, Kuwait, and South Yemen (PDRY).

Soviet policy toward the Gulf stemmed from both its rivalry with the United States and the priority accorded its immediate neighbors. In the 1970s, the oil decade, the context for the advancement of Soviet influence appeared mixed.

Although under the shadow of the Vietnam War the United States was not anxious to assume new commitments and sought to limit them in the Nixon Doctrine, developments in the Gulf offered only limited grounds for Soviet optimism. The regional powers, particularly Iran and Saudi Arabia, enriched by oil revenues, were building up their military and cooperating politically (despite rivalries) to assure regional stability.

The USSR could support the Dhofar Liberation Front (later PFLOAG) against Oman or Iraq in its border dispute with Iran, even at the cost of neglecting more important regional ties. Soviet support for these rather marginal states continued but in a rather lackluster, more ritualistic way. In Dhofar, when Iranian-UK military support to the sultan in 1975 raised the stakes, Moscow did not seek to match them. In the subcontinent, Horn of Africa, and later in the Gulf war, the Kremlin also used a policy of seeking to supply arms to both sides—directly or indirectly—in order to maintain the basis for some influence. The same approach characterized the USSR's policy toward Iran and Iraq during their war (1980–1988) and after the July 1988 cease-fire.[4]

The late 1970s created new opportunities and risks for the USSR that posed classic problems, even dilemmas, which have become more apparent a decade on. The buildup of Soviet military power capabilities, on the one hand, and the variety of constraints operating on the US use of force, on the other, seemed to encourage a more activist Soviet Third World policy in general. This may have encouraged both an excessive faith (and investment) in the efficacy of arms in diplomacy and an ill-founded optimism about the future of Soviet power in all its dimensions.

For reasons discussed below, the USSR on the threshold of the 1990s has changed its perception of threats and its priorities. Problems of managing the reform process within the USSR now take precedence over the extensive and costly geopolitical rivalry thought necessary by the ideological predecessors of Gorbachev.

Much of the new thinking that seems eminently reasonable from outside may turn out to be empty for the Soviet people if it cannot deliver a better life, economically and in terms of pluralism and even enhanced freedoms. It is sufficient for our purposes here to note that there are many pitfalls on this path; economic failures, generalized nationalist agitation threatening the integrity of the country and a right-wing/Soviet backlash, civil war—none of these can be ruled out. A radical departure from current policy stimulated by one or more of these would affect policy toward the states on the USSR's southern flank. Currently the emphasis in relations toward these countries is on maintaining a balance, whether toward Iranian, Afghan, Turk, or Arab (republican or monarchical). Emphasis continues to be on the immediate bordering states not so much because they pose a potential *military* threat, but rather because in the new ethnic/Islamic map they are clearly a priority. These bordering states are more important than the noncontiguous ones further afield. Good relations with them constitute a sort of insurance policy insofar as they could contribute to stabilizing (or at least not exacerbating) disruptions that take place within the USSR. Insofar as Moscow enjoys good relations with its immediate neighbors to the south, it may count on them to help in insulating its domestic unrest and assist in containing them. The theme today is one of cooperation—in cross-frontier trade and in transparency that promotes cultural and individual contacts and on a degree of decentralization from Moscow.

The implication of this is that Moscow expects some loosening from the center and some local interaction to increase the leeway for its reforms. Moscow now implicitly and even explicitly sees its neighbors as potential allies in stabilizing its minority and nationality problems. This was the clear implication of Gorbachev's reception of Iranian President Rafsanjani's visit in June 1989. In this visit, not only was the Iranian president encouraged to make a side-trip to Baku and deliver a short sermon at a mosque, but the ensuing communiqué included a "declaration of principles," the most notable of which was a reference to noninterference in each other affairs—superfluous except as an emphatic reflection of Moscow's primary concern. Reciprocity being the base of the understanding, the implication was clear; the USSR would be as sensitive about Iran's primary concerns as Tehran showed itself to be about those of the USSR.

How durable will this new approach be, how successful can it be, and what happens to it if there are strong pressures for the USSR to revert to past practices, which, though not necessarily successful, were at least tried and true in some respects? To these questions there are no clear answers at the time of writing. Even without a brandished military threat, Soviet power will remain latent. The USSR is still in a position to supply arms on favorable terms from its vast stocks and to do so quickly, across the board if necessary, for hard currency or for barter. Some such agreement confined to Iran's "defensive needs" was agreed on during the Rafsanjani visit, although the terms and scope have yet to be published.

The new pragmatic emphasis has already borne fruit. Iran has more or less supported Soviet policy in Afghanistan since the departure of Soviet troops in March 1989 and has been exceedingly restrained about Islamic activities in the USSR. In both November 1988 and December–January 1989–1990, Iran has been careful not to let its relations with the USSR be harmed by outbreaks of nationalism in Azerbaijan. In the latter case, Tehran has consulted closely with Moscow and, despite some rhetoric about Islam in some quarters, was cautious. Perhaps Tehran sees an area of potential common interest in containing any nationalist contagion in the USSR that results in the disintegration of that state.

There is always the risk that the USSR will revert to reliance on the military instrument in foreign as well as domestic affairs, that it might again define its security in ways incompatible with the sovereignty of its neighbors, and that it will once again see in the existence of the capitalist world, and especially the United States, a continuing threat to its security and ideological cause for rivalry. If such a reversion takes place, which seems doubtful, it will more likely do so as a result of the failure of internal reforms than from revived geopolitical competition. On the other hand, if these reforms are to prove successful, they will require time, probably at least a decade. The problems that the success of Soviet reforms might pose for Western interests in the Gulf thus need not concern us here.

Soviet Policy in the 1980s

The USSR on the threshold of the 1980s could contemplate its prospects in the Gulf with optimism and concern; hope sprang from the weakening of pro-Western regimes in the region, the blow to Western interests and US credibility, and the sensitivity of the region for the West's economy, and concern stemmed from the unpredictable nature of Islamic fundamentalism, which might turn out to be two-edged sword. A larger question raised by the Soviet invasion of Afghanistan, but implicit in all US-Soviet relations, and now more pressing than ever, was the degree to which the USSR was willing to carry competition with the United States in the Third World to the point that it affected the stability (and benefits) of the central relationship itself. This was to be clarified in the course of the 1980s.

A prime consideration in that decade was to prevent the re-entry of the United States into the Gulf, either as a result of a regional crisis or as a consequence of strategic realignments within the region. In this respect Soviet policy toward the Islamic revolution in Iran and the Gulf war was clear: to prevent Iran from drifting back into the Western camp and to forestall any US military intervention in the stalemated and inconclusive conflict between Iran and Iraq.[5] While seeing the region primarily in terms of rivalry with the United States, the Soviet Union increasingly shared some concerns with the United States. One area of admittedly limited convergence was the desire to see no victor emerge from the war and no fundamental change in the strategic landscape take place as a result of a battlefield decision. Another was the similarity of view regarding Islamic fundamentalism as a dangerous and destabilizing phenomenon, not necessarily to the benefit of either superpower. A third area of overlap more discernible now than in the recent past was the Soviet stake in stability, in this case border security.

While paying lip service to this in the past, Soviet policy had been more anxious to promote anti-Western trends than to stabilize forces that might threaten its own interests. A recent indicator of this attitude was the Soviet response to the Iranian revolution. The USSR had encouraged the radicals in Iran, aggravated the hostage crisis, and posed as the "protector" of the revolution to the clerics in Iran. (On November 18, 1978, Brezhnev had publicly "warned" the United States against intervention when Washington had shown no such inclination, precisely to position the USSR to claim that its warning had "saved" the revolution. Such posturing could also enhance the position of Soviet protégés within Iran who could argue that the young revolution would need such Soviet protection in the future. The Iranian Communist party, the Tudeh, survived longer than any other party.[6])

The USSR then offered arms and a security relationship to revolutionary Iran and provided that country with overland transit facilities for goods destined for Europe. Slow to condemn international terrorism, the USSR sought to exploit and benefit from Western difficulties whatever their source. This slowly changed as Iran's radicalism and rhetoric came to embrace the USSR as well. Starting from 1983, the USSR showed a firmer hand in dealing with Iran, recognizing that the Islamic revolutionaries had "nowhere else to go," having limited their room for maneuver and their options by so effectively antagonizing the United States. Moscow's tougher, less solicitous stance toward Iran correctly reflected tacit recognition that Iran was isolated diplomatically and mired in an inconclusive war as the *demandeur*.

Soviet conservatism in the Gulf war increased the attraction of the USSR as a diplomatic partner for the Gulf states. Oman and the UAE announced the establishment of diplomatic relations in late 1985, and Qatar followed in 1986. Contacts with Saudi officials in Moscow and the kingdom increased, and tacit cooperation on OPEC policies emerged. The Soviets did not hide their expectations that after a suitable interval their withdrawal from Afghanistan would be rewarded by the resumption of diplomatic relations with Saudi Arabia.

In keeping up its large-scale arms supplies to Iraq, opening doors to Saudi Arabia, and condemning unequivocally the continuation of the war (i.e., by Iran), Moscow demonstrated a firmness toward Tehran that put Moscow's interest first. Soviet policy toward the United States remained competitive but less antagonistic. In spring 1984, when the United States had increased its naval deployments to the Gulf (at the start of what was to become the "tanker war") Soviet commentaries had been shrill and hostile. In contrast the Soviet reaction to the revelations of "Irangate" and to the US decision to reflag Kuwaiti tankers, in 1986–1987, was relatively moderate, especially when one considers the United States' (anti-Soviet) rationale for the latter move, as stated by Defense Secretary Caspar Weinberger. In the later part of the war, Soviet policy warned of the dangers of a major US military presence in a war zone and was concerned about attempts by the United States to exploit the hostilities to improve its strategic infrastructure on the Arabian peninsula and access to the region, but it was neither threatening nor unremittingly hostile. The USSR instead emphasized multilateral alternatives, cooperated somewhat grudgingly in the United Nations Security Council in the passage of Resolution 598, and proposed a UN fleet as a replacement for the US and later US-European naval detachments.

If the tone and content of Soviet policy was different, it was not because of a radical change in its view of its rivalry with the United States. Soviet aims still remained the exclusion of US power from the Eurasian periphery, including the Gulf, and the extension of Soviet power and influence in its place. Soviet policy now was more "reasonable," with an emphasis on international approaches to security, the dangers of regional conflicts, and the need for multilateral and cooperative solutions. Behind this change remained a continuing Soviet interest (notably articulated by Brezhnev in December 1980) in becoming an internationally recognized power in the Gulf. A formal acknowledgment of such a role, an historical departure, would imply not only responsibilities but also rights, and a presumption that its interests must be taken into account.

The shift in Soviet policy toward the Gulf is not directly traceable to a watershed year (such as the accession of Gorbachev in 1985) but is rather a matter of degree. Nonetheless, after 1985 the confrontational rhetoric declined and areas of potential cooperation assumed greater prominence. In the course of the 1980s, the limitations of the reflexively competitive view came under scrutiny and it was found wanting. Competition persisted, as in the different interests of the superpowers in how the Gulf war was ended, that is, whether it would be through the agency of US naval power or through Soviet involvement in a UN fleet. Each superpower continued to be preoccupied by its own net standing in the region, and to assess this primarily with reference to that of its principal adversary.[7] But the acute sense of rivalry, crisis, and urgency that had characterized superpower relations at the start of the decade had diminished by its close.

The reasons for this are worth enumerating for their possible bearing on future relations. Competition stabilized in part because of the communication of the unmistakable importance the United States attached to the area. The Carter Doctrine, the development of the Central Command force, the willingness to deploy and maintain ships into the Gulf during the crises (especially in 1984 and 1987–1988) and to take casualties during that war all testified to the seriousness of the US commitment to the region. The USSR for its part found that its interests were not unalterably opposed to the United States. It also became aware that closer to the homeland, and potentially more dangerous to its interests than the military-strategic threat the United States posed, there was an "independent threat"—namely, the Islamic fundamentalism it was encountering in Afghanistan and that was beginning to fester in the internal empire itself. An interest in stabilizing the border regions was assuming greater prominence in thinking than exploiting putative opportunities against the United States.

By 1989 it had become clear that Soviet foreign policy as a whole had been radically revised. This started with a change in the definition of national security, which was now seen as less military and more a product of diplomacy, conscious of interdependence and common security. As a result, the earlier insistence on military superiority, which implied political dominance, had given way to the concept of "reasonable sufficiency." Faith in and reliance on the military component of power was being replaced by a less unidimensional view of power. More emphasis was being put on areas of special Soviet weakness and inadequacy, especially economic performance. One consequence of this was an unwillingness to expend unlimited resources in a futile quest for military security while the economic system deteriorated. A corollary of this was a new unwillingness to underwrite wasteful allies or to take on new and potentially expensive commitments. Foreign policy was no longer seen as an area of primary concern but rather more as a means of buying time. A "predictable" external environment was needed to assure the critical process of restructuring at home.

The upshot of this was a regime more tolerant of change and diversity, less reflexively ideological, less automatically zero-sum in its approach to relations with the United States. Formerly virulent relations could thus become more "normal," not hostage to accidental crises. The central relationship was increasingly valued and returned to a "central" position, unlikely to be risked by peripheral activities or challenges. An important outgrowth of this new thinking was a change in the way "opportunities" are defined. Crises are no longer automatically seen as ways to weaken the adversary or to pursue unilateral advantage. The tendency toward damage limitation appears to prevail over that toward exploitation.

A concomitant of this—which is reflected in the United States as well—is a diminished sense of vulnerability, a sense that both superpowers are adequately armed, that the military balance between them is stable and insensitive to marginal shifts (up or down). With this came a reduced sense of encirclement and strategic threat from abroad and greater concern for domestic problems. In the case of the USSR, the problems of empire, including the nationalities question and, specifically, the potential Islamic problems in Azerbaijan and Central Asia,[8] mean that there can be no sharp dividing line between external and internal. But clearly this class of potential "security" problem is not a classical military threat, nor does it derive from the United States, both reasons for redirecting security priorities to the proximate and real questions confronting the Soviet state.

The significant changes in the Soviets' world view, priorities, and competition with the United States should not obscure continuities that will persist and condition superpower rivalries in the Persian Gulf and elsewhere. The USSR will continue to seek allies and influence and support for its interests and aims and to see as rivalry other powers' attempts to expand their influence. Geopolitical considerations will give the USSR a stake in the politics of its immediate neighbors and in establishing as solid a relationship of influence with them as possible. It will continue to view US influence in these regions (which includes Iran, Turkey, and borders on the Gulf) as competitive, harmful, and potentially threatening. To that extent it will continue to try to block US influence, particularly the extension of US access to military facilities in the region. And it was this consideration among others that motivated a Soviet reluctance to support quickly or without reservations the extension of US military power into the Gulf, or its early endorsement of force use by the United Nations in the crisis unleashed by Iraq in August 1990. This will mean a regional diplomacy that seeks to weaken local states' links with the West. As a maritime power, the United States will be unwilling to acquiesce in any situation in which the USSR becomes the principal power, or security guarantor, for the Eurasian states; it must therefore remain vitally interested in the politics of these regions and provide the countervailing power necessary for these states to assure their independence.

Because defense of its homeland is a vital interest, the USSR is bound to be concerned about the security of its borders. This will entail a continued willingness to invest heavily in these regions, however much retrenchment becomes inevitable for more distant commitments. War plans will have to include contingencies that envisage offensive moves that seize, harass, and neutralize possible US bases and maritime assets nearby and that deny the areas near Soviet borders to hostile powers. This planning would include provision for denying the resources of the Gulf to a potential adversary.

There are other reasons for expecting continued Soviet involvement in the region that would have a competitive dimension with the United States. One is the possibility of independent threats from the region, threats that constitute challenges for Soviet security and stem from regional politics rather than the United States. Islamic fundamentalism is an example. Consider the impact on the USSR of a regional or adjacent state's directly encouraging Soviet Islamic tendencies to oppose Moscow.[9] Threats emanating from beyond its territory but affecting national integrity and stability in the southern republics would foster a diplomacy that sought to offset whatever leverage the Islamic factor gave to regional states, by the acquisition of counter-leverage. Military power and diplomatic leverage would be useful in this regard, and they could come principally from continued involvement in the region's affairs.

Another factor making for Soviet involvement in the region stems from the catalytic effect of sudden and intense conflict. The proliferation of long-range missiles and the potential for the spread of chemical weapons and nuclear capabilities, would, in a more distant region, encourage decoupling rather that involvement. Here, both because of the range of the weapons systems and the proximity to the USSR, Soviet involvement is likely. Soviet Foreign Minister Eduard Shevardnadze alluded to Soviet concern about these weapons systems in his tour of the Middle East in February 1989, and numerous Soviet statements suggest a deeper concern about the general questions the growth of such capabilities pose for the superpowers when they are themselves reducing arms expenditures, eliminating categories of weapons systems, and converting large numbers of conventional weapons.

Despite past Soviet-US rivalry in the Middle East, the nature of the Arab-Israeli dispute and shifts in US-Soviet relations together with the advent of these new weapons systems make more collaborative approaches likely. In relation to these weapons systems there is already a bilateral dialogue that will soon see—in all probability—the entry of the USSR into control regimes such as the missile technology control regime (MTCR) and the conclusion of chemical weapons conventions, which could increase the pressures for adherence by other states. This is an obvious area of future cooperation between the superpowers because, as superpowers, they share a common interest in preventing both the erosion of the taboo of nonuse nuclear weapons of the past forty-five years and the lowering of the threshold of use.

Soviet-US rivalry, which will persist however modified, is a general factor separate from the region itself, which will encourage continued Soviet involvement. To the extent that the Gulf region remains or becomes a key US interest, Soviet presence and influence in it provides Moscow with an important source of leverage on the United States. In the Iraq-Kuwait crisis of 1990 the USSR's policy amply supported this interpretation. For while Moscow was not itself directly affected by Iraq's seizure of Kuwait, it was clear that the United States and the West would not stand for it. As a result of a decision to pursue the matter in the United Nations and to seek Soviet support, Moscow was given the choice between acting cooperatively and maintaining and improving its good relations with the West or acting obstructively and weakening them. The decision to support international sanctions and to use diplomatic pressure on Baghdad directly and through a summit declaration in Helsinki in September revealed the degree to which Moscow valued its newfound relations with the West. At the same time, for reasons of amour propre and competition, the USSR was unwilling either to provide the United States with a military carte blanche or to terminate its own quasi-military relations with Iraq. Insofar as the crisis would require military action eventually, the USSR supported a resuscitation of the military staff committee of the UN, in which it would at least be assured of some formal role.

Quite apart from considerations of rivalry with the United States, the USSR will seek to maintain and expand its diplomatic presence in the region, for it cannot discount the possibility that other competitive powers (like China) will enter the region in a major way, or that it will not itself become more interested and even possibly dependent on the region's resources.

Thus, by the end of the 1980s, if it was clear the US-USSR rivalry was to be less extensive in the Third World, it was also evident that residual competition would persist and that it was unlikely to exclude the Gulf. The persistence of geopolitical rivalry and limited cooperation will see a pattern of "competitive cooperation" similar to that evident in the closing stages of the Iran-Iraq war.

Toward the Year 2000

The Soviet leadership is no longer as exercised by the need for absolute military dominance or parity with a combination of foes, and is correspondingly less conscious of military vulnerability itself. It is instructive to contrast the Soviets' outrage and exaggerations about US strategic intentions in the Gulf in the 1970s, when Iran and Saudi Arabia first embarked on building modern armed forces,[10] with the more relaxed view taken in the infinitely more dangerous period of the 1980s.[11]

Islam and Security

For the USSR the Muslim question is becoming both an important political issue and potential security question.[12] Demographically, it is from this pool of the population that the bulk of the military manpower will have to be drawn. This may in turn raise the question of representation and the disproportionate number of Slav officers for the mainly non-Slav forces. A broader issue on the horizon is how the Muslim population of the USSR will react to economic reforms, political liberalization, and greater tolerance of religion. A form of religious revival has taken place in the southern republics of the USSR in recent years, especially evident in the activities of unofficial clerics, "underground" mosques, and formal religious observance. The southern republics cannot remain unaffected by the sweep of religious revival in the adjacent Islamic countries, even if they may have remained unimpressed by the economic and social performance of those states.

It was in part to prevent the infection of the Soviet republics that the USSR a decade ago sought to nip in the bud the Muslim counterrevolutionary "insurrection" in Afghanistan. It was also in part due to the effects of that war on its own Muslim population as well as on the wider Muslim world that the USSR decided to withdraw from Afghanistan. Without accepting an exaggerated version of the Islamic revival/contagion thesis, which posits a disintegration of the USSR, it is still possible to accept the argument that Islam is a potential political-security problem for the USSR. Increased cultural and religious consciousness will stimulate interest in the activities of neighboring states and in making contacts. This will affect Soviet policy toward the regions lying to its south.

In order to have influence on the Islamic states in a position to threaten Soviet interests, it is necessary to be in a position to provide them with incentives and sanctions as encouragement and punishment for acts or contemplated policies. In this way bilateral understandings can be fashioned, quid pro quo agreed upon, and compromises arrived at that take into account the realpolitik of the situation. Such an understanding may account for Iran's relative restraint vis-à-vis Central Asian and Azerbaijani Muslims in the USSR and also Tehran's quick acceptance of the USSR's decision to withdraw from Afghanistan.[13]

The Oil Dimension

Western reliance on Gulf oil and the relative proximity of that region to the USSR have given rise to fears for the security of access to the region and the unobstructed flow of oil. In the past two decades local instabilities rather than Soviet policies have contributed to the sense of insecurity. Besides the oil embargo and the revolution in Iran in the 1970s, there was a prolonged war in the 1980s, and the 1990s have started out with a major crisis in which Iraq has annexed its smaller neighbor. The Iran-Iraq war saw the use of mines and surface-to-surface missiles against oil installations; the current crisis in the Gulf (whose outcome remains uncertain at the time of writing) threatens to dwarf earlier events in the magnitude of consequences and intensity of destruction. Particularly notable about this latest crisis is the unabashed effort by one state to steal another's resources, however couched in historical claims.

Despite all this, with admittedly sudden price jumps, the price of oil in real terms before the Kuwait-Iraq crisis in 1990 was less in real terms than that of the early 1970s. In addition, supply has been abundant and Western nations have been better prepared to deal with supply disruptions and less vulnerable to them. Nor have Soviet oil shortages become such as to force the USSR onto the market for imports or to look for ways of controlling supplies.

All of this may change in the late 1990s, with the Gulf again the main source of world oil (other higher-cost areas having been exhausted), demand in the industrialized world up, and Western dependence on the region again significant and possibly vital. In these circumstances the threat of a prolonged interruption of oil supplies again assumes strategic importance, as does the possible role of the USSR.

The most serious strategic threat to the West would be the physical control of oil supplies by the USSR. This, to be effective, would require the occupation of one or more major oil producers, such as Iran, Iraq, Kuwait, or Saudi Arabia. Besides the military difficulty, there are the political costs and repercussions of such a policy for the USSR. As long as the United States retains a credible deterrent force, this scenario will remain a very remote prospect outside of a general war. In wartime, however, one must plan for likelihood of a Soviet attack in the direction of the oil fields, to seize assets, deny oil to the West, and to divert Western forces from other sectors.

Other possibilities of Soviet involvement in the oil equation stem from its own potential needs, i.e., when it is forced onto the market as an importer. If Soviet energy resources do decline, exports are stopped, and new sources are inaccessible, the USSR may become an importer. Under these conditions Moscow would become interested in the Gulf for specific reasons having to do with national or self-interest. It would have every incentive to seek advantageous arrangements, e.g., in being able to import oil without paying in hard currency, perhaps by barter.

The situation with respect to gas is somewhat different. Iran, with the second largest reserves of gas, has no natural or proximate market for its product. The USSR, in turn, has a need for gas supplies in its southern regions, which can be met by Iran's natural gas transported by pipeline. After ten years of interruption, Tehran has again decided to revive the supply of gas through the existing pipeline, IGAT 1, and develop another, IGAT 2, for further supplies. Of particular interest in this arrangement, the terms of which are unclear other than that it is a barter deal, is the likelihood that it includes a component of arms transfers on the Soviet side. This finesses the problem of payment rather nicely, for whereas Iran needs arms and cannot afford hard currency for them, the USSR would not have hard currency to pay for Iran's gas. Some such pattern is likely in future energy deals between the Gulf states and the USSR.

Four Scenarios for the Year 2000

The principal motivation of Soviet policy in the Gulf for the near future will remain the nature and intensity of Soviet-US rivalry. The USSR certainly has in this region interests that stem from relative proximity and geography, but how these would be pursued will be determined largely by Soviet-US relations. How the Soviets would define their security, their degree of strategic nervousness, the extent of their claims in the region and beyond would be influenced by the depth and antagonism of this central strategic competition. Therefore assessments of probable future Soviet policies must start with assumptions about US-Soviet relations.

A related assumption concerns the role of any other major power, such as China, competitive with the USSR in the region. This also would provide a motive for Soviet policy. The third variable is the regional environment, which could provide a permissive context for interference or act as an obstacle for outside powers. Here we assume different regional settings while holding superpower (and third-power) rivalry constant at the level of those prevailing in 1989, that is, at a reduced and muted level of antagonism.

Political Stability

Assuming a region that sees a period of unaccustomed political stability after a decade of turmoil, what would be Soviet policy? There is no reason to suppose that the USSR, absent a compelling strategic motivation such as intense rivalry for clients or bases in the region, would have its interests served by instability. Soviet response to a tranquil region would therefore be one of relief and encouragement. A quiet backyard would be doubly welcome for the lack of opportunity it would give others to meddle in the area and the time it would buy for the USSR to concentrate its energies on domestic restructuring.

Political Radicalization

Political instability stemming from rapid change, social dislocations, and radical ideologies (including nationalism or a variant of Islam), while not inevitable, have tended to characterize the politics of the Middle East and may come to dominate it again in the coming years. A coup by a radical faction in an existing important conservative state may accelerate the spread of extremist ideologies, tilt the regional balance of power, and invite and increase superpower involvement and competition. For our purposes, the causes or sources of this potential for instability are less important than the probable reaction of the USSR to it.

Past policy—even at its most competitive with the United States—has shown the USSR risk-averse and unwilling to side unequivocally with local radical forces either against more moderate regional forces or the United States. If the USSR has hedged support for radical states and movements, in recent years it has also moved to diversify its relations, to get into the mainstream rather than remain on the margins of regional politics.[14] It is also too early to say with certainty that the USSR has become a status quo state or that ideology no longer plays *any* role in its foreign policy or in its domestic legitimacy. Competition with the United States will still motivate the USSR to support forces hostile to US interests and the extension of US influence, even though this support will be less reflexive, more modulated, and more conditional.

For the moment Soviet interests seem to be served by the stabilization of regions, for a breathing spell in foreign policy in which few demands are made on it either of time or of resources. In this period Soviet efforts are being expended to show a new face, a willingness to cooperate in stabilizing regions and to buttress international organizations.[15] In the Gulf region this policy is doubly important to the extent that it reduces the US military presence in the region and contributes toward a reduction in indigenous tensions making for conflict.

Besides *promoting*, *disowning*, and *reacting* to radical movements, there is another theoretical possibility—acting to *suppress* them, singly or in tandem with the United States. It is possible that in this decade radical movements are confronted by "holy alliances" bent on maintaining regional order. The GCC currently cooperates (though not completely) on the question of terrorism. Britain and France and Germany assist individual countries in this area. In May 1989 the United States and USSR agreed to discuss potential methods of cooperating on this issue. The USSR may in coming years have a vested interest in promoting such cooperation because of domestic political dissidence and the spread of armed movements for secession within the USSR itself. The clarification of the rules of asylum, sanctuary, and the conditions of extradition would then assume added importance.

New Regional Conflicts

Soviet policy toward wars taking place in the Gulf have been different from those pitting the Arab states against Israel. In the latter, polarization makes some choice necessary, and Arab numbers made the particular choice inevitable. In the Gulf there has been no such easy choice. Soviet policy in the Gulf war is an imperfect guide regarding future wars in that the exact circumstances are not likely to be replicated.

In the past the USSR has used the threat and option of supporting internal dissidents (tribal, ethnic, or political) as a lever on the central government. It has not generally been Soviet practice to promote these movements as an alternative to existing governments—the partial exceptions being Soviet support for the Gilani and Azerbaijani secessionist movements in 1921 and 1945 and the Kurdish republic of Mahabad in 1945–1946. In the future the USSR, as it experiences fissiparous tendencies within its republics, will be more sensitive to this issue. The links with "liberation movements" in adjacent countries will become a two-edged sword as able to be turned against the USSR as become a useful instrument of policy. Links with the Islamic world and with Iranian, Turkish, and Iraqi Kurds may continue, but Soviet support for a Kurdish state or individual insurrections will be less than enthusiastic.[16]

The specific conditions of each future war will determine the nature of the Soviet response. Another round of war between Iran and Iraq, depending on how it started and on the US reaction, is unlikely to see a response different from the last one. A war between Saudi Arabia (and, implicitly, the GCC) and an Iran similar to the present regime might encourage the USSR to resolve its internal debate about the relative weight to attach to Iran versus the Arab states. In this eventuality, it would not be surprising to see a Soviet tilt toward Riyadh. Similarly, an Iraqi war against Kuwait might well see the USSR diplomatically behind the GCC.

If the USSR seeks to exploit regional conflicts, it will be for its own influence, which in the 1990s may not exclude taking the same side as the United States. Lesser wars will see the USSR following the GCC. In such cases, the USSR will seek to be useful and relevant, as protector or mediator rather than bystander or adversary. New conflicts, in short, would increase or maintain the importance of the USSR in Gulf diplomacy without creating the kinds of opportunities that would significantly alter Soviet standing in the area.

Growing Soviet Influence

A relative newcomer to the Gulf, the USSR has made slow progress in establishing ties and influence in the region. But the experience of the 1980s was such as to encourage a more balanced relationship between the superpowers. Kuwait had shown the value of having diplomatic options. It was not overlooked that one of the US principal motives for reflagging Kuwaiti tankers had been fear that the USSR might otherwise do so. Questions about the future of the US commitment in the absence of a strong Soviet threat was thus a logical concern. So, too, was the value of a US security relationship that made the purchase of arms a humiliating exercise and the durability of that guarantee suspect in that it was popularly (and sometimes officially) tied solely to the flow of oil from the region. This tended to dilute the commitment and demeaned it, making it appear subject to fluctuations in the latest statistics of barrels imported.

A regional context in which even a weakened Soviet Union is more present in the politics of the Gulf in the year 2000 is thus conceivable. With retrenchment from costly distant entanglements, the USSR will still have incentives to remain actively engaged in the countries on its southern periphery. This area is simultaneously a Third World area and border-security issue. This, together with the increased salience of the Muslim question in the USSR, would increase Soviet incentives to be actively engaged in regional politics, both to acquire leverage and deflect pressures against it.

Any significant growth in Soviet influence in the Gulf (i.e., beyond the development of normal ties) is likely to come not from Soviet assets but from US weakness or, if you will, adjustments. It is possible that the USSR will focus most of its external energies on that sector of its border that it cannot stabilize by agreement (contrast China and NATO). By reducing the visible military threat across the board, the USSR may precipitate a rapid decline in US military spending. It may also loosen the domestic consensus undergirding postwar US foreign policy and support for costly overseas deployments.

The USSR might be ready to step in when the United States withdraws. Offering arms on concessional terms to the now poorer Gulf states, or treaties of protection, the USSR might be able to exploit such a void. In the 1990s it may seek a special military relationship with Iran modeled on that of the US-Iranian tie in the 1970s. As the major arms supplier to Iran and Iraq, it would be in a stronger position to influence the outcome of future wars. Soviet advantages in a competitive situation are not impressive. But it would be prepared to barter goods or oil for arms more quickly than its Western counterparts. It might offer terms that the West could not match; in the case of Iran's gas exports, it is in the unique position of being the logical and even sole market.

None of this adds up to a triumphant USSR gaining unsurpassed or uncontested influence in the Gulf at any time soon. There are too many constraints on Soviet resources and energies, too many regional obstacles and complexities, too many competitors. But the period of virtually exclusive Western influence in the region has almost been conceded. The outlook is thus for a more balanced superpower presence in the Gulf, less intensely competitive but also more complicated if only by the rise of indigenous issues and threats.

Uncertainties, Caveats, and "Extreme" Cases

Three major conditions (or variables) could cause a dramatic shift in the more benign Soviet attitude toward the Gulf discussed above: (1) those originating in the US-Soviet relations, (2) those reflecting a major change in the USSR itself, and (3) those coming from the adjacent southern region. We shall take these up in turn, not as predictions but as illustrations. In each case the result would be a more insecure USSR, more willing to contemplate the use of force to assure its security and more inclined to defend its security expansively even if "defensive" in motivation or intention.

1. A principal conditioner of Soviet security policy has been rivalry with the United States. Renewed bitter rivalry with the United States, which heightens the sense of a zero-sum competition and Soviet insecurity, could see more Soviet incentives to use force or its threat (actual use or coercive diplomacy) to extend Soviet influence and weaken that of the United States. Without assigning a high probability to this, we must be sensitive to the scope for influencing Soviet policies (for good or ill) by US policies.

For example, a lessening of US military capabilities to project power, a shrinkage of access rights, a weakening of the consensus to stay globally involved, would all contribute toward a revised estimate of US commitment to the region. It could also radically alter the cost calculus currently prevailing in respect to the use or (in)efficacy of force.

A revival of a US strategy of forward defense through the reactivation of a CENTO-like pact, especially if it is based on Islamic fundamentalism and oriented against the USSR, could see a sharp Soviet response.

US unilateralism—global or regional—could stimulate a revision in Soviet thinking and policy; consider US interference in Eastern Europe, or attempts to pursue the Reagan Doctrine. US policies that seek to "rub in" the Soviet decline, that do not reciprocate Soviet "moderation," and that hurt Soviet interests may precipitate a reversal. Similarly, unilateral US resorts to force may cause a turnaround in policy. In the 1980s the United States resorted to force for punitive purposes in Grenada, Panama, Libya (twice), and Iran (at least twice). If continued, this type of behavior (e.g., in Cuba) could erode the norms against the use of force and encourage equivalent Soviet policies.

2. A second set of factors that could see a reversal in Soviet security policies originate within the USSR. The Soviet Union is in the throes of major political and economic reforms whose course is likely to be as unpredictable as their outcome is uncertain. It is doubtful whether a clear verdict on the economic fruits of *glasnost* will be available before the end of the 1990s. At the same time the political forces released by liberalization may come to challenge the basis of the communist state and the Soviet dominance of it.

History provides few examples of great powers accepting gracefully their ineluctable decline without a last effort to stem or reverse it, usually by force of arms. The Hapsburg analogy is hardly reassuring, and awareness of the sensitivity and volatility of Soviet policies under analogous circumstances will be necessary.

The destabilization of Eastern Europe, together with growing and unacceptable nationalist demands first in the Baltic states and later by the Muslim states in the southern republics, could spark a renewed emphasis on military force, secure borders, and compliant neighbors. A Soviet backlash to the demands of the various nationalities would see a much firmer line toward religion, including Islam, and toward attempts by nearby states to encourage an Islamic revival in the USSR. In the extreme case, the increasing claims of various nationalities threatening to unravel the USSR by a chain reaction would focus attention on the nexus between the inner empire and the adjacent areas, encouraging a more conservative definition of border security and a greater willingness to use force to maintain it.

3. The decision to invade Afghanistan was inconsistent with Soviet policy since 1945; both the decision to enter *and* to withdraw were essentially unforeseeable. Consider a crisis in which Soviet state and ideological interests (which, however reduced, remain a distinguishing feature of the USSR as a power) coincide. A civil war or succession struggle in Iran is illustrative. A request by factions friendly to the USSR for aid against a reactionary despotic regime that threatens its neighbors (including the USSR) would pose an unpredictable risk, perhaps bringing the United States onto the doorstep of the USSR. On the other hand, it provides the USSR—perhaps with limited risk—an opportunity to remove the threat and improve its own security legitimately without harming its image or affecting perceptions of its ideology. This may be the extreme case, but

it is a corrective to any premature assumption that there are no regional contingencies in which the USSR would be willing to resort to force.

Implications for US Policy

Soviet-US rivalry, especially in its military dimensions and in its crude, zero-sum automaticity, has declined in salience in superpower relations. Competition will persist but with larger areas of dialogue, restraint, understanding, and possibly cooperation. In part this is because of the systemic crisis of the USSR that has seen an eagerness to relinquish excessive overseas commitments and to put its central relationship with the United States back where it belongs. But it is also because of a recognition that the Third World in general is not a vital stake or important enough to justify indiscriminate or unlimited military competition. And this view is reinforced in both superpowers by the sense that the military balance is essentially stable and that there are other more pressing claims on economic resources and domestic issues clamoring for attention.

If the beginning of the end of the cold war is the result primarily of Soviet exhaustion and reassessment, it is also the result of a US willingness to stabilize the relationship. Still, because neither the success of the Soviet experiment in restructuring and its ultimate outcome is clear, nor the stability of policies in the transition guaranteed, there are incentives for caution on the part of the West. US policy in particular must reflect an understanding of reduced tensions and the resources adequate for this less hostile (but not yet benign) competition.

The degree of US involvement in the Gulf is sensitive to assumptions about three questions: (1) the degree of US dependence on oil imports, hence vulnerability in a general sense to disruptions; (2) the incidence and intensity of regional conflicts; and (3) the future Soviet role in the Gulf.

It seems prudent to assume as base points for policy the following answers: (1) growing dependence relative to the past decade, (2) some conflicts not necessarily limited, and (3) growing, possibly defensive and benign, but volatile.

Assuming that the United States is able to secure domestic political support for keeping intact its base structure, permitting timely access and a presence near the region operational (for the traditional goals of access and denial), what should US policy be? In the first place, the change in rationale for US policy should not be overdone; denial may appear less urgent today, but its importance, however remote the probability of outcome, requires anticipation. A failure to plan for this contingency makes it less remote, and more probable.

Cycles of activism and withdrawal, exaggerated threats followed by detachment, have done nothing to make the US public (or indeed informed elites) conversant with appropriate US policies *absent* an overwhelming Soviet threat. The past decade of relative abundance of oil supplies may also have encouraged an ill-founded complacency about the tolerance of US interests for regional instability. There is no assurance that US dependence on oil will be sufficiently secure to undergo with equanimity a rerun of the Iran-Iraq war in the 1990s and beyond. There are two reasons, cumulatively persuasive, to argue for the continued diplomatic engagement of the United States in the security of the Persian Gulf, even in the absence of an acute USSR threat.

First, regional conflicts can be anticipated in the future with a chance that the violence will be intense and local disruptions extensive. Such conflicts could provide openings to the USSR, threaten oil supplies, and spread. Second, the Gulf lacks a stable, indigenous security system conducive to peace. There is unlikely to be a spontaneously activated or self-sustaining structure capable of maintaining security in the region. Just as the superpowers and the United Nations were necessary to help end the Gulf war, outside forces will be necessary to underwrite the peace and manage security for some time.

US policy in the Gulf should be one designed to prevent the outbreak of conflicts as much as to manage them once they have erupted. Such a policy requires anticipating and forestalling rather than reacting to crisis.

These lines written before the Iraqi seizure of Kuwait underlined the failure of US policy in the Gulf, especially in the period July 1988–July 1990. After the reflagging exercise in support of Kuwait and the cease-fire in the Iran-Iraq war, no further attention was paid to the region. Doubtless because of the cataclysmic events in Eruope and the end of the cold war, as well as the distaste felt by many toward the unattractive regimes in Baghdad and Tehran, US policy reverted to one of neglect—a neglect that some justified by the failure of the two adversaries to move beyond a cease-fire, and by their obvious deficiencies in areas such as human rights. Insofar as there was a policy at all, it was based on erecting a multilateral technology-denial regime in relation to ballistic missiles, and the promotion of a chemical weapons convention that would ban not only the use (as in the Geneva Protocol) but also the stockpiling of such devices.

No attempt was made to strengthen the cease-fire or to use the Security Council's proper role as the formulator of SC 598 to seek a stabilization of the military situation in terms of regional security, as suggested in that document. There was no attempt to come to terms with the insecurities in the region. It apparently escaped notice in Washington that Iraq was busy building up its weapons stocks on all levels despite the absence of any proximate military threat or competitor. Washington was in the throes of a period of detachment, neglect, or abstinence that was to lead not only to a misreading of Iraqi intentions but also a poor signaling of its own position. The upshot has been a military involvement that paradoxically appears easier to activate than a corresponding but sustained political engagement.

This diplomacy is more akin to "gardening" (in Harold Nicolson's terminology) than the "fire-brigade" characteristic of some approaches to crisis-management. It also suggests that equating "technology denial" or "restraint regimes" in relation to certain weapons systems is short-sighted and unlikely to be effective. The United States cannot and probably should not choose among the various states of the Gulf. None is a natural ally of the United States or shares its values. But this does not mean that certain norms cannot be pursued in the region.

Disrupters of the regional order, states who pursue policies of coercion against their neighbors, promote subversion, rely on military might to intimidate their neighbors, can be discouraged.

The United States should promote these principles by supporting "regional" groupings like the GCC. Despite the shortcomings of this institution, which is less a regional institution than an alliance against Iran, and despite the weakness of the GCC (which required US involvement before the Gulf war could be ended) it still remains a useful yardstick and touchstone for regional policies.

A US role as ultimate guarantor, as a supplementary if essential prop for the GCC, is essential. But there is no reason why it will have to remain exclusively a US role. The experience of allied cooperation in the Gulf in 1987–1988 was the most impressive example of "out-of-area" activity ever seen. In the future, burden sharing may become more pressing, and as Europe becomes more economically unified, there will be pressures for multilateral deployments. The United States will and should encourage this.

In the event that the USSR becomes a more benign power in the Gulf and the superpowers' common interests in stability in that area become more pronounced, there is scope for some cooperation between them. Broadly, there are three types of possible cooperation. The first is in the management of their own competition, in the establishment of "rules for the road." The second is in the scope for reducing the prospect of confrontation by the decoupling (formal or tacit) of crises from their relationship; this could cover "agreements" to acknowledge the other side's primary interest ("a free hand"), or to agree mutually to remain uninvolved. The third possibility covers the range of active rather than passive policy choices, from agreement on joint guarantees to "enforcement action" as envisaged under Chapter 7 of the UN Charter.

These are theoretical possibilities, and it may be too early to contemplate them as live policy choices at present. A weakened USSR, for example, would be in a poor position to demand concessions, whereas a reformed USSR might turn out to have interests in the region largely compatible with those of the United States. So the possibility of a new role in the Gulf merits Soviet consideration for the future.

Notes

1. For a more extensive discussion and documentation, see my report, "The USSR and Its Southern Neighbors in the 1990s," for the Office of Net Assessment, Department of Defense (Washington, DC: May 1989).

2. For a recent discussion, see Bruce Allyn, James G. Blight, and David Welch, "Essence of Revision: Moscow, Havana, and the Cuban Missile Crisis," *International Security*, vol. 14, no. 3 (Winter 1989–1990): 136–174.

3. See my *Iran's Foreign Relations* (Berkeley: University of California Press, 1974), and Bruce Kuniholm, *The Origins of the Cold War in the Near East* (Princeton, NJ: Princeton University Press, 1980).

4. On which see my "Hedging in the Gulf: Soviets Arm Both Sides," *International Defense Review*, no. 6 (June 1987): 731–735. For a more general discus-

sion, see Mark Kramer, "Soviet Arms Transfers to the Third World," *Problems of Communism* (September–October 1987): 52–68.

5. See Shahram Chubin and Charles Tripp, *Iran and Iraq at War* (London: Tauris, and Boulder, CO: Westview Press, 1988).

6. See my "The USSR and Iran," *Foreign Affairs*, vol. 61, no.4 (Spring 1983): 921–949.

7. See Norman Cigar, "The Soviet Navy in the Persian Gulf: Naval Diplomacy in a Combat Zone," *Naval War College Review*, vol. 42, no. 2 (Spring 1989): 56–89, and Frank Fukuyama, *Gorbachev and the New Soviet Agenda in the Third World* (Santa Monica, CA: RAND/Arroyo Center, R-3634-A, June 1989).

8. See Geoffrey Hosking, *The Awakening of the Soviet Union* (London: Heinemann, 1990); Zbigniew Brzezinski, "Post-Communist Nationalism," *Foreign Affairs*, vol. 68, no. 5 (Winter 1989–1990): 1–25; Ludmilla Alexeyeva, "Unrest in the Soviet Union," *Washington Quarterly*, vol. 13, no.1 (Winter 1990): 63–78; and Paul Goble, "Soviet Ethnic Politics," in *Problems of Communism*, vol. 37, no. 4 (July–August 1989): 1–14.

9. Elements still animated by zeal and ideology in Iran's leadership wanted this to be government policy in late 1989 and early 1990 when there were disturbances in Soviet Azerbaijan. Hints in some Azeri quarters that they sought unity with Iran seemed to be an attempt to get Tehran's support rather than reflective of a general Azeri sentiment or goal.

10. See my "Soviet Policy Toward Iran and the Gulf," *Adelphi Paper* no. 157 (London: IISS, Spring 1980).

11. For a contrasting view, see Michael Mccgwire, *Soviet Military Objectives* (Washington, DC: Brookings, 1987), and "Update: Soviet Military Objectives," *World Policy Journal*, vol. 3, no. 4 (Fall 1987): 723–731.

12. Especially as it interacts with nationality and economic issues; for some recent studies, see the issue on Central Asia of the *Middle East Journal*, vol. 43, no. 4 (Autumn 1989); William Fierman, "Religion and Nationalism in Soviet Central Asia," a book review in *Problems of Communism*, vol. 38, no. 4 (July–August 1989): 123–127; Tamara Dragadze, "The Armenian-Azerbaijani Conflict: Structure and Sentiment," in *Third World Quarterly*, vol. 2, no. 1 (January 1989): 63–69; and Amir Taheri, *Crescent in a Red Sky* (London: Hutchinson, 1989).

13. To which Foreign Minister Eduard Shevardnadze recently alluded when discussing the Geneva accords of April 1988 that allowed Soviet withdrawal from Afghanistan. He wrote: "And, of course, the agreement would hardly have been possible if Iran's position had not been well-disposed." Text of an article in *Izvestiya*, February 15, 1990, in *BBC Summary of World Broadcasts*, Su/0694/A3/1, February 21 1990.

14. See my chapter 7, "The USSR in Southwest Asia," in *The Soviet Union and the Third World: The Last Three Decades*, eds. Andrzej Korbonski and Francis Fukuyama (Ithaca, NY: Cornell University Press for RAND/UCLA, 1987).

15. See Jonathan Haslam, "The UN and the Soviet Union: New Thinking?" *International Affairs*, London (1989): 676–684.

16. Unless—and we can only mention it here—Moscow accepts the secession of the Transcaucasus states and then seeks to fashion a belt of independent states in their place.

9
The European Community and the Gulf
Philip Robins

It seems increasingly reasonable to group the twelve members of the European Community together for the purposes of analysis in international relations. First, eleven of the countries belong to the European landmass; and the United Kingdom, which is geographically part of Europe, is soon physically to be linked to the Continent through the Channel tunnel. Second, the twelve have passed through more or less similar experiences with regard both to state formation and the broad development of their economies. Third, they are now in any case bound together in membership of the EC. Though the debate over deepening and widening the community continues,[1] there is no doubt that the EC is in many ways becoming a more coherent body. The creation of a single European market and other reforms planned for the 1990s suggest that, whatever the eventual size of the community, the deepening process will continue at least among a core group of countries.

Inscribed on the other side of the coin are a number of qualifications. Whatever the ultimate economic and political complexion of the EC, for the next decade at least the community will be made up of states that are more individually than corporately sovereign. The members will continue to organize their own armed forces, formulate their own foreign policy, and compete with one another in the world market. Moreover, whatever breakthroughs are made in terms of central institution-building, such as the creation of a European central bank, the prospects for the forging of a common foreign policy will be limited. Indeed, it is important to remember that the EC is not equipped with the legislation to pursue a single foreign policy, nor with the mechanisms with which to implement it were a hypothetical policy to exist. Periodic meetings of EC ambassadors in foreign capitals may now be established practice, but still the ambit of EC missions in the field is confined to economic reporting and the implementation of aid. The best that can be hoped for in the 1990s, from an integrationist perspective, is further tentative and incremental progress on the "harmonization" of policies where a broad consensus among EC members already exists.

Undoubtedly the UK has had the deepest exposure to the Gulf.[2] The importance of the area to the British stretches back to the opening up of Persia as an additional market for British exports bound for India. The Gulf then became important to the lines of communication between Persia and the UK. It must be remembered that the early relationship between the UK and the Gulf was driven by the security preoccupations of the British. The need to pacify the Gulf was paramount and was attained through the eradication of piracy in the area. Once the UK had seen off its international competitors and had pacified the Gulf, the British enjoyed an exclusive relationship with the area between 1890 and 1970. The twin turbines of a security and economic interest in the region also led the British to take an active interest in the domestic politics of the Gulf. It is therefore no coincidence that the United Kingdom was active in Kuwait in 1961 in protecting the established order (albeit from an external threat), and in Oman in 1970 in changing it.

None of the other eleven member states has the historical continuity of length or depth of the United Kingdom in the Gulf. For most of them, an active interest in the area rose to the surface only in the 1970s. The other members were obliged to take an interest in the affairs of the Gulf because of their dependence on oil from the region and the attractive commercial prospects offered by the enriched states there.

The second reason for the intrinsically different ways in which the EC states view and interact with the Gulf is their varying economic structures and the degrees of their intercourse in the region. These are best gauged by examining the quantitative nature of the economic interaction among the EC states and individual Gulf states. The most apparent element is whether an individual EC state can be described as being in any way dependent on Gulf oil and, second, whether it is an exporter of goods and services sought by the individual Gulf states. Again, the twelve find themselves at different points along a continuum. In 1987 seven of the eleven (taking Belgium and Luxembourg together) EC states had a trading deficit with the Gulf; this was in spite of the rapid decline in the price of oil in the middle of the decade. For instance, in 1987 the Netherlands imported over 52.9 percent of its energy inputs from the littoral states of the Gulf. Italy, France, and Spain were also heavily involved in the purchase of energy needs from the Gulf.

The varying capacities of the EC states in the economic domain may be judged using three yardsticks: the size of the potential country markets for oil and downstream exports and willingness of that country to import such downstream products from the Gulf; the ability of EC states to satisfy Gulf demand for exports; and, in certain cases, such as Iraq, the provision of credits. Predictably, the size and relative sophistication of individual EC member economies determine the extent to which each state scores in the first two areas. One exception in the category of potential oil purchases is the United Kingdom, which has an important domestic oil industry of its own, based on the North Sea. Though there will be an overall decline in the output of the North Sea fields through the 1990s, the UK oil industry will remain the primary source of local energy needs throughout the decade. However, even in the case of Britain, large purchases of Gulf oil are made. These are likely to grow as a result of the countertrade element involving oil incorporated into the large-scale and open-ended al-Yamamah contract, under which the UK will sell advanced weaponry and backup services to Saudi Arabia. In the area of credit provision, France, the United Kingdom, and West Germany all extended sizable lines to Baghdad. The bilateral debt is largest with Paris, the size of the civilian debt alone being estimated at some $2 billion in March 1988.[3] The Iraqis have a varying record when it comes to debt repayment to these three EC states, based on the nature of the credit. Along with the United States, Britain has enjoyed a favored status with Iraq so far as debt repayments have been concerned mainly because of the nature of its commitments, which are chiefly in the form of government-guaranteed debt. Baghdad has been less conscientious toward France, where the private sector has had a much higher profile in the extension of credit. Iraq does at least view as loans the money extended to it by all relevant EC states in contrast to the considerable finance that was forthcoming during the war from the Gulf Arab states, which Baghdad considers as grant payments for defense.

The third reason for having to treat EC members separately is their different executive capacities in the domain of foreign policy implementation. The United Kingdom and France are both permanent members of the Security Council, therefore it is clearly more worthwhile for other states to cultivate relationships with them than with the remaining members of the EC.

On the military front, the varying capabilities of the EC states were well illustrated during the latter stages of the Gulf conflict, when a number of European states established a naval presence in the area. By the beginning of winter 1987, five EC states had deemed it desirable to establish a military presence in or near the Gulf. These states were Belgium, France, Italy, the Netherlands, and the United Kingdom. Due to the domestic sensitivity of involvement in any military activity, West Germany did not play a direct role in the Gulf. It did, however, send four ships to the Mediterranean to take over NATO duties, thereby allowing other vessels to be diverted to the Gulf.

Belgium, the Netherlands, and Italy did not respond with a naval force until areas of the Gulf waterway had been demonstrably mined. Consequently, Belgium and the Netherlands sent only minesweepers to emphasize the limited and overtly peaceful nature of their mission. Their contribution has been described as "more a symbol of Allied solidarity than a decisive contribution to the security of the region."[4] The Italians dispatched three frigates to establish a more pronounced presence. The United Kingdom and France were the most militarily active in the area. The British had sent a naval force, the Armilla Patrol, to the southern Gulf almost at the very outset of the conflict, reflecting its historical and commercial connections with the area. The Armilla Patrol started out in October 1980 with one frigate, one destroyer, and a Royal Fleet auxiliary tanker. Yet in September 1987, at the height of the naval conflict, the British presence had only grown slightly. This indicated both the diminished capability of the Royal Navy and a reluctance to take steps that might be interpreted as an escalation of the conflict. Nevertheless, in escorting well over 1,000 merchant vessels in 1987 and 1988, the Armilla Patrol accompanied more than the total of vessels protected during this period by all the other Western navies combined. France was the EC state with the largest naval contingent in the Gulf area, reflecting in part the proximity and efficacy of its naval base at Djibouti. France's nine-ship contingent between Djibouti and the Arabian Sea included an aircraft carrier and was backed up by a six-ship Indian Ocean fleet.

It has perhaps become clear from such a survey that one may immediately group together the smaller members of the EC when looking at the EC states and the Gulf. This group of states may be said to include Belgium, Denmark, Ireland, Luxembourg, and Portugal. They are small in terms of population and in terms of the export and import capacities of their economies. They have negligible historical relations with the Gulf and, moreover, have little inclination or ability to play a diplomatic role on the world stage. One may next identify an intermediate group of countries in the community that have a more substantive relationship with the states of the Gulf. This group may be said to consist of Italy, the Netherlands, Spain, Greece, and Germany (whose inclusion in this category is of course controversial). The relationship is primarily confined to the commercial field, either to their purchases of Gulf oil or their importance as an export market. In many ways France, Germany, and the United Kingdom are the three leading states of the community. However, two factors tend to exclude Germany from the third category. First, it has not and cannot play any sort of naval or wider military role in the Gulf region. Second, Germany's diplomatic prowess is qualitatively less than that of the United Kingdom and France owing to the latter two countries' permanent membership in the UN Security Council, a forum that has been of unusual importance in the context of the Gulf conflict. It may well be the case, especially now that unification has taken place, that Germany is destined to be a comparable actor to the UK and France in the Gulf. This development is, however, likely not to take place in this century, when the expanded German state will have a greater economic challenge at home. Consequently, the third category can include only the United Kingdom and France as the two European countries that are the most important with respect to the Gulf.

EC States and Oil Dependence

Estimating whether Europe will become more reliant on Gulf oil for its energy sources in the 1990s, and the extent to which this might take place is an inexact science—indeed, not a science at all. Two elements have to be taken into consideration in a discussion of such a subject. The first is the likely demand structure within the EC states, placed against a backdrop of global demand. The second is the availability of alternative supplies of oil. Before considering either of these it will be useful to look at the pattern of oil trade between the EC and the Gulf at the moment.

In the decade following the 1973 oil crisis, the EC members made a determined effort to reduce their dependence on OPEC in general and the Gulf in particular. The uncertainties caused by the Iranian revolution, the Gulf conflict, and most recently Iraq's invasion of Kuwait have underlined the importance of reducing such dependency. The success of this effort is illustrated by the oil import figures. In 1973 the EC imported 43 percent of its oil from the Gulf. By 1987 that level had been reduced to 36.5 percent. The lower oil prices of the mid-1980s have not appreciably encouraged the EC states to halt their diversification away from oil as an energy source in general and Gulf oil in particular.

Imports of Gulf oil tended to fluctuate in the mid-1980s. The move away from government-to-government contracts, together with rapid changes in the price of oil, were important contributors in this respect. The figures still show, however, that Gulf sources have a significant profile in the oil imports of the EC states. The share of the Gulf exporting countries in the major European importers appears to be moving between the 30 to 45 percent mark. Altogether three EC states, including the Netherlands and Greece, received over half their oil imports in 1987 from the Gulf. Germany and the United Kingdom are the EC states whose imports of Gulf oil are significantly below the rest. Germany relies on Libya, Nigeria, and Venezuela for the bulk of its supply, while the United Kingdom's import profile is dominated by Norway.

Table 9.1 Gulf Oil Imports as a Percentage of Total Imports, 1986

	Saudi	Iran	Iraq	Kuwait	Qatar	UAE	Gulf
Belgium	12.4	11.1	10.1	0.1	—	—	33.7
Denmark	2.9	—	—	55.0	—	—	57.9
France	12.3	8.1	12.5	1.9	0.1	—	34.9
W. Germany	7.7	2.3	5.2	0.8	—	2.6	18.7
Greece	31.6	3.5	18.2	9.2	—	—	62.6
Ireland	—	—	—	—	—	—	—
Italy	9.9	3.5	10.5	4.6	1.8	6.5	42.1
Luxembourg	—	—	—	—	—	—	—
Netherlands	16.7	18.2	4.0	12.0	—	1.9	52.9
Portugal	20.1	—	12.0	—	—	12.1	44.1
Spain	9.5	10.0	9.5	0.9	—	1.7	31.6
UK	2.3	4.7	11.6	1.4	0.6	0.9	21.5

Source: Eurostat, *Energy Statistical Yearbook*, 1987.

Next it would be useful to look at the likely pattern of energy demand within the EC states in the 1990s. In spite of the flatness of oil prices in the 1980s, it seems likely that demand within the EC will, in general, do no more than stagnate, and may indeed decline, during the 1990s. A decline in the profile of oil in energy consumption is certainly the conclusion of the most authoritative survey of future energy trends produced by the EC Commission when looking at the two largest importers of Gulf oil, namely, Italy and France. In Italy oil consumption as a proportion of total energy use looks set to fall from an expected 57.3 percent in 1988 to 51.7 percent in 1995. In France the demand for oil is expected to fall from 85 million tons per annum in 1986 to 74 million tons per annum in 1995. This means that by 1995 oil will have lost its first place in the French national energy balance to primary electricity generated by hydro and nuclear sources. Levels of imported oil in Italy look set to fall by around 6.5 percent up to 1995 and some 8 percent by the end of the century on a base year of 1986. The fall in France is expected to be even more pronounced, with a decline of over 10 percent to the middle of the 1990s and 11.7 percent to the year 2000.[5]

Table 9.2 Net Oil Imports into Major EC States Importing Gulf Oil

	Million tons			
	1986	1990	1995	2000
Belgium	22.85	20.9	21.0	21.0
France	81.54	76.4	73.3	72.0
Greece	12.14	12.1	13.5	14.0
Italy	81.65	80.0	76.3	75.0
Netherlands	29.69	29.4	31.5	31.5
Spain	38.50	41.1	45.6	47.5
W. Germany	115.51	121.6	118.2	117.0
Total	381.88	381.5	379.4	378.0

Source: Commission of the European Communities, *The 1995 Community Energy Objectives*, Brussels, 1988.

If the situation in Italy and France is atypical of the other EC members, it is not because most of them will be rapidly expanding their use of oil. West German energy consumption was expected to be nearly constant until the end of the century, although this prediction is now under review in light of German unification. Its use of oil rose in the second half of the 1980s but is expected to fall slightly in the 1990s as oil demand slumps below 40 percent of total energy demand in the country. Only Spain of the large or medium consumers of oil in the EC is likely to increase its use of oil at anywhere near a rapid rate. Oil consumption is expected to grow at approximately 23 percent between 1986 and the year 2000, with the rise in the first half of the 1990s alone being some 11 percent. Rises, though only incremental ones, are expected in the consumption of oil in the smaller EC states such as Belgium and Greece that also import oil from the Gulf.

Of course, stagnating oil demand in Europe does not automatically mean that demand for Gulf oil will stagnate or decline within an overall context of diversification. Of vital importance will be the availability of non-OPEC oil. Foremost in this respect will be the resources of the North Sea, which are significant to the United Kingdom as well as to Belgium, the Netherlands, and Ireland. There is broad agreement that British oil production will continue to fall in the 1990s. A crucial date could be 1995, when the UK will progressively have to scout around for other oil sources, which could at least arrest the drop in Gulf oil exports to Europe. Otherwise, considerable uncertainty surrounds the likely availability of non-OPEC oil in the second half of the 1990s.

Two broad scenarios may be offered for non-OPEC oil to the end of the decade. The first scenario is that one or a combination of factors will ensure that this source of oil does not significantly decline to the end of the century. The decrease may not occur if there are major new finds of oil, for instance in mainland China; breakthroughs in technology, especially in satellites or computers, which enable oil to be extracted at much reduced cost; a sustained high oil price that renders economic a number of crude oil and oil shale fields that currently cannot be commercially exploited. Although the first factor and particularly the second factor may be important in the 1990s, the third possibility is far less probable, owing to a variety of built-in responses in the oil market. Under this broad scenario, Gulf oil would be likely to increase its profile within EC oil imports.

The second scenario is based on the steady decline of non-OPEC oil, making the supply of OPEC oil more important. An adjunct to this could be that within OPEC, non-Gulf oil will in turn be of waning importance because of the apparently smaller resource endowments and larger populations of states such as Algeria, Indonesia, and Nigeria. Only Venezuela of the non-OPEC Gulf countries has proven reserves on a par with the major Gulf producers. According to this scenario, the states of the EC would have to look increasingly to the Gulf producers within OPEC to replace oil imports from the non-OPEC oil exporters.

Both scenarios include persuasive arguments. Either could well become a reality in the later years of the 1990s. In the face of such uncertain variables it is perhaps important to say that the very possibility of the second scenario must be of serious concern to the states of the EC. The likelihood of scenario two rather than scenario one taking place is too great to leave the whole issue of energy dependence to chance.

Relations with Iran

During the Gulf war many EC member countries continued to enjoy thriving economic relations with Iran. Italy has consistently been the EC state that has purchased the largest amount of Iranian oil. The Netherlands, West Germany, Spain, and, curiously (given its role as a major arms supplier to Iraq), France[6] have also been consistently large purchasers. The willingness of Tehran to sell oil to a former imperial power that has been so closely identified with its main adversary illustrated the extent to which, when it comes to a policy area as crucial as that of oil, politics is in general not permitted to intrude in Tehran.

The other side of the trading coin, namely exports, has been rather different. West Germany has dominated bilateral trade with Iran. Between 1981 and 1987 West Germany was the largest single supplier to Iran, even ahead of Japan. The high point of the relationship was in 1983, when Iran purchased over $3 billion worth of German exports. Four years later this had dropped by nearly half, although this decline conformed to the general trend in Iranian imports from the industrial countries, as the fall in oil revenue impaired Tehran's effective demand. Because of the lower profile of German oil purchases, the trade balance stood at $1.08 billion in favor of Bonn. This large deficit with West Germany contrasted with the pattern of Iranian trade relations with the other EC states that buy large quantities of its oil. Iran enjoyed large surpluses with Italy, France, Spain, and the Netherlands.

Germany was not the only EC state with a substantial trade surplus. The United Kingdom experienced large, though fluctuating, surpluses as a result of being a negligible oil trading partner. Until 1987 UK exports to Iran had not fallen beneath the $500 million mark. A relatively large trading profile had been maintained by the revolutionary regime in Tehran, regardless of the extensive involvement of Britain in its economic and political affairs up to a little more than a generation ago. Similarly, the low-key presence of the Armilla Patrol in the Gulf since 1980 appeared to be no impediment to the continuation of flourishing trade ties. Political problems have recently threatened to impair the quality of economic relations with Britain, mainly because it is in this area that Tehran presumably believes it has greatest leverage. Iran vowed to reduce its volume of trade with the United Kingdom in autumn 1987 following a political dispute that saw the downgrading of diplomatic relations and the forcible closing down of the Iranian Goods Procurement Office in London. However, business trading organizations in London report that, despite such actions, actual trade levels for the most part have been unaffected.

Iran seemingly values its relationship with some half dozen of the EC states. It enables it both to have access to major markets for its oil and to import modern goods and services from the West. Its relationship with states such as Italy and Germany is on the whole free of any political cost. In relation to states like the United Kingdom and France, where bilateral relations are far from smooth, the Iranians show themselves to be pragmatic when their national interests are believed to be involved. This approach to the EC states has been put under greatest strain during the Salman Rushdie affair.

Iranian involvement in the Rushdie affair perhaps came about for reasons of domestic politics and pan-Islamic affairs. On the one hand, those personalities in Iranian politics generally labeled as radicals in the West saw in the Rushdie affair an opportunity to seize the political initiative from their rivals, who had used their ascendant position to advocate improved relations with the West. On the other hand, the Iranian leadership, and in particular Ayatollah Khomeini, viewed the affair as a chance to reassert some authority over the world community of believers, its credibility having been badly damaged as a result both of the scenes at the 1987 pilgrimage in Saudi Arabia and Iran's meek acceptance of a cease-fire in the war with Iraq. The rhetorical vitriol aimed at the Germans in the aftermath of the withdrawal of the EC heads of mission points to the degree to which Iranians had been stung by the German action.[7]

The EC states and Iran enter the 1990s with their relations having been given a sharp jolt. It is unlikely that the psychological effects of this will wear off easily. The greatest breach has been between the United Kingdom and Iran. The reaction of the British government to Khomeini's death threat against Rushdie has further reawakened Tehran's historically recurring suspicions of the United Kingdom.

The relationship between the other five or so EC states that trade heavily with Iran is not analogous with that of the United Kingdom. Their relations have not been affected so profoundly. Indeed, the other EC states returned their envoys to Iran within four months of the original dispute. It seems unlikely that Iran will try to discourage trade between itself and Italy, France, Spain, and the Netherlands, with all of which it enjoys a healthy trade surplus. Iran's desperate need to sell its oil precludes any rash actions in this direction. On the European side, however, the Rushdie affair will not have raised confidence in the stability and reliability of Iran. Italy's oil policy had in any case been "directed . . . to securing a greater diversification of supply as a counterweight to the high overall level of dependence and, in a crisis, as a guard against interruption of supplies."[8] The experience with Iran will have encouraged Rome in this policy, which had already seen a steady reduction in imports of Iranian oil.

Japan is already Iran's second-largest supplier. A shift in trading emphasis from the EC to Japan would lead increasingly toward one-country dependence. It is therefore unlikely that trade between Iran and the EC states will completely collapse barring all but the most profound of contingencies.

The Arab-Israeli Dispute

Since the oil crisis in the wake of the 1973 Yom Kippur war, the Arab-Israeli dispute has been an important factor in trade and political relations between EC states and the Gulf. In October 1973 the Gulf-dominated members of OAPEC decided to reduce their production of oil by 5 percent per month. The then nine members of the EC were extremely vulnerable to such a move, being reliant on the Gulf states for 68 percent of their total oil imports.[9] Indeed, the new power relationship was made more alarming by the decision of OAPEC to single out the Netherlands of the EC states for a total ban. The reaction of the EC states was to make the political compromises necessary to gain exemption from the reduced production levels. The EC, in its Joint Resolution of November 6, called on Israel to end the territorial occupation it had maintained since the 1967 war, and for the recognition of the Palestinians' "legitimate rights." In placating the

Arab producers on a political level, the EC countries also established the precedent of independent European action on the Arab-Israeli issue, though it may be at variance with the political position of the United States. Washington, recognizing the pressing national interests involved in the saga, accepted the need on the part of the EC states to act in such a way. In turn, the Europeans, in order to reduce the potential friction that might have occurred with the United States, emphasized their role as a bridge between the United States and the area.

Since those desperate days of 1973, the degree of political involvement by the EC in the affairs of the area has been, by and large, a function of the oil market. It is no coincidence that the other great foray of the EC states into the politics of the Palestinian issue was in 1980, when the Venice Declaration was adopted at the height of the second oil price shock. By the same token, interest in the Arab-Israeli problem has never been as strong as in the days of a weak oil market. Witness in this regard the demise of the Euro-Arab dialogue in the early 1980s. With oil prices falling and the importance of OPEC greatly reduced, Europe lost interest and was prepared only to go through the motions of a substantive dialogue. The European side was ultimately not unhappy to see the dialogue fail with the row over whether Egypt should be a participant. Against the backdrop of oil, the depth of interest of the EC states in the Arab-Israeli issue has risen and fallen, although two important precedents have been established and remain in place in the wake of 1973: first, the principle that the EC states hold views and take positions on the issue at variance with those of the United States; second, the notion that the EC states make political concessions in order to secure economic objectives.

In the late 1980s the position of the Gulf members of OPEC was clearly not a strong one. By 1988 the share of Gulf producers in the world trade in crude oil stood at 43.2 percent. On the political front, strains owing to the Arab-Israeli war have been lessened for two reasons. On the part of the GCC states, the naval role the five EC states and the United States played in the Gulf war has increased the faith the six have in the West's willingness to render material protection in time of physical threat. In the future the GCC states are likely to value their relationship more earnestly with the West. Then, too, the United States' beginning a substantive dialogue with the PLO has removed a chief source of criticism of the United States by the EC states and the littoral Gulf states alike. There is now rather less need for the EC states to emphasize the policy gaps between Europe and the United States, although the Europeans will of course seek to maintain their right to differ. Similarly, for the moderate Gulf states the need to distance themselves from the United States is no longer so great, although for reasons of asserting sovereign independence, it has far from disappeared.

That some variables may not even be known illustrates the difficulty of prediction. The "new conventional wisdom" among oil analysts is that "any tightening of world oil markets, characterized by rising real prices and a much greater call on OPEC oil, will be delayed to the late 1990s, or even the early part of the next century."[10] If one assumes that such a trend does take place at some time, it will do so against a likely backdrop of greater influence within the organization of the principal Gulf producers, namely Saudi Arabia, Iraq, Iran, Kuwait, and Abu Dhabi. These five Gulf polities all enjoy large reserves of crude oil, ensuring that they will remain producers well beyond the life of the oil industries of other OPEC members and most of the non-OPEC producers, such as the United Kingdom. Were such a trend to be established at the end of the 1990s, it is reasonable to assume that the EC states, as in 1973 and 1980, will become once more sensitive to the political issues of the region. Furthermore, the United States, with its withering domestic oil sector and growing reliance on imported energy sources, could also come to be increasingly reliant either directly or indirectly on the Gulf.

If Gulf oil does become of growing importance sometime after 1995, it is likely that it will do so with changes having taken place in the Arab-Israeli theater. Three broad scenarios may be offered. First, some form of peace negotiations may have taken place involving Israel, the Arab states, and Palestinians and brokered by the five permanent members of the UN Security Council or within a superpower condominium. Transitional arrangements may already be in place for a solution to the Palestinian problem, and individual peace treaties may have been forged between Israel and the remaining Arab frontline states. With the occurrence of such developments, the Arab-Israeli dispute may be largely neutralized as a factor in EC-Gulf relations. Despite the encouraging diplomatic changes that took place in 1988 and 1989, such a scenario looks less than likely.

A second scenario may be that a conflagration takes place in the Occupied Territories in the early 1990s. Israeli actions in attempting to restore order to the Occupied Territories may result in increasing casualties. This could lead to a change in strategy on the part of Palestinians, who may put emphasis on action against the lives of Israeli soldiers and settlers and a more concerted attempt to sabotage economic targets within Israel proper. This in turn may result in Israeli moves to "transfer" large numbers of Palestinians to neighboring states, notably Jordan. This would no doubt increase the bloodshed and may destabilize the kingdom. Should such a scenario take place, it would be even less possible than in the past for the Gulf states to ignore the Palestinian issue. Reactions to such developments in the Gulf would be made on the following broad bases. First, ideological considerations would necessitate a strong reaction in both Iran and Iraq, the former on the grounds of pan-Islamic solidarity, the latter on the basis of the pan-Arabist faith. Second, considerations of regional power politics and the desire to play a leadership role in the Arab world would again lead to a strong reaction in Iraq and Saudi Arabia. Third, reasons of domestic stability would motivate the smaller Gulf states, especially those, such as Kuwait, with a large Palestinian expatriate population, to take a similarly strong stance.

Both of these scenarios, though far from fanciful, are on balance less likely to take place. The most likely scenario, I would argue, is that the present historic opportunity to achieve substantive movement on the Arab-Israeli front is lost, but that it does not lead to such apocalyptic happenings. The *intifada* may lose some of its energy as the inhabitants of the Occupied Territories become exhausted, or, indeed, in its violent form at least, it may collapse. The Israelis may be able broadly to contain the situation. A situation analogous to that in Northern Ireland might replace the current strife. Such ideas can only remain at the level of speculation. What such a scenario would mean is that the Arab-Israeli conflict would continue to be a festering wound in the affairs of the region. The Gulf states could not afford to ignore such an issue and would be preoccupied with it at a time when Gulf oil would be returning to center stage within the world energy balance. It could then once more be the main political issue over which the EC states have to offer some conciliation as insurance against future crises.

The extent to which the EC states might have to make further political concessions akin to those of 1973 and 1980 will depend on a number of factors. For one, there is the question of the existing political stances EC states individually hold on the issue. A minimum requirement to appease the Gulf states might be the EC's adoption of a common policy to improve the clout of the individual states' positions. Then, too, it will depend on the regional political situation in the Gulf and how the major oil producers, such as Saudi Arabia, perceive their national interests. Ultimately, the degree to which the Arab Gulf states are keen to cultivate rather than to alienate the EC states will probably rest on the perception of external threat. Finally, it would depend upon the quality of relations between the United States and the Gulf states. Had the former ended its dialogue with the PLO and returned to a position of uncritical support of Israel it might make the Gulf states more eager or desperate to open up a gap between the policy of the United States and Western Europe. On the other hand, if the US position were regarded as beyond the pale by the Gulf states, it would make it easier for the EC countries to impress the littoral states with relatively minor concessions.

While the EC states would probably have no compunctions about scoring points with the Gulf states at US expense, there are definite limitations beyond which they would be extremely unlikely to go. The green line would be the extent to which an independent EC policy might affect EC-US relations in other substantive areas. Chief among these would be in the area of protectionism and defense cooperation. The current "bonfire of certainties" in the domains of security and foreign affairs notwithstanding, it is difficult to imagine that Western Europe and the United States will not be close allies by the end of this decade. The importance of the US market, and US military capability, together with long-term reservations about the internal fortunes of the Soviet Union, make it highly likely that the United States will still be Western Europe's major ally by the year 2000. If such a relationship remains intact, it is difficult to envisage a scenario in which any of the EC states would abandon the United States in the event of an oil embargo aimed exclusively at the United States for its support of Israel. It is inconceivable that the EC states would, for instance, refuse to honor its International Energy Agency oil-sharing arrangements, even if they were to be threatened with inclusion in such an embargo.

It is, in turn, rather unlikely that any combination of the Gulf states would proceed down that road. The formation of three definite groups in the Gulf (Iran, Iraq, and the GCC), together with the legacy of suspicion in the aftermath of the Iran-Iraq war, and that which may safely be expected following the crisis of the Iraqi invasion of Kuwait, makes the coordination of political strategies among them very difficult. Moreover, the existence of the GCC cannot be taken as proof that the six smaller Arab states would act in concert on such a vital issue. Should there be any attempt to galvanize a boycott of oil sales to the United States or the West, there is absolutely no possibility of European naval power being harnessed to secure the continued supply of oil from the region. The only exception to this clear position would be if there existed a violation of international law, such as an attempt to interfere with the oil production of states in the area or to block the Straits of Hormuz. Only in the case of such development would a military option occur to the United Kingdom and no doubt the other states in the EC.

The Gulf and 1992

The attitude toward 1992 and the creation of a single European market on the part of most of the GCC countries has been similar to that held in Japan and the United States. There is a strong feeling of uncertainty as to exactly what will be the implications of 1992 for them, and a tendency to think the worst will happen, with their exports either being excluded from Western Europe or subject to prohibitive tariffs. This anxiety and the consequent defensive posture adopted is not helped by the inability of the EC to clarify the situation in certain important fields. The fact is that even the EC members do not know precisely what will be the outcome of the negotiations on the nuts and bolts of a single European market. And it is unlikely that all the regulations will have been thrashed out by the target date of 1992.

Though the concern in the Gulf is similar to that in the United States and Japan, its focus is much narrower, reflecting the structure of the respective economies. In the Gulf the worries are almost exclusively confined to the petrochemical sector. This means that the real concern in the area is limited to those states that have large-scale petrochemical industries and have tried to penetrate the European market, which effectively means just Saudi Arabia. The Saudis in turn have enlisted the support of the GCC as an organization in an attempt to try to broaden their campaign. Other GCC states, such as Bahrain, which have much smaller petrochemical industries, are only marginally interested in the issue, though they tend to support the Saudi position for political reasons. The exception is Oman, which is not only unaffected materially by the situation but which resents that Riyadh appears to be prepared to prejudice wider relations with the EC through lack of flexibility on this issue. The Omanis are quick to appease individual EC states on the subject of implications for bilateral relations.

The deep concern the GCC countries feel over the issue of 1992 has been manifested in the persistence with which the council as a multilateral organization has sought to conclude a cooperation agreement with the EC. The first stage of the agreement was sealed in June 1988. In addition to a trade component, the first stage also included a political statement. The inclusion of the latter was by no means automatic in such agreements and was an attempt to allay the broader concerns of the GCC about the establishment of a fortress Europe. It appears to have been of little comfort to the GCC, which has been eager to conclude a second stage to the agreement. The EC is presently studying the possible scope of the second stage, which will provide for greater trade liberalization with mutually acceptable safeguards for both parties' petrochemical industries. The Iraqi invasion of Kuwait has given a greater boost to the speedy conclusion of such an accord as the EC tries to bolster the GCC as a multilateral organization with weight.

It seems unlikely that the studies will be concluded quickly for two reasons: first, because the European commissioner for Mediterranean affairs, Claude Cheysson, who was responsible for the first stage and who was a keen advocate of the agreement, has retired from his position; second, because of entrenched material interests on the part of certain EC states. The chief objectors are obviously the United Kingdom and the Netherlands, which are the two EC states with the most advanced petrochemical industries. Because of the effect on their own industries, they are loath to discontinue the high petrochemical tariffs currently in place and thereby open up the EC to Gulf downstream products. Crude oil inputs into the European downstream industries are, needless to say, much more expensive than in the Gulf; in the event of free competition between both outputs, Gulf petrochemicals would be expected to be marketed more cheaply than their counterparts from Europe. Other EC states are markedly less dogmatic on the issue. France, for instance, which has a much less well developed sector, is more conciliatory. Greece, which has no fear of competition but is happy to use the issue to improve relations with the Arab world, is positively enthusiastic about opening up the EC, to the great irritation of the United Kingdom.

It seems likely, however, that the British and the Dutch will be successful in ensuring that the EC continues to procrastinate over the issue of protecting the European market from Gulf petrochemicals. From the UK point of view its economic interests are unlikely to change before the end of the century. Even voices in the British business establishment that have close commercial ties with the Gulf take the line that the Saudis should make greater efforts to market their petrochemicals in countries that do not have an indigenous downstream industry. Kuwait, though it has an important petrochemicals sector, has not sought to market its products within the EC, instead plumping to develop markets elsewhere. The British and the Dutch also point to the unfairness of the Saudi position in singling out the EC for specific criticism on the issue. They point out that the community has in the past admitted certain levels of Saudi petrochemicals duty-free under the EC's generalized scheme of preferences. That preference level may be a very small one, but it is better, so the argument is made, than the US and Japanese policy of unrelentingly subjecting Saudi imports to punitive tariffs and quotas. The Europeans also accuse the Saudis of wanting to have their cake and eat it, claiming that although they seek a free trade agreement, the Saudis have not the least intention of removing the growing number of GCC protectionist barriers of between 20 and 25 percent to nurture embryonic manufacturing industries.

The EC generally welcomes vertical integration and direct investment in its member countries. Such involvement is regarded as embodying a positive approach toward 1992 and of course means economic benefits for the host countries. But not all examples of direct financial involvement are viewed as being so constructive. The large equity stake the Kuwait Investment Office acquired in British Petroleum in 1987 and 1988 was viewed with increasing discomfiture by the British government. Eventually, the KIO was obliged to sell the majority of its stake. The motivation for such a decision, which apparently contradicted the espoused values of private ownership and the unrestricted movement and investment of capital, was a strategic one. The British government believed that it was against the national interest for a major oil-producing and OPEC member country to have a major stake in Britain's largest oil company. Aware of the delicacy of the situation, the Kuwaitis went along with the requirement without permitting it to spoil broader bilateral relations. The discretion and sensitivity of the Kuwaiti government make it unlikely that another attempt would be made to build up a high-equity profile in an EC-based company of strategic importance. In addition to national oil companies, major defense manufactures would come into the same bracket. It is also unlikely that other Gulf states would mimic the KIO's BP operation.

EC Arms Sales to the Gulf

There are perhaps few other areas of relations with the Gulf in which the individual EC states compete with one another more robustly than that of arms sales. This is primarily because of the lucrative export market they offer and the desire on the part of individual EC states to profit from them. The chief focus of arms sales competition is between the community's two main arms producers, the United Kingdom and France. Competition between the two states has been sharpened by the falling away of the United States as an arms supplier in the 1980s. Occasionally healthy competition between the two degenerates into mutual denigration; negligible cooperation, either formal or informal, takes place between both countries in this area.

Though the competition between the two countries is often fierce, there seems every possibility that both countries will continue to benefit from a lucrative arms business in the Gulf in the 1990s, assuming, of course, the ability of potential purchasers to fund such procurement. The principal reason for this is the desire of all the states of the Gulf to expand and diversify their arms procurement. Historically, the two superpowers have dominated arms sales to the area, the United States supplying the bulk of the demand in Saudi Arabia and prerevolutionary Iran, the Soviet Union supplying the Iraqi market. All three countries have at one time or another suffered as a result of an over-reliance on one supplier. Iran found it impossible to buy spares in the wake of the revolution. The Soviet Union has thrice reduced arms supplies to Baghdad to a trickle for political reasons. Saudi Arabia has suffered because of growing domestic objections in the US Congress to transfers of advanced weapons systems. In the 1980s France, in the case of Iraq, and the United Kingdom, in the case of Saudi Arabia, stepped in as both those Gulf states sought to diversify. Iran has turned more to China and the Third World.

In seeking to diversify their supply of arms, the Gulf states neither want to lose contact with previous suppliers nor do they in turn want to remain dependent on one country, simply exchanging one monopsonist for another. It is therefore misleading, for instance, to see Saudi purchases of British military equipment as evidence that Riyadh is no longer interested in buying supplies from the United States. The Saudis, especially King Fahd, have not wanted to see an end to the defense industries' relationship with the United States, as they no doubt believed that this would lead to a dilution of US interest in Saudi Arabia. The fear has in turn been that Washington might devalue the importance of the kingdom in the Gulf area, although this now seems unlikely, given the provision of basing facilities to the United States in the aftermath of Iraq's invasion of Kuwait. One may thus look at the Saudi emphasis on offset investment as more than simply a desire to increase the activity and sophistication of the domestic economy. Both the US-supplied Peace Shield program and the British al-Yamamah defense deal may also be regarded as an attempt on the part of Riyadh to force a direct economic interest in Saudi Arabia by those two countries long after the military supplies element of the contract has been completed.

Similarly, Iraq has sought to diversify its arms suppliers and has found Europe a convenient shopping place, although the Gulf crisis has shown the limitations of such diversification in the post–cold war era. The EC states have the advanced weapons systems and general levels of technology that Baghdad needs in order to maintain the qualitative edge over the Iranian military. This is likely to provide the crucial deterrent to ensure that Iran does not restart the Gulf war a generation or so into the future. At the same time the Soviet Union is unlikely to be too alarmed by Baghdad's turning to Western Europe, especially in the context of the "new thinking" in the foreign policy going on in the Kremlin. The Soviet Union can live with Iraq's diversifying in the direction of the EC states, whereas purchases of US equipment would no doubt be viewed with considerably greater suspicion. On the other hand, while Iraq seeks advanced aircraft and air missile supplies from France, and ballistic missile technology from private sources in West Germany, it is unlikely to turn its back on the supply of more basic equipment from Moscow. The Iraqi armed forces are geared up to the use of lower-level Soviet technology and that is the equipment with which the army in particular is familiar. Diversification again does not necessarily mean turning one's back on one's main supplier.

In spite of some caveats, it is true to say that the United Kingdom, in particular, and France stand to develop closer procurement links with the states of the Gulf region. The two-stage al-Yamamah contract concluded in 1985 and 1988 looks set to establish a strategic relationship between Saudi Arabia and the United Kingdom to the end of the century and beyond. The potential value of the Saudi relationship to the United Kingdom and (within Panavia) its German and Italian partners can only be guessed at. Large sums have already been mentioned. In fact procurement and payment will be spread out fairly evenly over a number of years and may even involve the provision of credit should Saudi Arabia's balance of payments current account difficulties persist. The announcement of such large contracts does not therefore mean that the money has already been received. It still has to be earned, with the United Kingdom, for instance, having to show that it has the capacity to offer the training and maintenance for such a large project. The decision of Jordan and Oman to postpone and cancel, respectively, its orders for Tornado aircraft, because of financing difficulties, illustrates that declarations of intent cannot be taken as certainties of purchase.

A possible gremlin in the to-date smooth evolution of the Anglo-Saudi arms supply relationship is the offset investment dimension. There was considerable foot dragging on the part of the British before an agreement in principle was made to reinvest a proportion of the payments for the enterprise. Since then there has been a marked lack of enthusiasm by the British private sector at the project identification stage. This is despite the Saudi offer that offset investment may be made anywhere within the GCC and the possibility that third countries, such as Turkey, could be included in a triangular relationship. British tardiness on the issue of offset investment will no doubt continue to irritate senior Saudi government officials, who regard such procrastination as churlish, given the size of the contracts involved. In spite of the hard bargaining and exasperation caused to both sides by such a painful process, it is unlikely that problems in this area could jeopardize the whole project or major parts of it. It will take an issue of greater fundamental importance than petrochemical exports to the EC or teething problems over offset investment to knock the emerging relationship between the United Kingdom and Saudi Arabia seriously off course.

Assuming that the relationship proceeds smoothly, it will represent a new plane for Anglo-Saudi relations. For all Britain's long association with the Gulf, Saudi Arabia is not a state with which it has developed special ties. Indeed, Saudi-British relations were characterized more by suspicion than cordiality as late as the start of the 1980s. In earlier years Britain did not create a special relationship with Saudi Arabia, not least because of the paternalist links it had with the smaller Gulf states. The al-Yamamah project is thus a great opportunity to foster the type of intimate relations with Riyadh that have not existed before. The challenge for the United Kingdom in the 1990s will be to use the al-

Yamamah ties as a base from which to broaden the relationship to other sectors. The health sector and other areas of security cooperation are believed to be prime areas of potential. It is thereby hoped to consolidate the relationship between the two states. An important aspect of such a diversification process, as far as the United Kingdom is concerned, is the need to expand the range of personal contacts within the kingdom. In a polity where personal rather than institutional relations are of paramount importance, it is essential not only to strike up an intimate working relationship in the present, but to second-guess the emergence of tomorrow's elite. The broadening of functional relations, in addition to the deepening of strategic relations, is therefore fundamental to the continuation of a close and profitable working relationship well into the future.

Conclusion

For the duration of the 1990s the twelve members of the European Community will remain more individually than corporately sovereign. There will be EC positions adopted on economic issues, but these will be subordinate to individual national interest. In the important areas of foreign affairs, defense, and commerce, in particular, the states of the community will guard their prerogative. Harmonization of policy will increase, but only incrementally as the perception of common interest grows.

If observers will have to continue to think in terms of twelve policies toward the Gulf rather than one in the 1990s, they will notice two areas of more general relevance to the community. The first is oil. Even those states that purchase little or no Gulf oil are interested in the security of supply and broad stability of price. The profile of the Gulf states in the oil market still means that developments in the region can cause great volatility in the global market. A weak oil price has prevailed together with an abundant supply for most of the last decade. Such a situation may well characterize most of the 1990s as well. The Iraqi invasion of Kuwait has, however, shaken the EC states out of their somewhat complacent attitude. The crisis means that the EC is once again likely to become sensitive to the issue of energy security.

The second area of more general concern to the community would be if an issue or occurrence of great regional political importance, such as Iraq's invasion of Kuwait, threatened to disrupt trade and other interaction with the EC states. The Palestine problem is a second issue capable of eliciting both a deep and general response in the Gulf. A conflagration in the Occupied Territories involving the death or expulsion of large numbers of Palestinians could lead to such a situation. With the United Kingdom and France most earnestly involved, a new imperative could be given to EC policy on the Arab-Israeli problem. This could result in an EC policy that diverges further from that of the United States. The EC position, however, will be tempered by other, wider interests. The enduring strategic relationship between Western Europe and the United States will curb any thought of action that seriously impairs the interests of the United States.

As the twelve look at the 1990s, they see that their common international political agenda appears to be lengthening. For the EC, then, the Gulf as a regional subsystem is unlikely to be anything more than one key priority area among several. Even the United Kingdom and France, which have major and growing commercial interests in the region, will but fitfully be able to address themselves to the issues of the area. As the invasion of Kuwait by Iraq has shown, only in the event of a major crisis will the collective diplomatic thoughts of the EC states be brought to bear on the region in the next decade. Such a prospect offers little hope of anything more than crisis management and a passive diplomatic mode.

Notes

1. This is one of the most fundamental debates within the EC. It surfaces in a number of forms. For instance, applicants for EC membership, such as Turkey, are faced with the argument that the membership of the community cannot possibly be expanded until after 1992 and the creation of the single European market. In other words, in the short to medium term a strong argument is put forward for the increased consolidation of relations among the twelve prior to the admission of additional members.

2. The deepest association with the area but not the longest. The Portuguese were active in the Gulf area for much of the sixteenth century. The Dutch had the better of the British for significant periods in the seventeenth and early eighteenth centuries. However, this historical relationship has had little impact for these two European states on contemporary relations with the Gulf.

3. *Mideast Markets*, vol. 15, no. 5 (March 7, 1988): 13.

4. Dominique Moisi, "A European Perspective," in *Great Power Interests in the Persian Gulf*, ed. Paul Jabber (New York: Council on Foreign Relations, 1989), p. 60.

5. Calculations made from figures contained in Commission of the European Communities, *The 1995 European Community Energy Objectives* (Brussels, May 1988), p. 98.

6. The one break in French purchases of Iranian oil on noneconomic grounds was made by Paris. This occurred in 1987–1988 over the Gorji affair.

7. For example, see continued criticism of West Germany by the Iranian daily *Kayhan*. BBC/SWB/MW, March 15, 1989.

8. Commission of the European Communities, *The 1995 European Community*, p. 98.

9. Valerie Yorke and Louis Turner, *European Interests and Gulf Oil* (Aldershot: Gower, 1986), p. 6.

10. Philip Robins, *The Future of the Gulf: Politics and Oil in the 1990s* (London: Dartmouth 1989), p. 112.

10

Japanese-Gulf Relations Toward the Year 2000

Ukeru Magosaki
Yasumasa Kuroda

The success of Japanese foreign policy toward the year 2000 will depend on how well Japan is able to adjust to the changing international environment and on what initiatives it takes as these changes occur. Developments in Soviet and Chinese economic and political stances, US industrial and trade policies, and a united European Community and its impact on international trade and investment policies, for example, will affect Japanese policy directly. Nevertheless, joining the international community and establishing harmonious relations with other countries must remain top priorities for Japanese diplomacy.

In order to forecast Japanese behavior in the international community, particularly in the Gulf region, it is necessary to examine the external forces that will influence this behavior. Moreover, to understand Japan's motivation behind certain initiatives, it is necessary to study more intensively the process and logic of Japanese decisionmaking for its policies toward foreign countries.[1]

What Influences Japan's Gulf Policy?

Japanese policy toward the Gulf cannot be decided by one dominant factor, but rather by a combination of several elements. Key factors include the following:

1. To secure petroleum import from this region;
2. To gain access for development of Gulf countries;
3. To coordinate with other Japanese diplomatic priorities, particularly in relations with the United States;
4. To emphasize peace and to respect the wishes of the people of any region; and
5. To make active independent diplomacy that corresponds and appeals to the majority of the Japanese public.

One of the capacities to be expected of decisionmakers is a sense of balance. In the Ministry of Foreign Affairs, diplomats who have the most influence in deciding Japan's stance toward the Gulf may not necessarily be the most knowledgeable about the Gulf or petroleum, but they should be capable of making a balanced decision without being strongly influenced by just one factor.

Nevertheless, in some circles too much weight is given to petroleum and US influence. Some people argue that Japan's dependency on the Gulf distorts its policy toward the Middle East and that Japan will go against US pressure when the Japanese consider that the import of oil is vital to their survival. Others argue the opposite, that Japanese foreign policy is merely following instructions from the United States.

Taking into consideration Japan's position toward the Middle East as outlined above, we must examine all elements for decisionmaking in order to make an objective assessment of Japanese policy.

Japan's Dependence on Oil

Toward the year 2000, the supply and demand for petroleum will tighten worldwide. Such major oil-producing countries as the United States, the Soviet Union, and China, unable to meet growing domestic needs for petroleum, will look to foreign sources to supplement increased demand. Development of alternative energy sources, including nuclear power, will also occur, but in the shorter term this will be insufficient to meet world needs. Hence the share of Gulf petroleum in the world market will likely expand.

A petroleum price rise could come at any time. But Japan will be ready. Because today Japan, unlike other industrialized nations, is better able to absorb higher prices, its people will not necessarily feel the same sense of panic they might have felt at past oil price increases. Moreover, due to Japan's lesser dependence on petroleum as a major energy source, any restriction on output that OPEC might impose would be withstood much more easily than in 1973. Japanese power plants reduced dependence on petroleum from 71.1 percent in 1973 to 24.9 percent in 1988.

The worst-case scenario for Japan would be that of quantitative restrictions on output. But in many oil-exporting countries, including Iran and Iraq, together with other non-Gulf OPEC countries, there is the internal necessity to keep constant revenues from petroleum export. Therefore, long-term deterioration of petroleum export is unlikely. Furthermore, export-import relations create a mutual benefit. With clear appreciation of benefits on the side of export countries, it is unlikely that they will disregard their own long-term interests.

Certainly, there is a possibility for OPEC to reduce the flow of crude oil in order to force prices higher. But this problem could be handled through the use of reserve stocks of oil that have recently been created.

The Japanese are not likely to take any commercial measure against the market mechanism without an assurance of government compensation. During and after the energy crisis, some advocates called for the diversification of petroleum resources, and others wanted government involvement in securing the purchase of petroleum. Almost all measures taken by private companies against the market mechanism failed. For example, in 1974, immediately after the energy crisis, the Japanese government succeeded in establishing a government-to-government oil purchase agreement with Iraq but then had to send a special delegation to explain to the Iraqi government that it could not buy the contracted amount of oil because its price was slightly higher than the market price.

But the government is not likely to take additional measures. Because of its dependence on Gulf oil, however much reduced since 1973, Japan will continue to maintain good bilateral relations with the Middle East.

US-Japanese Relations

US-Japanese relations will change in the 1990s, mainly because of the change in Japanese economic power. In the past, objective foundations for the pursuit of "equal partnership" between the two nations were lacking. Economically, militarily, and politically, Japan relied on the United States. Under such conditions, it was natural that some Americans expected the Japanese to blindly follow. Some US officials, in fact, had remarked that a lack of close cooperation in the military and political fields might influence US-Japanese economic relations to the detriment of the Japanese.

But the situation has changed. With the growing strength of the Japanese economy, the one-sided dependence of Japan upon the United States has gradually diminished. As a result, the US expectation of a compliant Japan is disappearing. However, decreased dependence does not mean a decrease of importance of the US factor in Japanese diplomacy. On the contrary, the US position is likely to increase in importance as Japan increasingly seeks to formulate an independent foreign policy.

Historically, frictions have occurred quite often when a superpower in a given epoch felt that its power, whether military, political, or economic, might be challenged by another country. Although not all Americans share the view that the United States is challenged by Japan, there are, and will be, certain influential sectors in the United States that consider Japanese economic behavior threatening. In the face of serious problems that require internal sacrifices, it is easier instead to use outsiders as scapegoats. If the United States does not solve its economic problems sufficiently, for example, strong voices will claim that Japan is mainly responsible for the US trade deficit. Consequently, friction in US-Japanese economic relations is very likely, no matter how successfully the Japanese adapt to new US requests.

Facing such requests, Japan could have two different reactions. It might argue that US demands go too far. Or no matter how rational it considers its opposition, Japan might decide to seek compromise at any cost. The first reaction has already started to appear in Japanese public opinion.

In the future, with the possible fragility of Japanese government, voices in favor of strongly presenting Japanese views to the United States might grow louder. The spiraling effects of emotions in both nations might create a crisis larger than that justified by the objective circumstances. On the other hand, Japanese mainstream diplomats with the responsibility of planning and executing foreign policy will be keenly aware that they should smooth relations somehow and should find and exploit every opportunity to improve US-Japanese cooperation so as to promote confidence in mutual interests and a common destiny.

The Japanese policy toward the Gulf may offer a chance for such cooperation. First, however, each country will have to adjust its approach to a solution. In the case of Japan, long-term dominance by the Liberal Democratic party has created a situation in which any government feels it should honor the policies of the previous government and hesitates to take actions that contradict earlier ones. As a result, its policy decisions could survive changes in leadership. The US government, in contrast, finds itself rather free from the restrictions of past policies and sometimes even tries to emphasize a break from the practices of previous administrations.

These two approaches have sometimes led to differences in policies toward Iran. The belief in the importance of solid bilateral relations with Iran did not hinder the United States from taking a tougher line toward Iran when necessary. But Japanese decisionmakers were hesitant to take a policy that might cause deterioration in the long-term relationship.

Japan's Economic Relations with the Gulf

Economic relations is one of the key elements in the formation of bilateral relations. In the case of Japanese relations with neighboring countries such as the Soviet Union or China, military or political considerations are vital in the decisionmaking,

Table 10.1 Japan's Trade with the Middle East (in millions of dollars)

		1972	1975	1980	1985	1988
Iran	Export	322	1,854	1,520	1,348	808
	Import	1,490	4,978	4,101	2,505	1,164
Iraq	Export	31	819	2,169	1,305	406
	Import	6	396	4,339	1,260	828
Saudi	Export	238	1,351	4,956	3,890	3,142
Arabia	Import	901	6,135	19,538	5,205	6,348
Kuwait	Export	117	367	1,273	1,536	730
	Import	548	2,012	3,458	1,162	1,590
UAE	Export	112	543	1,356	1,164	1,286
	Import	231	1,802	8,190	8,916	5,327
Israel	Export	44	73	109	170	420
	Import	59	89	227	215	684

Source: MITI white paper, 1988.

but in Japan's relations with nonneighboring countries, economic factors are destined to play a greater role. Tables 10.1 and 10.2 show the trends in Japan's trade relations with the Middle East over the past two decades.

The tables show that the share of Japanese trade with the Gulf countries is closely linked to oil prices. In the years when oil prices were high, Japan's economic relations with the Gulf countries increased. But with the decline of oil prices, the share of West Asia in Japan's 1988 trade fell to the same level as in 1966. Saudi Arabia's share was consistently high, as was that of the United Arab Emirates. Iran's share was high in 1972, before the energy crisis. (The current level is below that of Saudi Arabia, the UAE, and almost equal to other Gulf oil-producing countries such as Iraq and Kuwait.) On the other hand, Iraq's share was low in 1972 but in the early 1980s became almost equal to that of Iran. In comparison with oil-producing countries, Israel's share was very low both in imports and exports. (In 1988 its share in West Asia was 5 percent in export and 3.5 percent in import.)

Japan's exports to the Middle East more than doubled (5 to 11 percent) in the years following the 1973 oil crisis, and by the eve of the second oil crisis, 1979, amounted to a tenfold increase of $10.7 million.[2] The figure jumped to $19.9 billion in 1983, making Japan the largest exporter of goods and services to the Middle East, sending 12.3 percent of all goods and services imported by the Middle East.[3] By 1987, however, the figure had dropped to $10.7 billion (8.5 percent),[4] as the United States once again became the largest exporter to the Middle East. Figures for 1988 show further decline in Japan's value of the yen over the dollar.

Table 10.2 The Share of West Asia in Japan's Trade (in percent)

	1966	1972	1975	1980	1985	1988
Export	3.6	3.7	10.0	10.0	6.5	3.2
Import	12.2	14.6	28.0	31.3	22.7	10.4

Source: MITI white paper, 1988.
Note: West Asia includes Asian countries from Iran in the east and Turkey in the west. In 1988 the share of oil-producing countries was 83 percent in export, 94.1 percent in import.

Total imports by the Gulf nations fell from a peak of $93.5 billion in 1983 to $59.8 billion in 1987. The percentage of imports from Japan (textiles, steel, machinery, cars, electric appliances, and electronic goods) by the eight Gulf states in the peak year of 1983 was 17.8 percent of total imports but plummeted to 13.3 percent by 1987.[5] In terms of dollars, the drop was even sharper, from $16 billion to $8 billion during the same period—about half of what it was in dollars and subsequently less when the figure is translated into yen. Japan's exports to the Gulf declined from 3,635 billion yen in the peak year of 1982 to a mere 1,044 billion yen in 1987. (The yen appreciated significantly starting in the fall of 1985.)

Unfortunately, Japanese trade with West Asia shows a decreasing tendency in recent years. From 1982 to 1988 Japanese exports fell every year. Some scholars argue that these drops should be attributed to the evaluation of the yen and, as a result, to the decline of competitiveness of Japanese goods, especially in labor-intensive fields such as construction.

But the above thesis, reasonable as it seems, does not represent the whole reality. Recently Japanese exports on a global basis have increased sharply in spite of the evaluation of the yen, in part because of the restructure of industry. The annual increase of exports in 1988 was 15.6 percent, and in 1987, 9.6 percent. Consequently, the Japanese share in total exports by twenty industrialized countries was up from about 10 to 11 percent in the late 1970s to 13.5 percent in 1988. The decline of Japanese exports to the Gulf countries occurred at the time when Japan enjoyed an increase of exports on a global level.

The export structures of Japanese commodities to the United States and to the Gulf are rather similar. For example, in 1988 exported transport machinery to the United States was 33.6 percent and to West Asia 26.6 percent; electric machinery to the United States, 21.3 percent, to West Asia, 20.1 percent; general machinery to the United States, 22.3 percent, to West Asia, 17.1 percent. Therefore, the decline of Japanese exports to the Gulf is to be explained not so much by the loss of Japanese competitiveness but rather by special reasons attached to the region.

In recent years the Gulf has seen some negative economic development. With the relative decline in oil prices, many Gulf countries have suffered a decrease of revenue. National economic plans have been reexamined, and many projects for industry and social welfare have been canceled or postponed. As a result, imports from foreign countries have decreased. During the Iran-Iraq war, considerable resources in Iran and Iraq were spent on war efforts, thus stultifying economic growth. (Although there exist several different assessments about war efforts, Iraq spent more than $5 billion a year.) Some Gulf countries also shared financial burdens during the Iran-Iraq war. Finally, due to accumulated debt, Western companies have become hesitant to export to Iraq, for example, even though demand is high.

In relation to other countries in the volume of Japanese exports in 1980, Saudi Arabia ranked number six (behind the United States, West Germany, the Republic of Korea, Taiwan, and China) and Iraq was number fourteen (just behind Canada). But in 1988 Saudi Arabia ranked number fifteen; United Arab Emirates, twenty-nine; Iran, thirty-four; and Iraq, forty-nine.

Some countries such as Iraq have serious debt problems; it is thus not yet advantageous to expand imports to these countries. Nevertheless, there is a possibility that Japanese-Gulf economic relations could return to the same level as in 1980. With the end or cease-fire of the Iran-Iraq war, resulting in shifting resources from military use to welfare and industry, and with the possible increase of revenue from a relative increase in oil prices, Japan's economic relations with the Gulf are likely to improve well into the 1990s and beyond.

*Under such circumstances, what and how much can we expect Japan to export in the future to the Gulf region? Even if the price of oil gradually rises in the 1990s, Japanese products are most likely to be able to compete against Korean and Taiwanese products in highly specialized products and high-end goods. Also being considered in Japan today is the export of secondhand, reconditioned cars to less-well-to-do nations.

The Japanese are not likely to change their policy of refusing to export items that have potential military application. Many items such as computer chips and trucks can be used for military as well as civilian purposes. The Japanese are becoming more wary of shipping anything that can become a target of criticism from abroad, especially since Toshiba Machines' sale of a sensitive item to the Soviet Union. What will make the Japanese reassess this long-standing policy is a difficult question to answer.

Radical changes, not only in Japan but also in the rest of the world, would be needed before Japan became a competitor in the arms trade. The Japanese would have to undergo drastic psychological transformation before the public would even allow the sale of military weapons abroad; the constitution would have to be amended. The weapons industry can be lucrative, but at the same time it is highly volatile and unstable. Japan has done quite well since the end of World War II without the sale of arms and weapons abroad. Why should it start now? There would be such a flood of criticism abroad that Japan would not be able to sell other products.

An alternative to military assistance to nations around the world is economic assistance. Japan has in recent years increased aid to Turkey, Egypt, Jordan, and Oman, probably in response to US wishes. In 1989 Japan became the largest donor of economic aid to less-developed parts of the world. Japan has increased its financial responsibility of defending itself as well as such regions as the Gulf through stepped-up foreign aid and subsidization of the cost of stationing US troops in Japan. Japan also gave $41 million to UN peacekeepers in April 1989. Much of this money was used in Lebanon, the Golan Heights, Iran, and Iraq.

These are ways in which Japan feels comfortable assisting nations. This type of cooperation with the United States and the United Nations will continue in the years ahead.

In 1987 the government of Japan decided to deregulate the oil industry over a period of five years from 1988 through 1992. Unlike Japanese banks in relation to other banks around the world, Japanese oil companies are no match for Western oil companies. Because of this relatively weak Japanese oil management structure, the process of deregulation must proceed with deliberate speed and care for the rationalization of Japan's oil industry to take place with minimum disruption and maximum benefit to all parties.

Between 1987 and 1988 there was a startling jump in the consumption of oil in Japan. Consumption rose only 0.3 percent from 1983 to 1984;[6] then it fell by 4.9 percent from 1984 to 1985 and in 1986 continued to fall by 0.5 percent.[7] It started to rise again in 1987 and 1988 by 5.6 percent and 6.5 percent, respectively.[8] Although the import of crude oil fell successively from 1984 to 1986, the import of petroleum products continued to increase every fiscal year from 1984 to 1988, during which it doubled. With the deregulation of the oil industry, it is likely that more products will be imported, including those from the Gulf region.

Japan's product imports are still regulated and controlled.[9] Japan's refineries are operating at 65 to 70 percent capacity at the moment. In spite of the rise in oil consumption, only about half of the service stations are showing profit, because of excessive competition.[10] The number of refineries and service stations obviously needs to be reduced as Japan deregulates and rationalizes its oil industry. Nevertheless, the import of liquefied natural gas has continued to rise, as has that of petroleum products.

Rationalization involves reducing the number of refineries in operation. In some cases, former refineries have been turned into oil shortage facilities to increase Japan's oil reserves, and refinery workers have been asked to stay at work. The growing demand for oil, however, has made planners cautious in the reduction of refinery capacities.

The Japanese seem to have made a remarkable adjustment to the increased value of the yen since autumn 1985; the nation's economy continues to expand. The rate of growth for the domestic supply of total energy between 1984 and 1988 confirms this trend: The figures were 4.8 percent, 0.3 percent, -0.6 percent, 4.7 percent, and 5.5 percent.[11] Government efforts to stimulate domestic consumer demand for public works (16.6 percent in 1988) appear to be stimulating the Japanese economy.*

Japan's Aspirations for Greater Political Involvement

*Will Japan go beyond simply being an economic superpower and start flexing political muscle proportionate to its economic status? Can Japan continue to play a major economic role in the region while claiming that this somehow can be divorced from politics and political-military matters? Will Japan in the coming years allow its defense forces to be deployed abroad? Will Japan ever be able to sell arms to the Gulf?

Japanese government officials have indeed indicated a willingness to shoulder a responsibility to be more active internationally and have followed up with increased foreign aid, now ranked as the largest in the world. Japan sent Foreign Minister Tadashi Kuranari to Tehran and Baghdad in June 1987 to assist in finding an end to the Iran-Iraq war. Economic aid to Egypt and Turkey has increased in the past decade, and Japan gave a $200 million loan to Oman and $300 million loan to Jordan in 1987. In addition, as already noted, Japan has contributed to UN activities in the Middle East in recent years. It has also increased its share of the financial burden of keeping US troops in Japan. There have also been more contacts with Israel, both at the government and business level. These actions seem to coincide with US interests in the region.

Japan refused to go along with the United States, however, in its attempt to sever trade relations with Iran. A justification for its refusal lies in its reasoning that Iran should not be placed under a circumstance in which its leaders have no choice but to look to the Soviets for possible assistance. Such a sanction only contradicts the shared objective of keeping the Soviets out of the Gulf region. In reality, however, perhaps an underlying reason for this incident may lie in Japan's characteristic eagerness to maintain ties with all sides in conflict, such as in China, for example. Japanese businesses argue that it is in Japan's economic interest to do so.

In a way, Japan's refusal to become militarily involved is its strength in dealing with parties in conflict in the Gulf. For example, both Iran and Iraq knew that Japan did not ship arms to either side. This position gives Japan credibility in peace attempts in the region. Japan also refused to send minesweepers in October 1987 when asked to do so by the United States. After heated discussion, the government decided to provide financial and material assistance in minesweeping operations, increased contributions to the United Nations, and economic assistance to the Gulf.

Japan's Policy of Equidistance Toward Iraq and Iran

Japan's policy toward Iraq and Iran during and after their war represents a typical Japanese attempt to be friendly to everyone. Japan has so far successfully maintained a policy of equidistance without alienating either side, much to US chagrin. Individual companies, however, may act on their own in what they perceive to be their own interests. At times corporations may barter, for example, in order to sell as much as possible to Iran—an opportunity that in the short run certainly seems more attractive than dealing with Iraq.

Several obstacles prevent Japan from expanding its relationship with both countries. Iranians still would like to see Mitsui and its associates, including the government of Japan, complete the petrochemical complex it started but never finished. The Japanese side has politely declined, citing several factors that make the project unprofitable even if it were to be completed.

Unless these problems are resolved, neither nation is likely to rapidly intensify its business relations. True, there has been some increase in barter trade between the two in recent years. Iraq, too, has its own lingering problem of nonpayments for goods and services rendered by Japan. There is no insurance available for trading with Iraq.[12]

Although Japan attempted to be evenhanded in its relationships with Iraq and Iran, trade figures indicate that Japan consistently bought more oil from Iran than from Iraq in the 1980s. Likewise, Japan consistently sold more goods to Iran than to Iraq. In 1987 Japan's exports to Iran were thrice those to Iraq. Many factors, including demography and geography, make Iran a larger business partner than Iraq. Still, Japan tries hard to be neutral and to treat both countries as evenly as possible. This policy is likely to continue.

One basic characteristic that separates Japan from the rest of the major world powers is that it has no strong attachment to any absolute political or religious ideology, save its aversion to war. The West and the Gulf nations have the conflicting ideologies of Judaism, Christianity, Islam, communism, and democracy. Even democracy cannot get the Japanese excited. Polls conducted in the 1960s and 1970s showed that of ideologies such as capitalism, socialism, and democracy, none is considered "good" by a majority of the Japanese. Democracy is, however, most popular, accepted by about 40 percent of the people.[13]

Japan thus has no ideology or religion to propagate abroad. Japan's key interest lies in its economic well-being. Since it has no natural resources to speak of, particularly petroleum, it needs to secure its supply from abroad at the lowest cost. It can do so best when there is peace and it maintains friendly relations with everyone.

Obviously, trade with Iran is more important to Japan at present than trade with Iraq. However, where the future is concerned, there are two reasons why Iraq is equally important or even of greater importance to Japan than Iran. First, Iraq's oil is likely to last longer than Iran's. Second, Iraq is an Arab country, whereas Iran is not. Japan is in no position to alienate Arab countries, particularly those located in the Gulf region from which it buys more than half of its oil.

Thus, Japan has most to gain by maintaining its policy of equidistance toward Iran and Iraq at the present as well as in the future. The Japanese rightfully consider this part of the world the only area where Japan does not have to worry about the ramifications of developing trade surpluses, since it imports so much oil from there. Hence, Japan is anxious to increase its exports to these two nations in particular, which are likely to be in need of reconstruction of war-torn industries, buildings, and various facilities. Japan sincerely hopes that the war will not break out again; because it does not sell arms, it has nothing to gain from conflict in the Gulf.

It was reported that in March 1989 several Japanese corporations succeeded in receiving orders for oil tanker facilities from Iran. There seems to be little doubt that Japanese corporations are interested in doing business there, but they are more cautious in dealing with these two nations because of the problems cited earlier in this chapter. The question that remains is risk of war. Of course, this is the reason for Japan's emphasis upon maintaining peace and stability in this region. Other industrial powers would benefit if these two nations were to go to war, but not Japan. Perhaps this is Japan's weakness as well as its unique strength: Unlike the Soviet or the Western powers, Japan has not occupied these or neighboring countries in the past. The two nations can trust Japan in that it has no interest in furthering their conflicts.

How is Japan likely to behave in the 1990s vis-à-vis Iran and Iraq? Japan will find equidistance most useful to its policy objectives. The United States, which is more apt to take sides, will likely be irritated from time to time by Japan's seemingly inconsistent policies in dealing with both nations.

Japanese Diplomacy Toward the Gulf

Whether Japan will go against US pressure to protect its own interests in the Gulf is a matter of debate. It would be possible under the right conditions—if a crisis were to develop. Consider the following scenario: A political upheaval occurs in the Middle East that the Gulf countries cannot ignore. The Gulf states take unanimous action against the West to protect their cause. The United States disregards this action. The Gulf countries decide to restrict oil export. At the time, Japan depends heavily on petroleum and considers the import of oil from the Gulf vital to its survival. If any one of these conditions should be absent in a crisis, it is unlikely that the United States and Japan will seriously disagree over policies toward the Gulf. And if all conditions are met? Just how close is the scenario to reality?

First, there is no question that political tensions in the Middle East are likely to prevail through the 1990s. The future of Iran-Iraq relations, for instance, is uncertain because of the status of the cease-fire. The cease-fire was not created by the agreement of two countries; rather, it was achieved by international pressure. Without this continuing pressure, the situation could take a turn for the worst, especially if Iran were to recover its military strength (through the import of arms) to contend with Iraq.

Other elements could disturb Middle East stability, such as the Islamic fundamentalist movement, which is influential in Jordan and Lebanon, and ethnic group movements. How these movements might serve to undermine Western and Japanese influence in the Middle East remains to be seen.

Second, we cannot assume that the Gulf countries will take unanimous action against Western countries, with which they may have close bilateral relations in the fields of oil export, financial affairs, and construction of industries, even though the issue of the Occupied Territories remains a bone of contention. Arab countries cannot oppose the cause to liberate the Occupied Territories and to create an independent Palestinian country. But there is a difference in how strongly they support this cause. Past experience shows that the PLO cannot gain as much support from the Gulf countries as it would like.

Third, the United States is not likely to disregard any concerted action that the Gulf countries might take to protect their cause. Too much is at stake. Although US-Israeli special relations play a great role, other factors such as increased US energy dependence on Gulf countries, US-Saudi relations, and US involvement in economic construction in the Gulf should not be overlooked.*

Fourth, it is not likely that such action taken by Gulf countries would also include large-scale and long-term quantitative restriction of oil export. There are different interests among the Gulf countries. Iraq, for one, would be hesitant to impose large-scale and long-term restriction of oil export because of its need for resources for building industry and enhancing the standard of living.

Furthermore, it is not easy for any country, including the Gulf countries, to reduce revenues dramatically for a long period. Any reduction would create dissatisfaction among powerful interest groups and invite domestic instability. Indeed, a further question is whether, as Western and Japanese dependence on the Gulf for oil increases, the Gulf countries' increase in revenues from oil will be sufficient to maintain social stability, not only in the region but in Egypt and Jordan as well. These countries depend on the revenue to ease their economic woes. In any case, this driving force—the increased dependence of the West and Japan on Gulf oil—is a necessary condition to the development of a politically and socially stable Gulf.

Fifth, since Japan has sharply decreased dependence on petroleum, it is less vulnerable in the case of a reduction in oil export. And as Table 10.3 shows, this trend will continue into the 1990s.

Table 10.3 Japanese Energy Consumption (in percent)

Energy sources	1973[a]	1987[a]	2000[b]	2005[b]
Coal	15.5	18.0	18.7	19.0
Nuclear	0.6	10.0	15.9	18.0
Natural gas	1.5	9.7	10.8	10.0
Hydro power	4.6	4.1	4.4	4.0
Petroleum	77.6	56.9	45.0	42.0

Source: Advisory Committee for Energy to Minister of Trade and Industry, 1987.
Notes: [a] Actual figures
[b] Forecast figures

If Japan manages to maintain a level of petroleum dependency below 60 percent, the crisis could be averted. The argument for this conclusion is as follows. First, the minimum level of energy supply necessary to keep the economy running enough to prevent an energy crisis is 80 percent. Second, Japan's petroleum dependency is 60 percent. Third, suppose the Middle East supplies about 80 percent of Japanese oil imports. In 1987 the level was 67 percent, with the Middle East's share of proved oil reserves at about 64 percent. So the 80 percent share provided by the Gulf could be a higher figure than is the actual case. By the above calculations, about 40 percent reduction in oil export by the Gulf area would be necessary to force a 20 percent reduction in Japan's energy supply. It is unlikely that the Gulf countries would precipitate such a large-scale reduction. Although Japanese vulnerability is frequently discussed, a Japanese energy crisis triggered by any political incident of this magnitude is rather remote, contrary to the general perception.

Japanese Political Activities in the Gulf

Japanese military involvement in the Gulf region, as noted before, is not likely to occur. Opposition at home and from the West would deter it. And there is only a slight possibility that Japanese military personnel would participate in international peacekeeping efforts. Japan instead will probably increase its political activities in the Middle East.

On the basis of popular support of independent diplomacy, the Japanese government will be keen to play an active political role. Initiatives undertaken during the 1980s exemplify this role. In 1987, when efforts to attain a cease-fire were crucial, the Japanese government provided the United Nations with special funds for a bilateral dialogue between Iran and Iraq. In the late 1980s, Japan also intensified its relations with both the PLO and Israel to prepare for the future contribution to the Middle East peace negotiations. With Japan's ever-increasing political role in Middle East affairs, the question arises how the Gulf countries and the West will react. As far as the Gulf countries are concerned, several factors must be weighed in formulating a position toward Japan. First, generally there exists a nonhostile Arab feeling toward Japan. Second, Japan had made considerable economic contributions, such as in finance and industrial construction. Third, Japan has played a limited political role in established international organizations, symbolized by its nonmember status in the UN Security Council. And fourth, a country with negative leverage in the export of arms to "the other side" cannot be overlooked.

These factors mean that, generally, the Gulf countries will not be hostile toward Japanese political efforts. But because of Japan's negative leverage and limited political role in established international organizations, the Middle East countries will probably not consider seriously any political efforts made by Japan in this region.

In the absence of any dominant country that can influence international affairs by itself, like the United States in the 1940s, 1950s, and 1960s, future actions will have to be carried out collectively to be effective. Usually, the most feasible international collective efforts are those by the Security Council. Probably, toward the year 2000, an effective political framework will be a combination of the permanent members of the Security Council and some regional countries. In spite of Japan's increased economic and financial potential, the climate to welcome Japan as a permanent security member has not arrived. If this situation continues, Japanese political activities will remain ineffective. Only when such financial issues as reconstruction of a region become a main agenda for international action will countries like Japan be asked to participate in joint political activities.

Balancing Interests

For the past two decades, Japanese policy toward the Gulf has attempted to coordinate efforts to secure petroleum imports and to gain access to Gulf markets, while emphasizing peace and respecting the wishes of the people of the region. At the same time, Japan has sought to maintain good relations with the United States yet pursue an active independent diplomacy in accordance with the wishes of a majority of the Japanese people. Though there now exist differences between US and Japanese policies toward the Middle East, the conclusion that Japan will automatically go against US pressure to protect its own interests (namely, oil) does not necessarily follow.

Differences in policy in the Middle East between Japan and the United States are ever-present. Quantitative differences in the amount of Official Development Assistance (ODA) to the Middle East in 1987, for example, to a degree reflect the overall policies toward this region.

The United States provided a much higher level of assistance in the Middle East, particularly in Israel, Egypt, and Jordan in 1987. In other years, Saudi Arabia was among the leading recipients of US development aid. Japan's ODA is more widespread and noticeably to countries that received no US support, such as Iraq and Syria. The inequalities in ODA are not the result of some carefully arranged division of labor between the United States and Japan. They are due to differences in policy.

If a political upheaval in the Middle East should occur and the Gulf countries take action against the West by restricting oil export, it would take at least a 40 percent reduction in oil export over the long term for Japan to break with US policy toward the region. But it is unlikely that the Gulf countries, dependent on oil revenue, would follow such a course of large-scale, long-term reduction in oil export. Japanese diplomacy therefore will continue to seek a certain balance between securing its own interests and respecting the interests of others.

Certainly, this diplomacy will not exclude already existing disparities in approach between US and Japanese Middle East policies. Broadly speaking, Japan seeks a more active independent diplomacy in the Middle East. But these differences will remain fairly narrow and well within the range of acceptable international diplomacy, so as not to undermine basic US-Japanese relations.

Notes

Two sections of this chapter begin and end with asterisks. These sections were written by Professor Kuroda, and they express views Mr. Magosaki does not share.

1. Japanese scholars, politicians, and businesspersons do not impact upon Japanese foreign policy in the way that is true for their US counterparts. Much confusion arises in US thinking about the conduct of Japanese foreign policy on these grounds, especially toward an area like the Gulf. Japanese foreign policy is, for the most part, the province of the prime minister, foreign minister, and practicing diplomats.
2. Keizai Koho Center, 1981, p. 28.
3. *Chutokeizai*, December 20, 1988, pp. 34–35.
4. Ibid., pp. 42–43.
5. Ibid., pp. 34–43.
6. Japan's fiscal year begins in April and ends in March.
7. *EDMC Energy Trend* (May 1989), pp. 14–15.

8. This figure for 1988 ending in March 1989 is an estimate as given in the May 1989 issue of *EDMC Energy Trend* (p. 9). The recent rise in the consumption of petroleum is attributable to the growing Japanese economy and the increased demand for goods and services, accompanied by the increased value of the yen, which lowered the price of oil in Japan.

9. A five-year plan initiated in 1988 to deregulate the entire oil industry in Japan will allow other nations to engage in downstream investment. There are opportunities in this process of deregulation for non-Japanese firms to get involved. However, breaking into the existing market in Japan is a difficult task for any new company and especially for foreign firms.

10. Japan has about 59,000 service stations that on average sell only about one-quarter of what service stations in the United States sell per month. The United States has approximately 120,000 service stations. Seikiyu Renmei (Petroleum Association of Japan), 1988, p. 42.

11. *EDMC Energy Trend* (May 1989), p. 8.

12. The Ministry of International Trade and Industry makes insurance available to any firm interested in foreign trade. Trading with Iran is more attractive to Japan because Iran, unlike Iraq, does not owe money to Japan. Thus, figures in Japan's trade with Iran and Iraq reflect financial considerations of Japanese corporations and are not derived from any political consideration.

13. Tokeisurikenkyujo kokuminseichosa iinkai, 1981, p. 341.

11
Gulf Security in Perspective
Charles F. Doran

In looking forward to the year 2000, this study does not pretend to predict the future, an impossibility explicitly eschewed by several authors in this volume. In a region as full of surprise as the Middle East, noted in particular by Limbert and Twinam, such an admonition is especially prudent. Forecasting likely trends, highlighting outstanding problems, and recommending policy in response to those trends and problems, however, are quite another matter. Taken up in this final chapter, the effort to analyze energy security policy for the decade of the 1990s has led to some rather clear conclusions about *possible* vulnerability of Western and regional energy security.[1]

The probability that this vulnerability will ever come about may be regarded as rather low. But if the costs of susceptibility are great, notwithstanding IEA sharing arrangements or stocks held in the strategic petroleum reserve, it is far from a negligible policy concern, especially if forecasts now are helpful in substantially reducing the future risk.

The thread of the argument that runs through this final chapter is as follows. It starts with a set of premises about economics and energy, namely, that eventually (we think in the latter half of the 1990s), barring unforeseen, massively important technological developments on the supply or demand side and set against continuing economic growth, the world oil market will tighten, driving up the price of oil. A particular concern is the joint occurrence of episodic price volatility (which adds to uncertainty, thus discouraging new industry and producer investment) together with substantially greater dependency of the West on petroleum from a single region, the Persian Gulf. Under these circumstances of severe energy dependence, the Gulf would become a focal point of renewed pressure internally and externally.

Cutting across this situation of heightened pressure on the Gulf are four moderating trends. First, domestic political stability of individual governments within the region, notwithstanding an occasional surprise, is likely to be more broadly evident, not less so. Second, despite rivalry and military buildup, no new predominant state capable of exerting its will over its neighbors is likely to emerge in the region. Third, the US-Soviet global and regional confrontation will have markedly decreased. Fourth, the US presence in the region, in spite of some slippage, will continue to count for a good deal, politically, commercially, and militarily.

But despite all of these positive developments, one anxiety prevails: recurrence of major war in the region. While at present [prior to the Iraqi invasion of Kuwait] the greatest threat is generally held to be from a resurgence of the still unresolved Iraq-Iran war, other scenarios and other belligerents are conceivable. The central problem is that the next war may not be as contained as the last war; indeed, there are good reasons to expect that the region's oil facilities next time may become hostage. Easily targeted, oil facilities could be destroyed or become the locus of an aggravated confrontation. And although the oil fields are dispersed and rather sizable, a scorched-earth strategy by a belligerent could knock them out for a long interval. If such an event occurred near the end of the decade, in the context of a tight market situation and greater Western oil dependence, the consequence would devastate Western economies.

Four implications for US policy follow. First, an attempt to safeguard US energy interests with an excessive preoccupation about the domestic political stability of Gulf producers is not warranted and is probably counterproductive. Second, diplomatic progress on the Palestinian issue would create a helpful spillover for US policy in the Gulf. Third [despite the collective military action following the Iraqi takeover], the United States must be prepared to augment its permanent forces in the Gulf with an air and naval presence adequate to confront regional military threats; indeed, a continuing presence is helpful in deterring serious confrontation among regional powers. Fourth, the United States ought to initiate a two-track arms control policy in the region at a time when arms proliferation of all sorts will make any future war in the region far more costly to the Gulf producers and ultimately to the West itself.

Economic and Energy Premises

All of the analysis regarding the politics of oil access contained in this study rests upon certain assumptions concerning the economics of such access. "Access" is itself divided into considerations of reasonable price and absence of supply cutoff. A further, somewhat less directly related issue is the extent to which the percentage of US imports of oil (and indeed all of Western supply) increasingly comes from the Gulf. For purposes of a common anchor, all authors were encouraged to consider seriously the trends depicted in the recent Department of Energy international forecast.

Taking up the last matter first, the conclusions here are pretty clear. By the year 2000, the United States and the West as a whole will import a far higher proportion of oil than at present, and most of this increase will come from the Gulf region. The reasons for this trend are quite simple. Barring a major new discovery in the South China Sea or elsewhere, non-OPEC supply, certainly at anything like current prices, is likely to do no better than remain at present levels to the end of the 1990s. US supply in particular is likely to go into a tailspin. Known, relatively low-cost reserves exist in the Gulf. Since the Gulf countries also have relatively low capital needs, they can afford to take a long view and raise prices gradually, provided that they expand their surplus production capacity to meet demand. Thus US and Western oil dependence on the Gulf is likely to grow rapidly.

Supply considerations are not so easily forecast. Supply determines price to some extent, but price or expected future price also determines supply. Will price increase rapidly enough, in sustained fashion, to bolster declining relative amounts of non-OPEC oil? In the 1980s, technological refinements enabled non-OPEC production in the North Sea, for example, to hold up remarkably well. But Mexican drilling decisions turn sharply on price considerations. Non-OPEC oil is for the most part higher marginal-cost oil, so price is likely to affect this supply more than it does Gulf oil. Will the expectation of future price increases, as well as internal investment decisions, encourage the Gulf producers to expand their production and distribution facilities in an appropriate fashion? The oil is in the ground. But will it be brought to market? OPEC has a long way to go before it bumps against previous upper supply limits (for Saudi Arabia, 9.5–10 million barrels per day) and OPEC seems ready to invest in increased production capacity. Until surplus supply capacity is exceeded, price should remain in the "reasonable" range, although given the price preferences of most producers, the overall forecast is for an upward price drift.

Demand forecasts are the most difficult and traditionally the least satisfactory. The situation in the 1990s will be no easier to predict. High prices in the late 1970s encouraged substantial conservation that affected industrial usage, heating oil requirements, and gasoline consumption. Uncertainty of supply also induced some permanent energy switching. But in a period of declining real prices for energy, consumption is again on the rise, most notably since 1988. Third World countries are supposed to account for the largest part of these increases, because of rapid economic growth and poor energy conservation. Yet these countries consume the smallest fraction of the total world oil supply. Estimating long-term "demand elasticities" is more an art than a science. This is where the greatest errors in forecasting could arise. Nonetheless, the assumption of this study regarding future energy demand is that it will gradually build back to where it was at its peak in the 1970s.

A premise of this study, in short, is that much higher Gulf energy dependence is likely to confront decisionmakers by the year 2000. Tighter supplies and higher prices will return. The only question is when. If gradual, such price increases are not injurious and are indeed necessary to bring on new non-OPEC as well as OPEC production. Although producer supply interruptions for political reasons do not seem likely, price spikes in a tightening market because of suddenly imposed price controls, hoarding, or other market imperfections are always a possibility. Sharply increased dependence on Gulf oil and the return of high prices are not so problematic in themselves. It is rather the combination of these factors and a sudden dramatic loss of access to Gulf oil that is most worrisome. Therefore, the analysis now turns to the problem of sustained oil access.

Trends

Persistent Domestic Stability

For much of the post-1945 period, a principal concern in the Gulf has been the domestic political stability of regimes, and with some reason (see Twinam). Despite the British presence, the interval through 1958 was torn by coup d'état and violent regime change, mostly elsewhere in the Middle East, as radical socialism and other forms of ideological difference shook much of the Arab and Muslim world. Since the 1970s, Shiite fundamentalism and other types of incipient unrest periodically came to the surface. Revolution in Iran was the key event that preoccupied US decisionmakers, not just because of the hostage crisis, nor because of the break in relations, but because the whole US strategy for dealing with Gulf security seemed in jeopardy. It is therefore necessary for analysts looking toward the end of the century to anticipate further major domestic political disturbances that may unseat regimes and disrupt long-standing political ties. Pressures from many quarters will arise to try to bolster regimes in apparent political trouble or to plan a strategy for access to Gulf oil around the capacity to sustain friendly governments in office. In an age of democratic government and socialist reform, monarchies in particular may seem anachronistic and vulnerable to internal overthrow. In the aftermath of the Iranian revolution, other countries in the area with large Shiite minorities as well as well-placed Palestinian and other communal groups, upon which societies have become very dependent, appear ripe for overthrow. In a word, the region to some analysts may look like a cauldron ready to boil over.

But from the perspective of this study, a very different set of implications emerges for strategy formulation. What impresses us, given the domestic violence and even revolutionary activity, is not that such challenges to authority take place but that they have declined in intensity and scope. There are many reasons for this relative deterioration, not the least of which is the maturing of governments. Increased capacity not only to claim the allegiance of many tribal groups and communities but to govern in such a fashion that forceful political overthrow becomes extremely difficult is also evident.

Throughout the Gulf region, governments have learned to use the vast oil wealth to co-opt domestic opponents and to placate potentially frustrated members of the nontraditional elites. Ruling families, despite personal and political difference among the members, have acquiesced in the need for a common front in dealing with outsiders. Instruments of control have become more sophisticated even as they have been applied with calculated efficiency by determined governments. The walkie-talkie and wiretap have replaced their more visible counterparts, the nightstick and the revolver. Coercion is neither more omnipresent nor more brutal in the Middle East than in other Third World regions, but it is effective.

Of course, a whole new generation of leaders and potential leaders, many of whom have been educated abroad, is coming to the threshold of power. These groups often have ambitious plans for modernization; they are less committed to traditional patterns of governance and have learned to criticize patterns of behavior that they may characterize as wasteful or corrupt. Too few positions in government, the army, the clergy, the professions, and the private sector are available to absorb the eligible and the talented. Thus the next years will face renewed effort by each Gulf government to find places for everyone and to placate, or intimidate, those who may remain dissatisfied.

Rapid modernization such as that occurring in the Middle East is always something of a destabilizing process. Aspirations are raised to a point where they cannot all be met. Frustration sets in and sometimes takes a violent route of expression. Blame is placed on existing governments when alternatives might be even less promising. Iran under the shah and then under Khomeini are clear examples of this pattern, illustrated by the Limbert chapter in terms of the attitudes of the Iranian middle class. We are not suggesting that elites in the region have learned to become more tolerant of their governments or recognize the disappointments that may follow on the heels of radical change. No large-scale pattern of learning about the fallacies of economic development via the sword is in the minds of the new generation coming to power today. Rather, what impresses us is the variety of instruments Gulf governments have at their disposal to pacify the dissatisfied and to identify, rout out, and isolate those elements that may oppose the political leadership.

Despite the sorry history of the Lebanese civil war, the capacity of an Asad to remain in power in Syria on a very narrow communal foundation, or the failure of the unfortunate Kurdish minority to put much of a dent in the mechanisms of control in Turkey, Iran, or Iraq, suggests the preponderance of strength on the part of central governments. From Oman, through the Emirates, to Kuwait and Saudi Arabia, regimes that a dozen years ago might have been regarded as vulnerable to tribal strife and communal disaffection seem remarkably stable by most overt measures of that concept.

We are not saying that events of domestic instability, whether on the *hajj* or against oil installations not adequately guarded, will suddenly disappear. Some forced changes of regime may also occur. But it is remarkable how thoroughly governments in the UAE, for example, have after a weak beginning become institutionalized. As Marr convincingly argues, Saddam Hussein is likely to remain in office for a long time because he is in good health both personally and politically. [Indeed, it is this absolute control domestically that facilitated his capacity for external aggression.] The democratic winds from Eastern Europe could blow toward the Gulf as well. But the cultural terrain is surely different in the Middle East than in Eastern Europe, and the transformation of authoritarianism inside some communist states is not the same as the elimination of authoritarian rule everywhere. Governments that have survived the lean years of financial cutbacks are likely to be even more politically resilient when the next wave of petrodollars arrives in a rising market.

In short, from the perspective of domestic politics and relative to Southeast

Asia or Central America, for example, governments in the Gulf region look conspicuously stable. The power transition from Khomeini to more collective Iranian leadership surprised some outside observers, yet that transition seemed only to be an element of the more general patten of comparative domestic political tranquility that has marked the region for at least a decade. Notwithstanding an attempted coup d'état or the overthrow of an army outpost on some isolated frontier, central governments within the Gulf, as a genre, have never looked more confident.

A Continuation of the Prevailing Balance of Power

At the beginning of the 1990s, the regional balance of power and interest is fluid and somewhat diffuse. In narrow terms of military hardware, especially aircraft, Iraq is the most powerful Arab country, second only to Israel perhaps among all countries within the entire region. Even though Iraq looked very strong in the last months of the war, in the aftermath of its use of chemicals and in the wake of the collapse of the Iranian war effort, Iran is scarcely a country to be forgotten militarily. With its large territory and population, its capacity for economic output, and its significant oil production, Iran is consequential. It does not have a large foreign debt, and it does have the educated manpower base, despite emigration and bad management at the top, to develop economically.

In terms of oil policy, Saudi Arabia remains paramount by a large margin. It will, if it chooses, set the tone of the oil market. Although Saudi Arabia gave up being the swing producer in 1985 and doesn't now intend to go back, circumstances would change abruptly if it built back its financial reserves. No other country, including Iraq with its prospectively large oil reserves, will challenge Saudi Arabia for this role. In addition to their roles as large oil exporters, Saudi Arabia, Kuwait, and the UAE also serve as bankers for the Arab world and much of the larger region. One should not underestimate the influence finance has on the politics of Jordan, Syria, the factions in Lebanon, and even Iraq (despite the reality that Iraq is not expected to repay its war loans to its Arab allies).

In the larger regional setting, Egypt, temporarily distanced from the Arab world by the Camp David Accords, has been re-accepted within the Arab League and throughout the region. The Arab Cooperation Council of Egypt, Jordan, North Yemen, and Iraq is not so much the measure of this new Egyptian acceptability as are the many deals and forms of interaction between Egypt and its regional neighbors. Egypt, because of geostrategic position, size, military capability, and capacity for leadership, continues to rival Iraq for diplomatic leadership over other states in the area, notably in matters involving Syria. Yet the Egyptian-Jordanian relationship with Iraq may also have helped keep Iraq on a moderate path [and may still do so, although it did not deter Iraq from invading Kuwait.]

In the new age of long-range missile capability and of air power, Israel, backed by homegrown nuclear weapons, is scarcely less militarily dominant in the region than at any time since its founding. Despite its bitter psychological withdrawal following its unsuccessful incursion into Lebanon, and despite its internal political convulsions over how to deal with the *intifada*, Israel is, in military terms, in a very strong position. Its involvement in various ways in the Iran-Iraq war demonstrates its capacity to affect the regional balance of power even without becoming an active participant in hostilities. Although its principal impact upon the balance of power diplomatically was through its bilateral peace arrangements with Egypt, Israel has other means to influence the balance in the region that can bode ill or well for Gulf energy security. Thus, in overall terms, the balance of power in the region is at once more diffuse and more fluid than it has been for a long time.

How will the balance of power and interest shift by the end of the decade? However important, this is a virtually unfathomable question. A few indicators do suggest trends. Iraq intends to become the second most important oil exporter. It says that it will play by OPEC rules, and its lack of finance assures this for the present [but Iraq, of course, used alleged Kuwaiti overproduction as a pretext for invasion when, in reality, Iraq, not other OPEC exporters, is likely to be the severe overproducer in the future, as it has been in the past.] Iraq, with external help from China or elsewhere, could purchase the technology to make nuclear weapons over the next five to ten years. Given its growing missile capability, this would solidify Iraq's military preeminence among Arab states. But would Iran be far behind in such acquisition, and might Israel attempt some preemptive action?

Iran is its own worst enemy in terms of attitudes toward economic development. If its religious fanaticism wanes and the private sector is allowed to flourish, it could generate a vital economy by the end of the decade. In the absence of renewed external threats or involvements, Iranian military capability is likely to lag for some time. But it will rebuild. Its manpower base remains an advantage in confrontations where large land armies count. For a time, at least, Iran seems prepared to participate in terrorist activity as a substitute for more conventional forms of influence. If Iran wants to reestablish relations with the West, it will have to reduce its terrorist impulse. Whether improvement of relations with the West will come at the cost of Iraq's relations with the West remains to be seen. There is no necessarily inverse correlation here, just as there is no necessary inverse of relations between the Soviet Union and these two states. The Soviet Union will continue to try to maintain beneficial relations with both Iran and Iraq.

A best estimate is that by the year 2000 no single state in the region will have attained the dominance that the shah, for example, enjoyed with external help. Each government in the region will probably be stronger internally. We are likely to see a region in which power balancing becomes far more real and effective than in an interval when external states had a greater capacity to shape the regional equilibrium by direct financial and military means. This more mature balance of power has two further consequences. Israel once again is likely to participate in the balance more than in the past, directly and indirectly through its interaction with Egypt. The regional balance of power will be more impervious to external diplomatic suasion by the superpowers. Whether these conditions lead to a more stable region politically is very much dependent on how much the actors focus upon their own internal economic development rather than upon foreign policy adventures and upon how skillful they are at playing balance of power politics.

Constructive Soviet Engagement

The Gorbachev reforms have had an impact upon the way Soviet diplomacy is conducted in the Gulf as elsewhere. Soviet diplomacy is attempting to use flexibility and formal government interactions where ideological rigidity and support for opposition groups in the past often seemed to get top billing in the Kremlin. Most rapid change here will occur with the moderate governments who were once fearful of Soviet intentions and style of behavior. Paradoxically, however, former Soviet protégés such as Iraq and Syria are likely to find fewer advantages in doing business with the Soviets, in part because the Soviets are very hard-pressed at home and have less with which to do business either militarily or in trade terms.

But the key consideration is that the Soviet Union has not proved itself of great security value to the Gulf regimes. Its behavior in the Iraq-Iran war could not have earned it many credits. It has tilted a bit in the direction of Iran but has scarcely determined military or political outcomes. After the war it again pursued closer trade ties with Iran but without changing its outlook toward Iraq. Notwithstanding the fervor of past and present ideological commitment, Iran has far more to gain from its association with the West than with its huge near neighbor. The logic of this geostrategic and trade/commercial interaction will surely make itself felt by the end of the decade.

As both Twinam and Chubin note, the very success of the US naval presence during the Iraq-Iran war, combined with the Soviet effort to reduce costs by cutting back its foreign fleet visits as much as 30 percent in the last year, has meant that the Soviets have decided to shift their diplomacy into high gear. Some of this effort will pay dividends, often at a cost to the United States. Yet the staying power of the US presence cannot be much in doubt.

Insofar as US-Soviet détente at the global level moves forward, there is, moreover, no reason why the two countries cannot find common ground in the Gulf. Indeed, a kind of test of the rumblings of rapprochement could be the formulation of Gulf security on a firmer footing. But what does this mean concretely?

At base, what US-Soviet cooperation in the Gulf means is recognition that the production and export of energy from the Gulf is essentially an economic enterprise, but an enterprise of importance to overall strategic stability. As long as the superpowers have as a mutual objective strategic stability, the unimpeded flow of oil from the Gulf ought to be at the top of the list of foreign policy priorities. Insofar as both producer and consumer see the importance of an unimpeded flow of oil from the Gulf, regional interests and the global interests of the superpowers can be mutually reinforcing.

With the US military presence dominant in the Gulf, and there being neither a US interest in nor a national preference for a joint US-Soviet presence, the type of concrete arrangement between the United States and the Soviet Union that could work, benefiting from improved relations at the global level, is a joint reinforcement of regional-level agreements concerning stability. The advantage here is that local actors will receive superpower support for whatever regional agreements are attainable. Superpower rivalry will be less likely to undermine them insofar as each superpower has also endorsed them. Resulting agreements are likely to be stronger and more durable when underwritten by both the Soviet Union and the United States than when only underwritten by a single outside power.

Finally, the era of good feeling between Moscow and Washington, as long as it lasts, might lead to initiatives that actually have their origin at the superpower level but that are eventually acceded to at the regional level. Such initiatives tacitly suggest that the superpowers not only want to remove the Gulf from the list of potential areas of future global tension between themselves: Such mutual initiatives would mean that Washington and Moscow also seek to diffuse future regional conflict stemming from within the region that could spill over elsewhere. Action to achieve such stabilizing agreement would start at the global rather than the regional level, even though governments at each level would eventually become adherents.

Qualified but Still Dominant US Influence in the Region

A kind of obverse effect is occurring with respect to US influence in the region. On the one hand, US military capability has proven itself in the Iraq-Iran war through its naval presence and especially through its capacity to destroy virtually the entire Iranian navy without taking casualties itself. This and its willingness to stay the course with its Arab friends has certainly turned some heads in the region. On the other hand, the undeniable effect of generational changes in the leadership, especially of the moderate states, has left US diplomacy in a somewhat more difficult position. States in the region are simply less willing to listen to Washington's remonstrances than in the past. Governments are increasingly led by well-educated technocrats who despite their Western (and often US) educations are less prone to follow the Western lead unquestioningly. Thus, the military prestige of the United States is in the ascendancy at a time when its diplomatic prowess may have dwindled somewhat, through no particular fault of its own.

At the same time, two other factors have contributed to the relative diminution of US diplomatic influence. US reluctance to sell arms to Arab allies that at some time might use them, or transfer them, in some imagined future war with Israel and the fear that sophisticated armaments might get into the hands of radical governments such as Libya have forced some of the United States' Arab friends to look elsewhere, with a resulting reduction of dependence upon the United States. (The irony of these arguments, of course, is that the arms are purchased from other governments less willing or less able to monitor their disposition in any subsequent conflict.) Some decline in dependence would have occurred anyway because of the natural desire of arms buyers to diversify sources. Complete independence will not occur if US arms remain of highest quality, and of greatest sophistication, since wealthy buyers will always seek the best. But Saudi Arabia feels an undeniable irritation when, for example, the level of trust is apparently challenged by the United States' periodic refusal to sell some types of arms, often in a very public display of acrimony in Congress. But US debate is vigorous and open and often will rankle foreign friends, even when their own interests ultimately prevail.

A second source of diminished relative influence is the rapprochement between many governments in the Gulf, with different degrees of enthusiasm, and the Soviet Union. Envoys have been exchanged, visits occur, and new routes of diplomatic negotiation are explored. At the same time, commercial competition from the enterprises of other countries, notably Japan, establish linkages that rival those of the US oil companies and other large US corporations long accustomed to doing business in the area. Despite the easy relationship that has been built up over the years between corporate representatives and counterparts in the Gulf region, the US economic presence may be relatively less visible than in times past. This translates somewhat imperfectly into less overall US influence. Yet the answer here is to be found in the larger question of US economic competitiveness and concerted effort to retain investment and trade ties rather than in some explanation of perfidiousness. The more US industry has to offer commercially to Gulf countries, the stronger will be the resulting overall trade, financial, and political ties.

In the long run, diplomatic influence tends to follow the upward or downward pattern of military and commercial capability. The difference by the end of the decade will be that the internal regional balance of power will become relatively more important, and the United States will need to learn how to read it, and to operate within the newer, less patron-client-oriented set of rules.

Crux of the Western Security Dilemma in the Gulf

Based on the findings of this project, perhaps the most worrisome implication for Gulf energy supply is the possible renewal of major war in the area of the principal oil fields. What makes this argument difficult for some to accept is that they are still fighting the last war, the Iraq-Iran war, which went on for eight years without seriously disrupting supply for even a week. How then could another war be problematic for supply if this one that lasted so long did so little damage?

The answer is that this war was curious in that neither belligerent had much military capacity to project the war beyond its own borders. That is why the war ended, after very large casualties on both sides, about where it started in territorial terms. But the next war, if it occurs, may be of a quite different character. In particular, the belligerents may have more strategic capability, more destructive power at their disposal, and more willingness to strike hard at nonmilitary targets, including the oil wells and infrastructure.

In terms of warfare, both the hardware and tactics are changing rapidly. As Dunn notes, chemical warfare and longer-range missiles, despite problems of accuracy, are transforming the nature of conflict in the region. Shortly, governments will be in a position to hold hostage each other's fields with missiles armed with powerful conventional warheads. Soldiers themselves will not have to penetrate defenses to destroy the fields. Since neither side will have the equivalent of "second-strike" capability in nuclear terms, each side will have a very large incentive for preemptive attack. One can hardly imagine a more destabilizing deterrent situation.

But why would governments want to destroy oil facilities and even fields? What strategic purpose could this policy of annihilation serve? The answer lies in the evolution of the last war. It became a war of attrition. Regional strategists undoubtedly will point out that the reason the war dragged on was that each belligerent could finance the purchase of armaments from the sale of oil, including, for Iraq, Arab oil more generally. A sudden preemptive strike, wiping out this oil capacity, if combined with, or presumed to be combined with a defense of the attacker's own production and distribution capacity, would shift the outcome of the war suddenly and permanently. This is the strategic thinking likely to dominate the next massive use of force in the region if and when it occurs.

A related motive for a scorched-earth policy in the oil fields, perhaps used as a post hoc rationale for an action that was unable to take and hold the fields and infrastructure intact for production, is that too much oil exists on the world market. Forceful removal of some of it on a semipermanent basis would drive up the price for all of the remaining producers, including the perpetrator of the scorched-earth policy. Although this policy might be regarded by the perpetrator as second-best to acquiring the fields for its own purposes, such a second-best policy from the military perspective might be much easier to carry out and therefore much more attractive to a willful aggressor.

The other part of the puzzle that governments are not prepared to discuss very openly is the time required to rebuild the fields and infrastructure from the bottom up *once the fighting has stopped*. Whether immediate cessation of hostilities is feasible, and whether immediate access to the fields can be obtained politically and militarily, is a separate matter. But assuming immediate territorial access to both sides of a very badly damaged set of oil fields, an unofficial estimate of the time required to get the fields back to production levels previously enjoyed would be anywhere between one and two years, or, depending upon circumstances, perhaps a multiple of this. This scenario assumes massive destruction to all facilities including wells, such that most would have to be redrilled.

Western governments have sufficient supplies to get by quite nicely for up to six months with comparatively little importation from the Gulf. Beyond that point, the pressure on consumption would be very great, necessitating major allocation of supply according to governmental fiat. If such a destructive war occurred during a slack market situation such as that in the late 1980s, considerable expansion of supply could occur among nonbelligerents over a period of twelve months. This expansion of supply outside the area of military destruction could probably tide the West, and the developing world, over until the old fields could once again be brought on line. But if this particularly destructive brand of warfare took place in the interval of a very tight market near the end of the decade, the amount of surplus production capacity would not be sufficient to enable the West to get by in combination with its storage capacity in the absence of severe economic hardship.

One of the most difficult aspects of this possible situation is that the problem could not be resolved through political means because the shortages would be technical. They could not be eliminated until old fields were fitted with new wells, and this process would entail a considerable period of concentrated drilling and reconstruction. No amount of post hoc political bargaining could change the situation of physical destruction in an interval as short as, say, six months. A gap would inevitably emerge between the world demand for oil and the available supply. This is the principal message that should be left with the reader when such a significant margin of the world's exportable oil is concentrated in so few fields in such a tiny geographical region. War there could be devastating to everyone's energy supply.

The answer is that a major war in the region must not to be allowed to occur. Countries inside and outside the region have a mutually similar interest in averting such a war. Yet how can we assure it is prevented? The prospect of devastating consequence is no guarantee that the risks of war will be reduced.

Iraq and Iran will continue to rival each other even after a settlement of the current dispute, which at this writing has not taken place [but which has been for the present overshadowed by the Kuwaiti dispute]. Neither state is a territorially satisfied power in the sense that Saudi Arabia or Egypt can be regarded. Although this potential dissatisfaction may not again spill over into the region in a foreign war within the decade, the probability is pretty high that either Iran or Iraq or both will once again become belligerents, if not directly against each other, then elsewhere in the region. The gap between aspirations for regional hegemony and the capacity to actually display that hegemony is quite wide for both Iraq and Iran. Saudi Arabia and Egypt in different ways will attempt to be the peacemakers in a set of alliance relationships that will continually shift.

A significant naval presence, despite recent redeployments, to convince any aggressor in the area of whatever origin that war would be totally unprofitable is perhaps the best deterrent to the situation above outlined. Only by convincing all possible belligerents that they will lose before launching a full attack can the stability of the region be assured. Hegemonic behavior in prudent hands is the past method of attempting to guarantee the peace. The problem is further complicated in that a war may slowly escalate, thus triggering no response from US forces, and then suddenly lead to an overwhelming attack, possibly mutual on both sides, against the oil fields that lay almost totally vulnerable. Under these circumstances of too little information, US forces, even if prepared to repel an attack, would not be in much of a situation to do so until too late.

The upshot of this study is that the oil fields of the Middle East are becoming more vulnerable, not less so, over time. We in turn are becoming more dependent upon this source of supply. A return to tight markets is also likely. A confluence of all of these circumstances may be regarded as a worst-case scenario. Unfortunately, it is also a scenario with rising probability during the coming decade. More than any other set of circumstances, this matter of the increasing susceptibility of the oil fields to destruction during a new war in the Gulf ought to receive careful study and proper policy action in advance of the possible occurrence of such a devastating sequence of events.

Implications of Gulf Energy Security for US Policy

Don't Base Gulf Energy Policy on Hypotheses Concerning Regime Stability

Suppose the trend toward enhanced domestic political stability, observed in this study, proves wrong. What policy implications for Gulf energy security follows? Even if major regimes in the area were to follow the fate of the shah, and even if domestic political instability were on the rise, either for indigenous reasons or because of foreign instigation, *access to Gulf oil is not likely to be much affected* by such events. The explanation for this line of reasoning is found in terms of the nature of the world oil market as much as in the politics of the Gulf area.

Removal of most single exporters from the market, for an interval, in most market situations can be absorbed by oil that is in the pipeline or in storage (reservoirs in developed countries, for example). The exception to this logic may be Saudi Arabia in a tight market situation where price is already relatively high.

But in the case of all governments, whether conservative or radical, there is a desire to sell oil. After a forceful takeover, the desire to change policy, whether in terms of modernization or consumption or security, costs money. A delay may occur in the first year, but production cuts can be made up elsewhere. The need to sell oil goes on unabated regardless of the nature of the societal leadership. The more ambitious the regime, the more it will seek a larger OPEC share if it possesses the underlying production capacity and reserve size. A problem may arise down the road if a radical regime tries to do without all foreign production, drilling, and market assistance, thus running down its production capabilities. But such mismanagement will take some time to cause a damaging result. As long as the production facilities remain in place and the oil is in the ground, a new government, whatever its complexion, will seek to produce and to sell all it can obtain.

Late in the production horizon of some of these fields, a government might indeed try for conservation reasons to limit output in order to extend the life of the fields. But in the decade of the 1990s, no country in the Gulf is likely to have to face such physical limitations on output. Perhaps Iran comes closest because of the age of some of its fields. Even under these circumstances, the regime itself would have to pay for expanded modernization, and the only way it could generate enough hard currency is to continue to export large quantities of petroleum.

Finally, the nature of the oil market is that no single exporter can control the direction of its oil export. Thus single importers heavily dependent upon a single Gulf country for oil are not likely to be damaged by a revolutionary government that for one reason or another tries to punish the buyer of its product. This does not mean that control of the Gulf oil fields by a single polity, particularly a state hostile to Western interests, is desirable or even tolerable. Markets prosper through competition. Emergence of a simple monopoly producer would have the capacity to disrupt markets and would therefore pose very serious potential security problems for consumer nations.

Even if the former two arguments were incorrect, to wit that domestic stability is more evident today and that oil is not likely to be cut off in a serious and continuing way by the overthrow of an exporter, it would not follow that a strategy of regime support or defense ought to be devised or imposed on energy grounds. The reasoning here is quite simple. The greater the US effort to try to safeguard Gulf governments from their own demise, the more visible the US presence, both militarily and politically. The more visible this presence, the more likely that such governments will find themselves in trouble. They understand this phenomenon very well, and that is why they continue to refuse basing rights and troops in larger dimension than already exist. [Despite the size of the allied military buildup, nothing in the nature of the possible consequence for local political order and governance has changed since the Kuwaiti affair; if anything, the danger is more severe.] Whatever the nature of secret contingency arrangements (which are necessary and should by all means remain discrete), the history of our ability to safeguard governments from overthrow is not happy. This does not mean that they should not receive timely intelligence information, nor that we should not cooperate in discouraging terrorist activity or designs on a friendly government. But the bulk of the responsibility for regime survival is on the regime, not on us. When we begin to confuse the comparative burden of responsibility, we endanger our own position and theirs.

We ought to worry less about internal regime stability and build our strategy for the 1990s around other issues that are more problematic for energy security and over which we may possess a slightly larger measure of control. Safeguarding friendly governments from external aggression is the correct focus for Western security policy.

Imperative of Diplomatic Progress on the Palestinian Issue

In a tight market situation, the United States may find that leverage is used against it in oil matters as some of the principal Gulf producers lag behind intentionally in their building of production capacity. The United States could well look at such a policy as blackmail, but from the producers' perspective the policy is designed to prevent blackmail from being used against them. A possible US response could be that the next time a difficult situation develops in the Gulf, the United States might not be so quick to come to the aid of the Arab producers. But this argument will not have much credibility because the United States has as much interest in keeping the sea-lanes open as the producers themselves, and they know it. Another possible response to leverage used against the United States is implied threats to the security of some of the obdurate producers themselves. Should this route be adopted, the legacy of trust built up over the decades would quickly evaporate.

Hence the United States under a return of tight market circumstances may find itself more vulnerable both politically and in energy terms, especially concerning the principal problem that is as serious for the United States as for Israel, namely, what to do regarding the Palestinian issue. What is most important for all concerned is that the sense of progress toward a reconciliation be maintained. Then no sudden shocks or efforts at leverage-creation would be likely, and the United States would not have to consider adopting tactics that would lead to an unraveling of its privileged position in the Gulf. If the United States can demonstrate that it is genuinely working with the Palestinians and Israel to achieve both the creation of a Palestinian homeland *and* full recognition of the right of Israel to live within safe and secure borders, the region as a whole will be much more relaxed, each Gulf country will experience less internal tension, and the proper relationship between the United States and the Gulf producers in terms of leadership and trust can be maintained. The key is to defuse a situation in which a tight market gives certain governments a feeling that leverage in the form of reduced growth in production capacity can be used to bargain with the United States on political matters. Steady progress will best suit everyone's interests as the Middle East enters the last decade of the twentieth century.

A final note on this matter stems from several of the chapters in this book. Robins and Kuroda indicate that Europe and Japan, respectively, are less willing to support present US policies on the Palestinian question than is perhaps generally understood in the United States. Unless the United States is quite careful, it could become rather isolated on this issue or be forced into precipitous action during a crisis. Japan and Europe are in no mood to trade energy security for a free hand to Israel on the Palestinian question. Thus for the United States to avoid isolation and eventual confrontation on the issue of Palestinian rights, it must demonstrate to all that the negotiations are moving ahead.

It may seem strange that an issue so apparently removed from the Gulf situation is nonetheless so relevant to that situation, and to reasonableness in terms of price and production. But that is the reality of Gulf politics. According to one specialist on the Gulf, "Without question, continuation of the Arab-Israeli conflict will prove to be the single most troubling factor in American-Gulf relations."[2] Unfortunately, progress on Palestinian matters will not necessarily resolve overall difficulties in Lebanon or elsewhere in the Arab world. The explanation, of course, is that in some places Shiite sensibilities are as much a concern as Palestinian, and now march to a quite different drummer. But for most of the Gulf producers, including Iraq with its very large Shiite population, the Palestinian problem is still the front-burner issue.

Looked at from a slightly different perspective, if the United States is able to achieve progress on the Palestinian question, it can in turn use this progress as an instrument to obtain from the Gulf producers a more rational energy production policy defined in terms of the broadest of producer and consumer interests. Politics in the Middle East, as always, is a two-way street. Those who seek progress in one area must be willing to demonstrate it in another.

Necessity of Maintaining a Regional Naval Presence

Despite the difficulty of maneuver in the narrow confines of the Gulf itself, and notwithstanding the appropriateness of winding down some of the naval presence in the aftermath of the actual fighting during the Iraq-Iran war, the unfortunate reality is that the United States must be prepared to maintain a significant naval presence and to redeploy an air presence in the region throughout the decade. To those critics who note that the reflagging operation was not a conspicuous success in the narrow tactical sense of convoying, it must be noted that the real purpose of safeguarding oil supply was achieved. That purpose was to prevent an expansion of the war, an effort that was attempted at one point by the Iranian forces and that was convincingly rebuffed by the US Navy.

Thus the objective of keeping the sea-lanes open should not be construed in narrow terms. The larger interest, and the more important one, is to deter a large-scale war in the region. If such deterrence should fail, the objective must be to provide a defense of the oil fields against aggression, or, at the very minimum, to provide a quick and emphatic restoration of those fields to working condition under the sovereignty of the respective regional governments.

Scarcely simplifying this task, the prospects for additional territorial access are not good. Thus, whatever arrangements exist will have to suffice. Blue-water capabilities and facilities at Diego Garcia and elsewhere will compensate to some extent for these supply and maintenance limitations.

It is imperative that the United States' friends in the area understand and support the principle of free and open supply lines as well as a stable equilibrium of power within the region guaranteed by the continuing US presence. US capability ought to be low-profile, but compelling, in terms of its readiness, electronic intelligence-gathering prowess, and capacity to move with precision. These tasks will probably not become easier as the decade progresses, although cooperation among the great powers themselves may reduce some of the risks for the United States.

In short, as one contemplates missions where US, Western, and regional interests are at stake in the next decade, it is hard to find a commitment that ranks higher than the preservation of Gulf energy security.

A Two-Track Gulf Arms Control Proposal

Not only the oil fields are vulnerable militarily in the Gulf region. Many of the populations, located in a few major urban concentrations, are likewise easily targeted. The findings of this study show that an extremely volatile arms race is under way in the Gulf. Large quantities of weapons are being stockpiled in Iraq, Iran, and the GCC countries, as well as in countries adjacent to the Gulf region, such as in Israel and Syria. Yet security is relative. No absolute amount of weaponry or military spending will guarantee that security. Each new purchase in one country drives up the stakes for the others, forcing them to try to match the level of acquisition of a near neighbor or potential rival.

Moreover, new types of weapons have been introduced into the region with even more worrisome implications for security. Chemical weapons and medium-range ballistic missiles of increased accuracy and sophistication are now part of the arsenals of several of the Gulf states. Nuclear proliferation may extend into the Gulf region. These weapons provide not so much a deterrent as a vehicle for offensive warfare and surprise attack. Non-second-strike nuclear forces are always likely to be on hair trigger because of the fear of preemptive attack. Thus the nature of the new weaponry is itself a cause of growing political restiveness in an area as confined and penetrable as the Gulf.

At a time when the East-West dispute has taken some of the momentum out of arms acquisition, firms and governments will be looking for new buyers. The Gulf countries may be expected to pick up some of the slack in sales, regardless of whether the source is China, the Soviet Union, Western Europe, or the United States. Such an atmosphere will make cooperation among suppliers to constrain sales all the more difficult. Indeed, Gulf countries might question whether—given the inability of Western allies in the past to come to agreement on arms, for example, the failure of the 1950s Tripartite Agreement—they should place their security at risk to any extent in hopes that arms control might work in the region. A Western credibility problem here does exist.

Moreover, the United States and the Soviet Union may have had success in European arms talks, but outside the test ban and nuclear nonproliferation treaties, they have had less success and surely less experience in arms control agreements involving themselves and Third World countries. But even if the superpowers could agree between themselves, a host of new sellers, such as Brazil and North Korea, are emerging and are eager to exploit arms markets that may open up because of oligopolistic arrangements, for whatever reason, among the principal sellers. Only leverage from Washington and Moscow on their respective allies would ensure a degree of success for such arms arrangements.

Finally, the difficult matter of negotiation between Israel and states that do not formally recognize it or that do not have diplomatic ties with it must be considered. No reason exists to believe that Israel would ipso facto be willing to negotiate on arms control matters with its Arab neighbors because it might not want to be bound by an agreement that forecloses privileged options with suppliers. But the new missiles and chemical warheads place Israel in a far different security position than previously. It now has more incentive to seek mutual, verifiable constraint. Without including Israel in such a set of agreements, Iraq, for instance, will continue to argue that its acquisition of chemical weapons is not specific to its own foreign policy interests but represents the interest of all Arab countries, a position that other Arab governments may not believe but will not feel they can challenge. So Israel must be included in any arms arrangement through parallel agreements with arms suppliers, brokered by the United States and the Soviet Union if more direct routes of negotiation prove impossible.

A word of optimism here is perhaps warranted, however. The aftermath of the Iraq-Iran war on the threshold of the 1990s is a watershed in Gulf relations [deepened and broadened by the Iraqi invasion and its aftermath, but certainly not negated by those events]. The time may be ripe to begin regional arms control negotiations. Fresh in the minds of all is the devastating impact of chemical weapons and of missile attacks on urban sites. Each Gulf state has the financial capability to acquire such weapons; each is also subject to their use. Thus the awareness that either the countries in the region grasp the opportunity now to control the buildup of these weapons or acquiesce in an uncontrolled arms race must be apparent to all.

The time was never better to obtain from both the United States and the Soviet Union an agreement to back up and to reinforce an agreement on arms control among Iraq, Iran, and the GCC. Not only are the superpowers among the principal suppliers of weapons to the region and therefore relevant to the arms control process on those grounds, but by acting as "guarantors" of a regional arms control agreement, they could add political legitimacy to such an agreement. Their adhesion to such an agreement would also increase the reprobation and punitive pressure should any of the signatories fail to observe the terms of the agreement.

A two-track arms control proposal would not deny weapons to friends of the United States. Nor would it halt arms sales in the absence of an agreement on verifiable, mutual restraint. What such a proposal would do is to insist that discussions begin regarding mutual limitations on certain categories of weapons. Or such discussions would be employed to introduce confidence-building measures into the region. Israel directly or indirectly would necessarily be a part of such a set of arms control talks. The objective would be to open up a dialogue that is presently lacking for arms control discussion as a compliment to acquisition, now the sole route to the attempted enhancement of nation-state security.

General agreement on conventional arms limitation in the Gulf. By focusing upon specific categories of weapons such as tanks, artillery, planes, and missiles, the Gulf states could perhaps fashion an agreement along the lines now being pursued between NATO and the Warsaw Pact on conventional arms. Completion of such an agreement in Europe would create the stimulus for a regional agreement among the three principal actors in the Gulf area. Moreover, experience with counting procedures, verification, and negotiating formulae in the East-West balance could serve the Gulf states well.

Situations in East-West and South-South negotiations are by no means identical. The larger number of sovereign governments in the Gulf might complicate bargaining. But the very reality that another major conventional arms control agreement is in the process of finalization should add impetus to the plausibility of such an arrangement in the Gulf. If the principal arms suppliers would add their support to the agreement so that the entire burden of enforcement does not rest on the Gulf countries alone, the agreement might become more feasible. Such an arms control agreement could rank as a milestone among Third World countries.

A ban on chemical weapons. If a general agreement on conventional arms control proves unworkable, perhaps Iraq, Iran, the GCC, Israel, Syria, Jordan, and Egypt could reach agreement on the banning of chemical weapons. Multilateral treaties already exist to which these countries might subscribe with the same end. Yet the Gulf countries are sufficiently unique in political and geostrategic terms, and the region as a whole is sufficiently self-contained so that they might prefer to sign an agreement binding among themselves.

Should such a ban be impossible to negotiate either because of a lack of political will or because of technical problems of verification, for example, at the very least the various Gulf countries and their neighbors might agree to a non-first-use arrangement that could become at a later date the foundation for a full-scale ban.

Arms control arrangements will increasingly become necessary, and possible, in the Third World. The Gulf oil exporters have so much at stake, and in common, that they might become the locus of the first major set of conventional arms control agreements based on South-South cooperation and a little help from outside powers.

In Conclusion

This study began with the premise that by the end of the 1990s world oil markets are likely to tighten and the declining ratio of non-OPEC oil to OPEC oil will put far greater pressure on the Gulf to supply the bulk of the world's exportable oil. Notwithstanding some confidence that a series of four moderating trends will continue with respect to Gulf security, the crux of the Western energy and security dilemma is that war may again break out. [This prediction has already been fulfilled.] Yet the likelihood is great that additional foreign war will again occur within the decade. This time, the fields, the infrastructure, and access routes may be at risk. That the fields were not held hostage during the Iraq-Iran war is a poor argument for believing that they could not become targets in the next major conflict, or that such conflicts are of reduced likelihood. If such destructive strikes or occupation occurred at a time when oil markets are tight and a far higher percentage of world oil consumption is supplied by the Gulf, a very serious crisis could result for the West.

Implications for policy that follow are first to concentrate upon the potential problem of managing external hostilities and vulnerabilities caused by the hostilities rather than focusing upon the matter of domestic political stability of regimes, which will tend to take care of itself and is in any case much less directly related to the primary energy security concern of the importing countries. Second, the United States must continue to maintain a stabilizing military presence in the Gulf region as it has done continuously since the end of World War II.

Third, this study strongly recommends that the US government, in conjunction with cooperating countries inside and outside the Gulf region, embark on a set of two-track arms control initiatives involving both arms suppliers and purchasers. The uncontrolled arms race in the Gulf threatens the security not only of the oil fields and of the infrastructure but of the concentrated urban population of each country in the region. The object is to begin to get the countries affected by Gulf energy security to talk to one another regarding the perils of the new rounds of the arms race. In the absence of an arms control dimension to Western policy toward the Gulf, all emphasis must be on attempting to maintain an equilibrium of power under circumstances of accelerated arms buildup. A consequence will be that without arms constraint, the next war will be much more devastating than the last. For the Gulf region, the time for a two-track arms initiative is now propitious.

Notes

1. This chapter contains the formal conclusions and recommendations of the MacArthur study. While a few amendments, now bracketed, were made subsequent to the Iraqi invasion, the analysis was written for the decade as a whole. Indeed, for this analytic approach to be valid, no single event should have the capacity to undermine the general conlcusions.
2. J. E. Peterson, "The GCC States After the Iran-Iraq War," *American Arab Affairs*, no. 26 (Fall 1988): 96–106. The quotation is on p. 105.

Epilogue

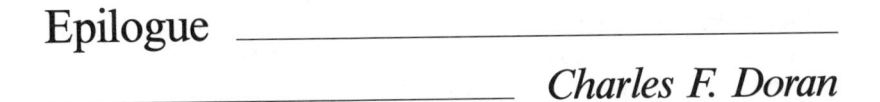

Charles F. Doran

Iraq made its bid for supremacy in the Gulf by invading Kuwait. What are the long-term consequences of this action for Gulf security?

First, a sense of realism has offset whatever complacency Washington and the world may have had regarding Gulf security. This unfortunate complacency of the Gulf states and the external powers seems unlikely to return. Iraq will remain a pivotal force in the Arab world, with or without the leadership of Saddam Hussein, because of Iraq's human, natural, and military resources.

Second, the question of alignment in the region must be reexamined in light of the Iraqi invasion. The apparent appeal of Saddam Hussein's confrontational rhetoric and policies among some of the Arab world's "have-nots," especially in Jordan and the Palestinian communities, highlights important underlying tensions. The role of the regional alliance structures also merits reexamination with the proven weakness of the Gulf Cooperation Council and the demise of the Arab Cooperation Council. The polarization of the Arab world around the Egyptian-Iraqi rivalry could provide the axis upon which future alliances will be determined.

Third, the proven vulnerability of Saudi Arabia and its oil fields does not bode well for either the long-term stability of the Gulf monarchies or US interests in the area. The United States must give priority to a postcrisis balance of power arrangement less dependent on a US military presence and more sensitive to the interests of the GCC states, Iran, and Iraq.

Fourth, the dramatic changes in the Soviet Union must also be factored into US policy considerations and should be a constructive factor. However, the general convergence of US-Soviet interests on the Kuwait crisis may not necessarily provide the basis for future collaboration in the region, especially if the Soviet empire continues to disintegrate. This could have an impact on Soviet policy in the Middle East because of the influence of the large Muslim population in the Soviet areas bordering the Middle East.

Nevertheless, the US-Soviet rapprochement on Gulf matters has proceeded further and faster than originally anticipated. This rapprochement makes the creation of regional security arrangements, as well as viable arms control negotiations, more achievable than before.

Finally, Iraq's invasion of Kuwait has highlighted the interrelationship between the Arab-Israeli conflict and security in the Gulf. By championing the Palestinian cause, Saddam Hussein has rallied popular support among Palestinians and non-Palestinians across the Arab world. They believe that the United States has followed a "double standard" by pressing for Iraqi withdrawal from Kuwait, but not similarly demanding an Israeli withdrawal from the Occupied Territories. The United States cannot afford to give Saddam a "victory" by officially acknowledging linkage between the two issues while the Gulf crisis continues. However, once the crisis is resolved or defused, the US government must give high priority to a just settlement of the Arab-Israeli conflict.

In short, the principal conclusions and policy recommendations of this study remain valid in the wake of the new threats and challenges to the region posed by the Iraqi invasion of Kuwait. A US military presence with a specific mission will be essential in the Gulf for some time. That mission is to deter threats to the region's oil fields and infrastructure and to keep the Gulf states from using force against one another in such a way that places these objectives in jeopardy. At a later date, arms control and other security arrangements to reduce tension should be encouraged. A new basis of regional political stability should also be developed that is not solely dependent upon the capability and nerve of a US president. Until the Gulf is no longer the focus of the exportable margin of world oil, these imperatives will remain the touchstones of US policy.

Chronology

G. Wade Wootan
John Schembari

1979

January 16. Shah Mohammad Reza Pahlavi leaves Iran for Aswan, Egypt.

February 1. Ayatollah Ruhollah Khomeini returns to Iran from exile in France.

February 11. Mahdi Bazargan replaces Shahpour Bakhtiar as prime minister of Iran.

February 14. An armed group attacks the US embassy in Tehran, killing an Iranian employee and wounding two US marines. About seventy US citizens are held captive.

March 12. Iran withdraws from the Central Treaty Organization (CENTO), which consisted of Turkey, Iran, Pakistan, and Great Britain.

April 1. The Islamic Republic of Iran is declared.

April 5. Iran cancels a $9 billion arms deal with the United States. The cancelled contracts include 160 F-16s, 7 AWACS, and 4 Spruance-class destroyers.

July 16. Saddam Hussein replaces Ahmad Bakr as president of Iraq.

August 23. Shiite demonstrators in Bahrain call for the establishment of an Islamic state.

October 1. US President Jimmy Carter orders the formation of the Rapid Deployment Force (RDF) to respond to potential military threats, especially in the Gulf.

October 22. After brief stays in Egypt, Morocco, the Bahamas, and Mexico, the shah is admitted into the United States for cancer treatment.

November 1. US National Security Adviser Zbigniew Brzezinski meets with Iranian Prime Minister Bazargan and Foreign Minister Ibrahim Yazdi in Algiers.

November 4. Iranian students occupy the US embassy in Tehran, taking sixty-six US diplomats and citizens hostage. The students demand that the United States extradite the deposed shah.

November 6. Iranian Prime Minister Bazargan and Foreign Minister Yazdi resign as a result of their meeting with National Security Adviser Brzezinski. The Revolutionary Council assumes official control of the government. Iran cancels the 1957 Treaty of Military Cooperation with the United States and the 1921 defense treaty with the Soviet Union.

November 8. The United States halts shipments of military spare parts to Iran.

November 12. President Carter announces an immediate suspension of oil imports from Iran.

November 14. President Carter freezes Iranian bank deposits and assets in the United States valued at $12 billion.

November 20. Gunmen belonging to an underground Saudi Arabian group seize the Grand Mosque in Mecca in an attempt to overthrow the monarchy.

December 4. The last of the gunmen who seized the Grand Mosque are captured.

December 27. The Soviet Union invades Afghanistan.

1980

January 23. President Carter declares, in what will later be termed the "Carter Doctrine," that the United States would use military force to protect its interests in the Gulf.

January 25. Abol Hasan Bani Sadr is elected president of Iran.

January 29. Canada closes its embassy in Tehran and secretly smuggles six US diplomats out of Tehran in the process.

March 18. After a breakdown in talks between the Soviet Union and Iran over gas prices, Iran halts both its export of 5 billion cubic meters of natural gas per year to the Soviet Union and the construction of the $3 billion Iranian Gas Trunkline 2 pipeline to the Soviet Union.

April 7. The United States severs diplomatic ties with Iran.

April 17. President Carter bans all imports from Iran.

April 21. The United States concludes an economic aid accord with Oman, wherein the United States supplies $100 million in aid over two years in return for access to military facilities in Oman.

April 24–27. A US military attempt to free the hostages fails when a helicopter and plane collide during refueling in Iran's desert. Eight servicemen are killed in the accident.

May 22. The European Economic Community embargoes trade with Iran.

July 27. The shah dies of cancer in Egypt.

September 17. Iraqi President Saddam Hussein abrogates Iraq's commitment to the 1975 Algiers Accord, thereby nullifying the Iran-Iraq border agreement concerning control of the Shatt al-Arab.

September 22. After months of increasing tensions with Iran, Iraqi forces invade Khuzistan province in southwestern Iran. Over the next few weeks, Iraqi forces overrun Khorramshahr and Abadan and move some 30 miles into Iran. The United States declares its neutrality.

September 30. Saudi Arabia accepts the deployment of four American AWACS planes on its territory.

November 12. Iran attacks a Kuwaiti border post in retaliation for Kuwaiti military and financial assistance to Iraq.

1981

January 20. Through Algerian mediation, the remaining fifty-two US hostages are released and leave Tehran as Ronald Reagan is inaugurated as president of the United States. The United States releases $2.9 billion of Iran's frozen assets. Approximately 4,000 claims for another $4 billion were to be addressed by a tribunal at The Hague.

May 25. Saudi Arabia, Kuwait, Qatar, Bahrain, Oman, and the UAE form the Gulf Cooperation Council to promote political, cultural, economic, and defense relations.

June 7. Claiming the reactor would be used to make nuclear weapons, Israeli aircraft bomb Osiraq, an Iraqi civilian nuclear research reactor at the Tuwaitha Atomic Center, located near Baghdad.

October 5. Ali Khamene'i is elected president of Iran.

October 28. The US Senate approves the sale of AWACS aircraft to Saudi Arabia by a vote of 52 to 48.

1982

February 26. The United States removes Iraq from its list of countries that support terrorism.

June 13. King Khalid of Saudi Arabia dies; Crown Prince Fahd becomes king.

June 29. Iraqi troops are forced out of Iran. Iraq proposes terms for a cease-fire but is rebuffed by Iranian authorities.

July 13. Iran takes the offensive in the war and invades southern Iraq.

September 4. The "tanker war" starts as Iraq begins attacks on Gulf shipping.

September 13. The US Commerce Department licenses Gates Learjet Corporation to sell to Iraq six small civilian jets valued at $21 million.

1983

June 23. France agrees to loan Iraq five Super Etendard fighter-bombers equipped with Exocet missiles.

July 23. Iran invades Iraqi Kurdistan, creating a second front.

July 29. Iran invades central Iraq, creating a third front.

December. The United States inaugurates "Operation Staunch," a program designed to stop arms shipments to Iran. US Ambassador-at-Large Richard Fairbanks visits several European and Asian capitals to enlist the support of other nations in the operation.

December 12. Terrorists in Kuwait bomb the US embassy, the French embassy, a US civilian compound, an oil refinery, the Electricity and Water Ministry building, and the airport control tower. Kuwaiti authorities arrest and try twenty-five Kuwaiti, Lebanese, and Iraqi nationals, all of whom appear to be associated with al-Dawa, a pro-Iranian group.

1984

January 23. The United States places Iran on its list of countries supporting terrorism.

January 25. Saudi Arabia signs a $4 billion contract with France to build the Shahine air defense system centered on AWACS purchased from the United States.

March 1. The GCC establishes the Gulf Investment Corporation (GIC) with capital of $2.1 billion. It was the first joint venture established under the aegis of the GCC.

March 5. Iran bombs Basra. Over the next two weeks, Iranian and Iraqi troops battle along the Baghdad-Basra highway.

May 13. Iran begins attacks on Gulf shipping.

May 28. US President Reagan approves the sale of 400 short-range anti-aircraft Stinger missiles to Saudi Arabia on an emergency basis to meet threats from the tanker war.

June 5. Two Iranian jets violate Saudi Arabian air space and are shot down by Saudi defense forces.

July 12. Kuwait purchases $327 million in arms from the Soviet Union.

August 2. Turkey and Iraq reach an agreement for a second Iraqi pipeline through Turkish territory.

November 26. The United States restores diplomatic relations with Iraq. (They were severed in 1967.)

November 28. The GCC announces plans to create a joint rapid deployment force to deter military threats.

Winter. The military situation in the Gulf leads to a peak naval buildup of forty-eight US ships in addition to eighty-two vessels from other Western nations.

1985

January 28. Iran, Pakistan, and Turkey ratify the Economic Cooperation Organization (ECO), a revised form of the Regional Cooperation for Development Organization.

March 11. Mikhail Gorbachev becomes general-secretary of the Soviet Union.

May 18. Saudi Arabian foreign minister Saud al-Faysal visits Iran. He is the first Saudi official to do so since 1979.

July. Saudi Arabia secretly purchases twenty nuclear-capable CSS-2 ballistic missiles from China with a range of 1,600 miles.

July 11. Bombs planted in two Kuwaiti cafes kill nine people and injure fifty-six others. The explosions result in the deportations of 4,000 people over the next fourteen days.

July 29. The UAE establishes diplomatic ties with China.

September 15. The US Congress rejects a proposal to sell forty-eight F-15 fighter planes to Saudi Arabia. The Saudi government responds by purchasing seventy-two Tornado jets from Britain.

September 24. France and Iraq conclude a deal to supply twenty-four Mirage F-1 aircraft.

September 26. Oman establishes diplomatic ties with the Soviet Union.

November 15. The UAE establishes diplomatic ties with the Soviet Union.

1986

February 2. Iraq destroys Iranian oil installations on Kharg Island.

April 26. Qatar seizes the Bahraini islet of Fasht al-Dibal but withdraws four days later.

May 7. Iran purchases Silkworm missiles from China.

May 25. US Lieutenant Colonel Oliver North, former National Security Council adviser Robert McFarlane, and Israeli intelligence officer Amiram Nir secretly visit Tehran to discuss trading arms for US hostages held in Lebanon.

July 3. Kuwaiti Emir Jabir al-Ahmad dissolves the National Assembly.

August 25. Iran and the Soviet Union agree to resume trade relations and reopen Iranian Gas Trunklines 1 and 2.

October 29. Saudi Arabian oil minister Sheikh Ahmad Zaki Yamani is replaced by Hisham Nazer.

November 20. Contradicting earlier reports released by the White House, Congressman Jim Wright issues a public statement saying that 2,008 TOW missiles and parts for 235 Hawk missiles were shipped to Iran via Israel.

November 26. The Saudi-Bahrain Causeway, the world's longest bridge, opens.

December 12. The Soviet Union and Iraq conclude a five-year economic cooperation agreement in banking, energy, steel, and transportation.

1987

January 6. Iran launches the Karbala-V offensive at Basra using the TOW and Hawk missiles secretly supplied by the United States.

May 6. The first superpower vessel, the Soviet freighter *Ivan Koroteyev*, is attacked by Iranian speedboats.

May 17. An Iraqi fighter plane accidentally attacks the USS *Stark* with two Exocet missiles, killing thirty-two US sailors.

July 17. France and Iran sever diplomatic ties during a dispute over the presence of Wahid Gordji, wanted in connection with a series of bomb attacks in Paris in September 1986, in Iran's Paris embassy.

July 20. The UN Security Council unanimously passes Resolution 598 calling for a Gulf war cease-fire. Iraq welcomes the action; Iran criticizes it but does not reject it.

July 22. US military forces begin escorting US-flagged Kuwaiti tankers.

July 24. The US-flagged Kuwaiti tanker *Bridgeton* strikes a mine in the Gulf.

July 31. In Mecca 402 people are killed when Saudi security forces move in to halt a political demonstration by Iranian pilgrims in front of the Grand Mosque at the start of the *hajj*. The dead include 275 Iranians and 85 Saudi security guards.

August 1. Crowds in Tehran storm the Saudi, Kuwaiti, and French embassies following reports of the riot in Mecca.

September 21. US forces in the Gulf attack the *Iran Ajr*, killing five crew members. The Iranian boat was laying mines off the Bahraini coastline.

October 3. Iran and Iraq officially sever diplomatic ties.

October 9. Iran hits the US-flagged tanker *Sea Isle City* with a Silkworm missile while the ship is docked in Kuwaiti waters.

October 19. In retaliation, US forces destroy two Iranian offshore oil rigs.

October 22. Kuwait's Sea Island oil terminal, the main Kuwaiti installation for handling supertankers, is hit by an Iranian missile.

October 26. US President Reagan declares an embargo on imports from Iran and prohibits US exports to Iran.

1988

January 7. In a letter to Iranian President Khamene'i, Ayatollah Khomeini says the government has the power to unilaterally revoke any lawful agreements that are "in contravention of the interests of Islam and the country." Khomeini's letter is in part a rebuke of statements made by the president on the limitations of government.

March 17. Iraq attacks the Kurdish city of Halabja with chemical weapons after its capture by Iran.

April 14. In retaliation for new Iranian mine-laying activities in the Gulf, the United States destroys two Iranian oil platforms, sinks a patrol boat and a frigate, and badly damages a second small frigate.

April 22. The United States announces it will expand its escort action in the Gulf to protect neutral shipping.

April 26. Saudi Arabia severs diplomatic ties with Iran. Reasons cited are the Mecca riots of 1987 and Iranian attacks on navigation in the Gulf.

May 4. The last three French hostages in Lebanon are released, following negotiations between the Iranian and French governments.

June 16. Following the release of French hostages in Lebanon, France and Iran resume diplomatic relations.

July 3. The USS *Vincennes* shoots down Iran Air flight 655 over the Straits of Hormuz, killing 290 passengers.

July 9. Qatar establishes diplomatic ties with China.

July 18. Iran accepts UN Security Council Resolution 598 calling for a cease-fire in the Gulf war.

July 20. Ayatollah Khomeini formally endorses the UN-sponsored cease-fire in the Iran-Iraq war.

July 22. Both Iran and Iraq agree to peace talks in Geneva.

August 1. Qatar establishes diplomatic ties with the Soviet Union.

August 20. The UN-sponsored cease-fire between Iran and Iraq goes into effect.

August 26. UN Resolution 620 is passed, condemning the use of chemical weapons and establishing sanctions for violations.

September 29. Kuwait and Iran resume diplomatic relations.

November 3. The United States extends more than $1 billion in export credits to Iraq.

November 10. Britain and Iran resume diplomatic ties.

December 18. Iran and West Germany sign a protocol on economic cooperation.

1989

February 14. Ayatollah Khomeini calls on Muslims to execute Salman Rushdie, British-based author of *The Satanic Verses*. Khomeini accuses Rushdie of denigrating Islam and the prophet Mohammad in his book.

February 15. In Tehran, some 3,000 Iranians demonstrate in front of the British embassy protesting the publication of *The Satanic Verses*.

February 26. Ayatollah Khomeini meets with Soviet Foreign Minister Eduard Shevardnadze in Tehran.

March 7. The Iranian Foreign Ministry severs ties with Great Britain over *The Satanic Verses* controversy.

June 3. Ayatollah Khomeini dies in Tehran. The Council of Experts elects President Khamene'i as Khomeini's successor.

June 20. *Majlis* Speaker Ali Akbar Hashemi-Rafsanjani visits the Soviet Union and signs a long-term protocol providing for economic, commercial, and technical cooperation.

June 21. Rail service is restored between Iran and the Soviet Union.

July 10. In Mecca, one person dies and sixteen are injured when two bombs explode during the *hajj*. Iran had boycotted the *hajj* because of restrictions placed on the number of pilgrims it would have been allowed to send.

July 27. Pakistan and Iran establish a joint commission for cooperation in military training and defense industries.

July 30. *Majlis* Speaker Hashemi-Rafsanjani is declared the winner of the July 28 Iranian presidential elections.

July 31. Soviet Foreign Minister Shevardnadze arrives in Tehran for a two-day official visit.

August 5. The agreement permitting Bahrain to retain US-made Stinger missiles is renewed.

September 21. In Mecca, sixteen Kuwaiti Shiites of Saudi Arabian and Iranian origin are beheaded in connection with the July 10 bombings in Mecca during the *hajj*.

September 28. The Bush administration announces it intends to sell 300 Ml-

A2 tanks to Saudi Arabia.

October 9. The Mitsui Company of Japan agrees to pay Iran $1 billion for withdrawing from the construction of the petrochemical complex at Bandar Khomeini.

October 13. Lebanese legislators meet in Taif, Saudi Arabia, to discuss ending the fourteen-year Lebanese civil war.

November 1. Gunmen kill Mohammad Ali al-Marzuqi, the last Saudi Arabian diplomat, in Lebanon. A pro-Iranian group takes responsibility, saying it is in retaliation for the September execution in Saudi Arabia of sixteen Kuwaiti Shiite Muslims convicted of a series of bombings in Saudi Arabia.

November 6. US officials announce that the government had agreed to return $567 million to Iran that had been held to pay claims brought by US banks following the 1979 revolution and the disruption of commercial agreements.

1990

January 6. An Iranian delegation goes to Moscow to sign an agreement easing travel restrictions across the border to defuse tensions in Soviet Azerbaijan.

January 8. In Kuwait, a political meeting at the house of former parliamentarian Ahmad Shraihan demands the restoration of Kuwait's elected national assembly suspended in 1985. Police disperse the crowd. Several people are injured.

January 20. Soviet troops enter Soviet Azerbaijan, killing at least ninety-nine Azeris in subsequent fighting. The Iranian Foreign Ministry issues a statement expressing "deep regret over such improper measures."

March 15. Iraq executes British-based reporter Farzad Bazoft, who was accused of spying for Israel.

March 28. Six people are arrested in Britain in connection with an attempt to smuggle krytons, nuclear trigger devices, to Iraq.

April 1. President Saddam of Iraq states that "we do not need an atomic bomb. ... We have the binary chemical. ... We will make fire eat up half of Israel" if Israel attacks Iraq.

April 12. British authorities impound steel pipes believed to be headed to Iraq for use as the barrel of a giant gun.

April 13. Sheffield Forgemasters, the manufacturers of the steel pipes impounded by British authorities, denies they could be used as a gun barrel and state that other shipments of the pipes had been approved by British authorities. The company claims the pipes were for use in the petroleum industry.

April 21. Greek officials charge a British truck driver with illegally transporting a giant steel tube that makes up part of Iraq's "super cannon."

April 22. The emir of Kuwait issues a decree establishing an interim national assembly.

April 22. Robert Polhill, a fifty-five-year-old professor at Beirut University College, is freed after being held captive for more than three years by Islamic Jihad for the Liberation of Palestine.

April 26. President Saddam of Iraq sends a letter to Iranian President Hashemi-Rafsanjani proposing direct talks to conclude a comprehensive peace settlement.

April 30. Frank Reed, a fifty-seven-year-old US citizen, is freed in Beirut after being held captive for more than forty-three months by the Islamic Dawn Organization. US President George Bush says, "We would like to thank the government of Iran for using its influence to help bring about this humanitarian step."

May 8. Eight Kuwaiti politicians are arrested for holding what government officials termed an illegal meeting to discuss a boycott of the June 10 general elections.

June 6. Iranian President Hashemi-Rafsanjani declares his nation is willing to discuss a peace agreement to end the Gulf war with Iraq.

July 18. Iraq accuses Kuwait of "stealing" Iraqi oil, building military installations on its territory and reducing its oil income through overproduction.

July 19. Iraqi President Saddam wins approval from the parliament for a revised constitution that would make him president-for-life in a legislative vote later in the year.

July 27. OPEC raises its target price for oil from $18 to $21 a barrel, and its members pledge that they will no longer surpass their allotted production ceilings.

July 27. The US Senate votes to impose sanctions prohibiting Iraq from receiving US-government-guaranteed loans for the purchase of US farm products.

July 30. Iraq concentrates nearly 100,000 troops close to its southern border with Kuwait.

July 31. Iraq and Kuwait hold talks in Jeddah, Saudi Arabia, to end the two-week-old political confrontation between the two nations.

August 2. Iraqi troops invade and overthrow the government of Kuwait.

Bibliography

Abir, Mordechai. *Saudi Arabia in the Oil Era: Regime and Elites, Conflict and Collaboration.* Boulder and London: Westview Press, 1988.
Ahrari, M. E., ed. *The Gulf and International Security: The 1980s and Beyond.* New York: St. Martin's Press, 1989.
Ajami, Fouad. *The Arab Predicament: Arab Political Thought and Practice Since 1967.* Cambridge University Press, 1981.
Al-Khalil, Samir. *Republic of Fear: The Politics of Modern Iraq.* Berkeley and Los Angeles: University of California Press, 1989.
Al-Yassini, Ayman. *Religion and State in the Kingdom of Saudi Arabia.* Boulder and London: Westview Press, 1985.
Albers, Henry H. *Saudi Arabia: Technocrats in a Traditional Society.* New York: Peter Lang, 1989.
Allen, C. *Oman: The Modernization of the Sultanate.* Boulder: Westview Press, 1987.
Amirahmadi, Hooshang, and Manoucher Parvin, eds. *Post-Revolutionary Iran.* Boulder: Westview Press, 1988.
Assiri, Abdul-Reda. *Kuwait's Foreign Policy: City-State in World Politics.* Boulder: Westview Press, 1989.
Axelgard, Frederick W. *A New Iraq? The Gulf War and Implications for U.S. Policy.* Westport: Greenwood, 1988.
Axelgard, Frederick W., ed. *Iraq in Transition: A Political, Economic, and Strategic Perspective.* Boulder: Westview Press, 1986.
Bakhash, Shaul. *The Reign of the Ayatollahs.* New York: Basic Books, 1984.
Bhatia, Shyam. *Nuclear Rivals in the Middle East.* London and New York: Routledge, 1988.
Bill, James A. *The Eagle and the Lion: The Tragedy of American-Iranian Relations.* New Haven: Yale University Press, 1988.
Bulloch, John. *The Persian Gulf Unveiled.* New York: Congdon & Weed, 1984.
Bulloch, John, and Harvey Morris. *The Gulf War: Its Origins, History and Consequences.* London: Methuen, 1989.
CARDRI staff, eds. *Saddam's Iraq: Revolution or Reaction?* 2d. ed. London: Zed Books, 1989.
Carus, Seth. *The Genie Unleashed: Iraq's Chemical and Biological Weapons Production.* Washington: Washington Institute for Near East Policy, 1989.
Casillas, Rex J. *Oil and Diplomacy: The Evolution of American Foreign Policy in Saudi Arabia, 1933–1945.* New York and London: Garland Publishing, 1988.
Chubin, Shahram, and Charles Tripp. *Iran and Iraq at War.* Boulder: Westview Press, 1988.
Claus, Burghard. *The Importance of the Oil-Producing Countries of the Gulf Cooperation Council for the Development of the Yemen Arab Republic and the Hashemite Kingdom of Jordan.* Berlin: German Development Institute, 1984.

Clements, Frank A. *Kuwait.* Oxford: Clio Press, 1985.
Cordesman, Anthony H. *The Gulf and the West: Strategic Relations and Military Realities.* Boulder: Westview Press, 1988.
Crystal, Jill. *Rulers and Merchants in the Gulf: Oil and Politics in Kuwait and Qatar.* New York: Cambridge University Press, 1990.
Doran, Charles. *Myth, Oil, and Politics: Introduction to the Political Economy of Petroleum.* New York: Macmillan, 1977.
Ehteshami, Anoushiravan. *Nuclearisation of the Middle East.* New York: Pergamon, 1989.
El Mallakh, M. S. *Qatar: Energy and Development.* Dover: Croom Helm, 1985.
Farazmand, Ali. *The State, Bureaucracy, and Revolution in Modern Iran: Agrarian Reforms and Regime Politics.* New York: Praeger Publishers, 1989.
Farouk-Sluglett, Marion, and Peter Sluglett. *Iraq Since 1958: From Revolution to Dictatorship.* New York: Methuen, 1988.
Fried, Edward R., and Nanette M. Blandin, eds. *Oil and America's Security.* Washington: Brookings Institution, 1988.
Ghods, M. Reza. *Iran in the Twentieth Century: A Political History.* Boulder: Lynne Rienner Publishers, 1989.
Golub, David. *When Oil and Politics Mix: Saudi Oil Policy, 1973-1985.* Cambridge and London: Harvard University Center for Middle Eastern Studies, 1985.
Grummon, Stephen R. *The Iran-Iraq War: Islam Embattled.* Washington: Center for Strategic and International Studies, 1982.
Hawley, Donald. *Oman and Its Renaissance.* Atlantic Heights: Humanities Press, Inc., 1987.
Helms, Christine Moss. *The Cohesion of Saudi Arabia: Evolution of Political Identity.* Baltimore: Johns Hopkins University Press, 1980.
Helms, Christine Moss. *Iraq: Eastern Flank of the Arab World.* Washington: Brookings Institution, 1984.
Hiro, Dilip. *The Longest War: The Iran-Iraq Conflict.* London: Grafton Books, 1989.
Holden, David, and Richard Johns. *The House of Saud.* London: Pan Books, 1981.
Ilgen, Thomas L., and T. J. Pempel. *Trading Technology: Europe, Japan, and the Middle East.* New York: Praeger Publishers, 1987.
Jabber, Paul, et al. *Great Power Interests in the Persian Gulf.* New York: Council on Foreign Relations, 1989.
Japan and the Arab World: Economic Development and Cooperation. Bahrain: Arab Banking Corporation, 1986.
Johany, Ali D., Michel Berne, and J. Wilson Maxon. *The Saudi Arabian Economy.* Baltimore: Johns Hopkins University Press, 1986.
Karem, Mahmoud. *A Nuclear-Weapon Free Zone in the Middle East: Problems and Prospects.* Westport: Greenwood, 1988.
Katz, Mark N. *Russia and Arabia: Soviet Foreign Policy Toward the Arabian Peninsula.* Baltimore: Johns Hopkins University Press, 1986.
Keddie, Nikki R. *Roots of Revolution: An Interpretive History of Modern Iran.* New Haven: Yale University Press, 1981.
Keddie, Nikki R., and Mark J. Gasiorawski. *Neither East nor West: Iran, the Soviet Union and the United States.* New Haven: Yale University Press, 1990.
Khadduri, Majid. *The Gulf War: The Origins and Implications of the Iraq-Iran Conflict.* New York and Oxford: Oxford University Press, 1988.
Khadduri, Majid. *Socialist Iraq: A Study in Iraqi Politics Since 1968.* Washington: Middle East Institute, 1978.
Khadir, Bichara. *The EEC and the Gulf: Relations and Stakes and the Gulf, Palestine and the West.* Louvain-la-Neuve, Belgium: Centre d'Etudes et de Recherche sur le Monde Arabe Contemporain, 1987.

Koury, Enver M., and Charles G. MacDonald. *Revolution in Iran: A Reappraisal.* Hyattsville: Institute of Middle Eastern and North African Affairs, 1982.
Kuniholm, Bruce Robellet. *The Persian Gulf and United States Policy: A Guide to Issues and References.* Claremont: Regina Books, 1984.
Kupchan, Charles A. *The Persian Gulf and the West: The Dilemmas of Security.* Boston: Allen and Unwin, 1987.
Lacey, Robert. *The Kingdom: Arabia and the House of Sa'ud.* New York: Avon Books, 1981.
Lawless, Richard I., ed. *The Gulf in the Early 20th Century: Foreign Institutions and Local Responses.* Durham: Centre for Middle Eastern and Islamic Studies of the University of Durham, 1986.
Lawson, Fred H. *Bahrain: The Modernization of Autocracy.* Boulder: Westview Press, 1989.
Long, David E. *The United States and Saudi Arabia: Ambivalent Allies.* Boulder: Westview Press, 1985.
Marr, Phebe. *The Modern History of Iraq.* Boulder: Westview Press, 1985.
McHale, Thomas R. *Saudi Oil Policy and the Changing World Energy Balance.* Boulder: International Research Center for Energy and Economic Development, 1986.
McNaugher, Thomas L. *Arms and Oil: U.S. Military Strategy and the Persian Gulf.* Washington: Brookings Institution, 1985.
Menashri, David, ed. *The Iranian Revolution and the Muslim World.* Boulder: Westview Press, 1989.
Milani, Mohsen M. *The Making of Iran's Islamic Revolution: From Monarchy to Islamic Republic.* Boulder: Westview Press, 1988.
Mottale, Morris Mehrdad. *The Arms Buildup in the Persian Gulf.* Lanham and New York: University Press of America, 1986.
Nakhleh, Emile A. *The Gulf Cooperation Council: Policies, Problems, and Prospects.* New York: Praeger Publishers, 1986.
Netton, Ian Richard, ed. *Arabia and the Gulf: From Traditional Society to Modern States.* Totowa: Barnes and Noble Books, 1986.
Nissman, David B. *The Soviet Union and Iranian Azerbaijan: The Use of Nationalism for Political Penetration.* Boulder: Westview Press, 1987.
Nonneman, Gerd. *Iraq, the Gulf States and the War: A Changing Relationship, 1980-1986 and Beyond.* London and Atlantic Highlands: Ithaca Press, 1986.
Nugent, J., and T. Thomas, eds. *Bahrain and the Gulf.* New York: St. Martin's Press, 1985.
Nyrop, Richard F., ed. *Persian Gulf States: Country Studies.* Washington: American University, 1985.
O'Ballance, Edgar. *The Gulf War.* Washington: Brassey's, 1988.
Olson, William J., ed. *U.S. Strategic Interests in the Gulf Region.* Boulder: Westview Press, 1987.
Peck, Malcolm. *United Arab Emirates: A Venture in Unity.* Boulder: Westview, 1985.
Perkins, Charles B. *Arms to the Arabs: The Arab Military Buildup Since 1973.* Washington: American Israel Public Affairs Committee, 1989.
Peterson, Erik R. *The Gulf Cooperation Council: Search for Unity in a Dynamic Region.* Boulder and London: Westview Press, 1988.
Peterson, J. E. *Defending Arabia.* London and Sydney: Croom Helm, 1986.
Piscatori, James. *Islam in a World of Nation-States.* Cambridge: Cambridge University Press, 1986.
Pridham, B. *Oman: Social and Strategic Developments.* London: Croom Helm, 1986.
Quandt, William B. *Saudi Arabia in the 1980's: Foreign Policy, Security, and Oil.* Washington: Brookings Institution, 1981.

Ramazani, R. K. *The Gulf Cooperation Council: Record and Analysis.* Charlottesville: University Press of Virginia, 1988.

Ramazani, R. K. *Revolutionary Iran: Challenge and Response in the Middle East.* Baltimore and London: Johns Hopkins University Press, 1987.

Ramazani, R. K., ed. *Iran's Revolution: The Search for Consensus.* Bloomington: Indiana University Press, 1989.

Rezun, Miron. *The Soviet Union and Iran: Soviet Policy in Iran from the Beginnings of the Pahlavi Dynasty Until the Soviet Invasion in 1941.* Boulder: Westview Press, 1988.

Rezun, Miron, ed. *Iran at the Crossroads: Global Relations in a Turbulent Decade.* Boulder: Westview Press, 1990.

Robins, Philip. *The Future of the Gulf: Politics and Oil in the 1990's.* Brookfield: Gower, 1989.

Rush, Alan. *Al-Sabah: History and Genealogy of Kuwait's Ruling Family, 1752–1987.* Atlantic Highlands: Ithaca Press, 1987.

Russo, Patricia. *Oman and Muscat: An Early Modern History.* New York: St. Martin's Press, 1986.

Safran, Nadav. *Saudi Arabia: The Ceaseless Quest for Security.* Cambridge and London: Harvard University Press, 1985.

Saivetz, Carol R. *The Soviet Union and the Gulf in the 1980s.* Boulder: Westview Press, 1989.

Salehi, M. M. *Insurgency Through Culture and Religion: The Islamic Revolution of Iran.* New York: Praeger Publishers, 1988.

Sandwick, John A., ed. *The Gulf Cooperation Council: Moderation and Stability in an Interdependent World.* Boulder: Westview Press, 1987.

Schulz, Ann Tibbitts. *Buying Security: Iran Under the Monarchy.* Boulder: Westview Press, 1989.

Sharif, Walid, ed. *The Arab Gulf States and Japan: Prospects for Cooperation.* London: Croom Helm, 1986.

Sick, Gary. *All Fall Down: America's Tragic Encounter with Iran.* New York: Random House, 1985.

Sicker, Martin. *The Bear and the Lion: Soviet Imperialism and Iran.* New York: Praeger Publishers, 1988.

Sindelar, H. Richard, III, and J. E. Peterson, eds. *Crosscurrents in the Gulf: Arab, Regional and Global Interests.* New York and London: Routledge, 1988.

Snyder, Jed. *Defending the Fringe: NATO, the Mediterranean, and the Persian Gulf.* Boulder: Westview Press, 1987.

Spector, Leonard S. *The Undeclared Bomb: The Spread of Nuclear Weapons, 1987–1988.* Cambridge: Ballinger, 1988.

Taryam, Abdulah O. *The Establishment of the United Arab Emirates.* London: Croom Helm, 1987.

Tetrault, Mary Ann. *The Organization of Arab Petroleum Exporting Countries (OAPEC): History, Policies and Prospects.* Westport: Greenwood, 1981.

Uthman, Nasir Muhammad. *With Their Bare Hands: The Story of the Oil Industry in Qatar.* New York: Longman, 1984.

Viola, Joy Winkie. *Human Resources Development in Saudi Arabia: Multinationals and Saudization.* Boston: International Human Resources Development Corporation, 1986.

Wilkinson, J. *The Imamate Tradition of Oman.* New York: Cambridge University Press, 1987.

Woodward, Peter. *Oil and Labor in the Middle East: Saudi Arabia and the Oil Boom.* New York: Praeger Publishers, 1988.

Wright, Martin, ed. *Iran: The Khomeini Revolution.* Essex: Longman, 1989.

Yager, Joseph A. *Nuclear Nonproliferation Strategy in the Middle East and North Africa.* McLean: Center for National Security Negotiations, 1989.
Yodfat, Aryeh Y. *The Soviet Union and Revolutionary Iran.* New York: St. Martin's Press, 1984.
Yoshitsu, Michael M. *Caught in the Middle East: Japan's Diplomacy in Transition.* Lexington: Lexington Books, 1984.
Zabih, Sepehr. *The Iranian Military in Revolution and War.* New York and London: Routledge, Chapman and Hall, 1988.
Zahlan, Rosemarie Said. *The Making of the Modern Gulf States: Kuwait, Bahrain, Qatar, the United Arab Emirates and Oman.* Boston: Unwin Hyman, 1989.

The Contributors

Charles F. Doran is professor of international relations at the Johns Hopkins University Paul H. Nitze School of Advanced International Studies. He was associate director of the Middle East Institute's study on "The Persian Gulf in the 1990s." He is the author of *Systems in Crisis: New Imperatives of High Politics at Century's End* (1990) and more than fifty scholarly articles and books on international politics, political economy, and energy policy.

Lucius D. Battle is president of the Middle East Institute and former assistant secretary of state for Near Eastern and South Asian affairs. He has served as ambassador to Egypt, senior vice-president of COMSAT, and chairman of the Johns Hopkins Foreign Policy Institute.

Stephen W. Buck is minister-counselor for political affairs, US Embassy, Ottawa. He served as deputy chief of mission/chargé d'affaires at the US embassies in Baghdad and Muscat, and as diplomat-in-residence at the Middle East Institute.

Shahram Chubin is professor of political science at the Graduate Institute of International Studies, University of Geneva, Switzerland. Dr. Chubin is the author of many books and articles on the Soviet Union and Middle East politics. One of his specialties is Iranian foreign policy.

Michael Collins Dunn is co-founder and senior analyst for the International Estimate, Inc. He is an adjunct professorial lecturer at Georgetown University and a frequent writer on Middle East defense and political issues.

Edward N. Krapels is founder and president of Energy Security Analysis, Inc. He is also executive director of Petroleum Economic Ltd. of London, president of PEL North America, and developer of STOCKWATCH oil market analysis service.

Yasumasa Kuroda is professor of political science at the University of Hawaii. He previously taught at both the University of Southern California and the University of California, Los Angeles. Dr. Kuroda has written extensively on Japan and the Middle East.

John W. Limbert is US consul general, Dubai, United Arab Emirates. He has served as a member of the US Foreign Service in Saudi Arabia, Iran, Tunisia, and Algeria. Dr. Limbert is the author of *Iran: At War with History* and many articles on Iran and the Middle East.

David E. Long is visiting professor of international relations at the US Coast Guard Academy and is currently writing a book on terrorism. He was previously diplomat-in-residence at Georgetown University. Dr. Long is the author of *Saudi Arabia and the United States: Ambivalent Allies* and many other books and articles on Saudi Arabia and the Middle East.

Ukeru Magosaki is a Japanese diplomat currently designated as minister in Ottawa, Canada. Having held a number of important posts throughout his career, including some in the Middle East, he writes knowledgeably of energy policy and overall Japanese foreign policy.

Phebe Marr is senior fellow at the Institute for National Strategic Studies of the National Defense University, and previously was a research associate at ARAMCO's Arabian Affairs division. She is the author of *The Modern History of Iraq* as well as many articles on that country.

Philip Robins is head of the Middle East Programme at the Royal Institute of International Affairs, Chatham House, London. He has taught at the University of Exeter and worked as a journalist in Jordan. Dr. Robins is the author of *The Future of the Gulf: Politics and Oil in the 1990s*.

Joseph Wright Twinam is John C. West Distinguished Visiting Professor of Government and International Relations at the Citadel. He served as both the first resident US ambassador to Bahrain and as deputy assistant secretary of state for Near Eastern and South Asian affairs.

Christopher Van Hollen is vice-president of the Middle East Institute and director of the institute's Islamic Affairs Programs and its Sultan Qaboos Center, and was a valued participant throughout the project. He has served as ambassador to Sri Lanka and the Republic of the Maldives as well as deputy assistant secretary of state for Near Eastern and South Asian affairs.

Index

Abdallah, Prince, 94
Abu Dhabi, 117, 120, 121, 163
ACC. *See* Arab Cooperation Council
Afghanistan: Soviet policy in, 212, 1, 134, 136, 141, 147
Agriculture: in Iraq, 53-54, 68(n10)
Ahl al-Aqd w'al-Hall, 94
Ahmad, Jabir al-, 215
Aid: Japanese, 179, 186; United States, 212, 186
Al-Aqsa, 96
Al Bu Said, 119
Al-Dawa, 214
Algeria, 115, 159; nationalism in, 95-96; oil prices in, 18-19
Algiers Accord, 213
Al-Khalifah, 119
Al-Yamamah contract, 155, 168, 169-170
Arab Cooperation Council (ACC), 64, 75, 194, 209; formation of, 79-80, 107-108
Arab-Israeli conflict, 126; and European Community, 161-165
Arab League, 116
Arabs, 126; nationalism, 95-96, 97; unity, 103-104, 163
Argentina, 6, 82
Armenia, 71
Armilla Patrol, 155-156, 160
Arms control, 205; agreements, 206-207. *See also* Arms race; Arms sales
Arms race, 6-7; Iraqi, 73-76. *See also* Arms control; Arms sales
Arms sales: by France, 74, 79, 167, 168; by Soviet Union, 214, 74, 75, 77, 114, 136; by United Kingdom, 215, 79, 167, 168, 169-170; by United States, 211, 213, 214, 215, 216, 218-219, 79, 99, 114, 197-198. *See also* Arms control; Arms race; Weapons
Asia, 178
Assassinations, 32
Azari-Qomi Bigdeli, Ayatollah, 37, 46(n6)
Azerbaijan, 219, 71, 134, 138, 151(n9)
Azerbaijani movement, 144

Baghdad Pact, 132
Baharnah, 119, 122
Bahrain, 211, 213, 215, 218, 117, 125, 127(n14); Gulf Cooperation Council, 8, 107, 109, 110, 111; leadership in, 119, 120, 124, 128(n24)
Bakhtiar, Shahpour, 211, 31
Bakr, Ahmad, 211
Bandar Khomeini, 219, 39
Bani Sadr, Abol Hasan, 212, 34, 35, 44, 46-47(n6)
Barzani, Mas'ud, 59
Ba'thists, 56, 57, 61
Bazaaris, 28-29, 46(n2)
Bazargan, Mahdi, 211, 212, 31, 36, 44
Bazoft, Farzad, 219
Beheshti, Mohammad, 31, 40
Belgium, 155-156, 158
Bombings, 218, 32
BP. *See* British Petroleum
Brazil, 6, 82
British Petroleum (BP), 167
Brzezinski, Zbigniew, 211, 212
Bubayan Island, 63
Buraimi Oasis, 117
Bush, George, 218-219, 220, 21

Camp David Accords, 96-97
Canada, 212
Carter, Jimmy, 211, 212, 13, 27, 28
Carter Doctrine, 212, 137
CENTO. *See* Central Treaty Organization
Central Command force, 137
Central Treaty Organization (CENTO), 211, 132
China, 215, 217, 6, 79, 82, 143, 159; and Japan, 174, 178; and Saudi Arabia, 80-81
Clerics: political, 31-32, 36-37
Common market, 109
Communism, 56, 95
Constitution, 37, 40
CW. *See* Weapons, chemical

Dar al-Harb, 97

Dar al-Islam, 97
Defense, d; Gulf Cooperation Council, 113-115.
    See also Security
Democracy, 182
Demonstrations. *See* Riots
Denmark, 156
Dhofar Liberation Front, 133
Dhofar rebellion, 119
Diplomacy: Gulf Cooperation Council, 115-117;
    Japanese, 183-184
Djibouti, 156
Dubai, 117, 120

Eastern Europe, 38, 147
EC. *See* European Community
ECO. *See* Economic Cooperation Organization
Economic Cooperation Organization (ECO), 215
Economy, 124, 135, 189, 193; European
    Community, 153, 154-155, 175; Gulf
    Cooperation Council, 103, 109-113, 120-
    121; Iran, 28, 38-39, 195; Iraq, 50, 55; Japan,
    176-180; Saudi Arabia, 88-91, 99
Egypt, 7, 64, 75, 100, 186, 195, 196, 200,
    207;Arab Cooperation Council, 79, 107,
    108; economy, 121, 180
Egyptian-Israeli treaty, 96
Egyptians: in Iraq, 54, 67(n7)
Elites: Gulf Cooperation Council, 119-120; in
    Iran, 35-37, 46-47(nn4, 6, 7); in Saudi
    Arabia, 93-95
Emami-Kashani, Hojjat al-Eslam, 37, 46-47(n6)
Embargos, 212, 217, 55
Energy, 24-25(nn 2, 4, 5); European Community
    use of, 154, 157-158; and oil demand, 13-
    15;security of, 201-207
Ethiopia, 100
Ethnicity, 70, 71; in Iraq, 58-59, 61
European Community (EC), 10; Arab-Israeli
    dispute, 161-164; arms sales, 167-170;
    economy, 153, 154-155, 175; function of,
    170-171; Gulf Cooperation Council, 110,
    111; Iran, 212, 159-161; military, 155-156;
    oil dependence of, 156-166; regional
    relations, 65, 165-167;United States, 164-
    165

Fahd, King, 213, 19, 20, 80, 97, 168
Fahd Plan, 97, 99, 115
Fairbanks, Richard, 214
Fasht al-Dibal, 215, 117
Faysal, Saud al-, 215
Federal Republic of Germany, 23, 144, 155, 156,
    169, 178; and Iran, 218, 10, 160; oil
    dependence of, 157, 158, 159
Foreigners: as workers, 111, 121, 124-125,
    127(n14)
France, 217, 3, 10, 67, 144, 154, 166; arms sales,
    74, 79, 167, 168; Iran, 4, 161; military, 155-
    156; oil use, 158, 159

GCC. *See* Gulf Cooperation Council
Genscher, Hans-Dietrich, 10
Germany, 67
Ghalib, Imam, 119
GIC. *See* Gulf Investment Corporation
Gilani movement, 144
Gorbachev, Mikhail, 3, 82; and Iraq, 66-67
Gordji, Wahid, 216
Great Britain. *See* United Kingdom
Greece, 156, 157, 158, 166
Gulf Air, 111
Gulf Cooperation Council (GCC), 213, 214-215,
    1, 63, 79, 107, 116, 144, 145, 150, 165, 166,
    167, 209; arms control, 206, 207; diplomacy,
    115-117; economy, 109-113, 120-121; oil
    policy, 7-8; ruling families in, 119-120;
    security, 113-115, 128(n25); Shiites, 122-
    123; structure of, 108-109; territorial
    disputes, 117-119; and United States, 125-
    127, 128-129(n27)
Gulf Currency Union, 110
Gulf Investment Corporation (GIC), 214, 111-
    112
Gulf University, 110
Gulf War. *See* Iran-Iraq war

Hashemi-Rafsanjani, Ali Akbar, 218, 220, 31,
    40, 37, 76, 77; leadership, 36, 46(n4), 47(n7)
Hashimites, 100
Hassan, Hussein Kamil, 74
Hawar, 117
Hostages, 211, 213, 215, 217, 220, 1
Hossein Dastgheib, Ayatollah Abd al-, 31
Hussein, King, 64, 80, 118
Hussein, Saddam, 211, 213, 219, 220, 36, 60,
    74, 96, 112, 209, 210; Israel, 65, 66; power,
    4, 56-57, 62, 73, 193

Ijma', 92-93
India, 71
Indian Ocean, 71
Indonesia, 18, 159
Industry: Iraqi, 53, 54-55
Infrastructure: regional development of, 109-110
International Energy Agency, 164
Intifada, 103, 163-164, 195
Investment, 169; downstream, 21-22, 187(n9);

Gulf Cooperation Council, 110, 111-112
Iran, 218, 1, 25(n7), 122, 126, 133, 144, 145, 151(n9), 193, 194, 195, 200, 206, 207; anti-Americanism in, 43-44; clerics in, 31-32; economy of, 215, 38-39; European Community, 159-161; government of, 41-42; and Japan, 181-183; military, 76-78, 83(n2); oil production in, 18, 51-52, 63-64, 163, 202; policies in, 27-28; politics of, 33-34, 45-46; power struggle in, 40-41; as regional power, 3-4, 61; revolution in, 28-30, 42-43, 108, 192; revolutionary council in, 30-33; ruling elite in, 35-37, 46-47(nn4, 6, 7); and Soviet Union, 132, 134, 135-136; as threat, 98, 100; United Nations Resolution 598, 115-116; and United States, 211, 212, 216, 45-46. *See also* Iran-Iraq war
Iran Air, 216
Iranian Communist party. *See* Tudeh party
Iranian Goods Procurement Office, 160
Iran-Iraq war, 213, 214, 216, 217, 220, 36, 56, 65, 72, 108, 149, 178-179, 190; Gulf Cooperation Council, 113-114; impacts of, 3-4, 5-6, 77, 198-199;and Saudi Arabia, 100, 101; UN Resolution 598, 217, 115-116, 137; weapons used in, 70, 74
Iran-Japan Petrochemical Company, 39
Iraq, 211, 68(nn10, 25), 132, 144, 145, 168, 193, 196, 200, 207; Arab Cooperation Council, 79, 107; economy of, 50, 52-54; foreign policy of, 61-67; and Iran, 63-64; and Israel, 64-66; and Japan, 177, 178, 181-183; Kuwait invasion by, 220, 3, 49, 70, 72, 104, 112-113, 115, 116, 140, 166, 170, 190, 209-210; leadership in, 57-58; military in, 52-53, 73-76; oil production in, 10-11, 18, 51-52, 163, 195; politics in, 56-61; as regional power, 3-5, 71, 108, 194; and Saudi Arabia, 96, 100, 101; as threat, 118-119; weapons use by, 217, 219, 52, 59, 65, 66, 67(n6), 69-70. *See also* Iran-Iraq war
Ireland, 156, 159
IRP. *See* Islamic Republican party
Isa, Emir, 120
Islam, 163; fundamentalist, 96, 135, 139, 146-147, 183, 192; political ideology of, 91-92; revolutionary, 32-33; in Saudi Arabia, 94-95, 97-98; in Soviet Union, 138, 140-141
Islamic Conference, 115
Islamic Dawn Organization, j
Islamic Republican party (IRP), 31, 32
Islamic Revolutionary Guards. *See* Pasdaran
Israel, 213, 96, 98, 104, 126, 186, 203; arms control in, 205, 207; European Community, 161-162; *intifada*, 163-164; Iraq's opposition to, 64-66; military in, 194-195; as regional power, 61, 71, 195-196
Italy, 154, 155-156, 158, 161, 169
Ivan Koroteyev, 216

Jabir al-Ahmad, Emir, 120

Jannati, Ahmad, 37, 46(n4)
Japan, 219, 10-11, 23, 81, 187(n9); diplomacy of, 183-184; foreign policy of, 173-174, 185-186, 203; and Iran and Iraq, 67, 160, 161, 181-183, 187(n12); oil dependence of, 174-175, 184; political involvement of, 180-181; trade with, 176-180; and United States, 173, 175-176
Jerusalem, 96
Jihad, 92
Jordan, 64, 75, 80, 118, 121, 183, 186, 194, 209; Arab Cooperation Council, 79, 107; arms, 169, 207; and Saudi Arabia, 100, 105(n7)
Judaism, 98

Karroubi, Mahdi, 37, 44, 46-47(n6)
Kashani, Ayatollah, 33
KDP. *See* Kurdish Democratic party, 59
Khalid, King, 213
Khalifa, Ali, 20
Khalifah, Emir, 119
Khamene'i, Seyyed Ali, 213, 218, 31, 34, 37, 39, 40, 76
Kharg Island, 215
Khomeini, Ruhollah, 211, 217, 218, 27, 32, 33, 37, 40, 77; Iranian revolution, 29-30; leadership of, 39, 47(n12); Rushdie affair, 160-161
Khor Abd Allah waterway, 62-63
KIO. *See* Kuwait Investment Office
Kirghiz, 71
Kuranari, Tadashi, 180
Kurdish Democratic party (KDP), 59
Kurdistan, 214
Kurds, 4, 56, 59, 78, 144, 176
Kuwait, 213, 219, 3, 25(n7), 49, 81, 110, 116, 120, 121, 125, 132, 145, 149, 154, 177, 193, 200; government of, 220, 123, 124; Gulf Cooperation Council, 8, 109, 111, 112, 115; Iran-Iraq war, 216-217; Iraqi invasion of, 7, 50, 60, 62, 63, 64, 69, 70, 72, 80, 101, 104, 112-113, 140, 166, 170, 190, 194, 209-210; oil production, 18, 19, 20, 21, 22, 23, 163; terrorism in, 214, 215
Kuwait Investment Office (KIO), 167
Kuwait Petroleum, 19

Index

Labor: foreign, 111, 121, 124-125, 127(n14)
Leadership: in Bahrain, 119, 120, 124, 128(n24); in Gulf region, 192-193; in Iran, 35-37, 46-47(nn4, 6, 7); in Saudi Arabia, 93-95
Lebanon, 215, 217, 219, 220, 183, 194, 204
Legitimacy, 92-93, 119-120
Libya, 22, 157
Luxembourg, 156

McFarlane, Robert, 215
Mahabad, 144
Mahallati, Baha al-Din, 31, 39
Mahdavi-Kani, Resa, 37, 44, 46(n4)
Maldive Islands, 71
Marxism, 98
Marzuqi, Mohammad Ali al-, 219
Mecca, 212, 216, 218
Meshkini, Ali, 37, 46(n4), 47(n7)
Mexico, 21
Middle class: in Iran, 29-30
Migration: in Iraq, 53-54
Military, 214-215, 70-71, 104, 132, 140, 185; European Community, 155-156, 165; Gulf Cooperation Council, 113-114; Iranian, 76-78, 83(n2); Iraqi, 52-53, 65-66, 68(n25), 73-76; Saudi Arabian, 78-81, 94, 105(n7); United States, 216, 69, 136, 145-146, 204, 208; Western, 81-82
Minorities, 134. *See also various minorities*
Missiles, 114, 139, 194, 199, 205; Iraqi, 66, 68(n25), 70; suppliers, 6-7
Missile technology control regime (MTCR), 139
Mitsui Company, 219
Mobil, 21
Modernization, 193
Mojahedin-e-Khalq, 32, 35, 44
Montazeri, Hossein Ali, 36, 43
Mossadegh, Mohammed, 33
Mousavi, Prime Minister, 37
Mousavi-Ardabili, Abd al-Karim, 31, 37
Mousavi-Kho'iniha, Hojjat al-Eslam, 37, 46(n4)
MTCR. *See* Missile technology control regime

Nasserism, 95
National Front, 29, 35
Nationalism, 59; Arab, 95-96, 97; Iranian, 32-33, 35; in Soviet Union, 71, 134
Nationalities, 134. *See also various nationalities*
Nazer, Hisham, 216, 21, 93
Netherlands, 155-156, 157, 159, 161
Nigeria, 18, 157, 159
Nir, Amiram, 215
Nixon Doctrine, 133

Non-aligned Movement, 115
North, Oliver, 215
North Sea: oil reserves, 159, 191
North Yemen: Arab Cooperation Council, 107, 108, 194; and Saudi Arabia, 100, 101
Norway, 157
NPT. *See* Nuclear Nonproliferation Treaty
Nuclear Nonproliferation Treaty (NPT), 79

OAPEC. See Organization of Arab Petroleum Exporting Countries
Occupied Territories, 163-164, 170, 183
ODA. *See* Official Development Assistance
Official Development Assistance (ODA), 186
Oil, 216, 71-72, 190-191; demands for, 13-15; European Community use, 154-155, 156-160, 162-163; Iraqi, 51-52; Japanese dependence on, 174-175, 179-180, 183-184, 187(nn9, 10); prices of, 18-20, 189; world supply of, 16-17, 24(n1); U.S. demand for, 17-18, 20-24, 25(n3). *See also* Oil policies; Oil production
Oil policies, 24-25(n2); Gulf Cooperation Council, 120-121; Saudi, 86-87, 102-103; Soviet, 141-142. *See also* Oil; Oil production
Oil production, 219, 220, 1, 3, 201-202, 207; Gulf Cooperation Council and, 7-8, 112-113; integration of, 21-23; by Iraq, 4-5, 10-11, 195; and war, 216-217, 199-200. *See also* Oil; Oil policies
Oman, 212, 213, 8, 117, 119, 120, 145, 154, 165, 169, 193; government of, 123, 124; Gulf Cooperation Council, 107, 109, 111, 115, 116; politics in, 121-122; and Soviet Union, 215, 133, 136
OPEC. *See* Organization of Petroleum Exporting Countries
"Operation Staunch," 214
Organization of Arab Petroleum Exporting Countries (OAPEC), 111, 161
Organization of Petroleum Exporting Countries (OPEC), 25(n7), 62, 63, 86, 87, 157, 174; and European Community, 162-163; and Gulf Cooperation Council, 7-8, 112; oil production, 16-17, 18-20, 191

Pacific Rim, 14
Pahlavi, Mohammad Reza, 211, 212, 28-29, 30
Pakistan, 211, 215, 70, 71
Palestine Liberation Organization (PLO), 103, 104
Palestinians, 64, 65, 190, 203-204, 209, 210; European Community's views of, 161-162, 163, 170; self-determination of, 96, 99

Palestinian state, 104
Pasdaran, 77
Patriotic Union of Kurdistan (PKU), 59
PDRY. *See* People's Democratic Republic of Yemen
Peace Shield program, 168
Peninsula Shield, 114-115
People's Democratic Republic of Yemen (PDRY), 96, 100, 101, 115, 132
People Who Bind and Loose. *See* Ahl al-Aqd w'al-Hall
Peshawar coalition, 70
PFLOAG, 133
Pipelines, 212, 214, 51
PKU. *See* Patriotic Union of Kurdistan
PLO. *See* Palestine Liberation Organization
Polhill, Robert, j
Portugal, 156
Power, 171(n2): Iraqi, 56-57, 71, 73, 108, 193; Israeli, 71, 195-196; regional balance of, 3-5, 61-62, 194-196; Soviet, 136-137

Qaboos, Sultan, 119, 120
Qasimi, 119
Qatar, 213, 215, 217, 122, 123, 136; Gulf Cooperation Council, 7, 8, 107, 111; leadership, 119, 124; territorial dispute, 117, 118
Qotbzadeh, Sadq, 35, 44

Rapid Deployment Force (RDF), 211
Rashid, Sheikh, 120
RCC. *See* Revolutionary Command Council
RDF. *See* Rapid Deployment Force
Reagan, Ronald, 213, 214, 27; and Iran, 217, 1; oil policy of, 21, 25(n3)
Reagan Doctrine, 147
Reed, Frank, j
Refineries, 21-22
Republic of Korea, 14, 178, 179
Revolution: Iranian, 27, 28-33, 42-43, 108, 192; Islamic, 32-33
Revolutionary Command Council (RCC), 58
Riots, 216, 29
Royalty. *See* Elites
Ruling families. See Elites
Rushdie, Salman, 160-161; *The Satanic Verses, 218*, 33, 43

Saad, Sheikh, 120
Sabah al-Ahmad, Sheikh, 120
Sadat, Anwar, 95
Satanic Verses, The (Rushdie), 218, 33, 43
Saud, King, 94
Saudi Arabia, 212, 214, 6, 25(n7), 51, 62, 72, 85, 110, 117, 133, 145, 200; arms sales to, 213, 219, 168, 169-170, 198; economy of, 88-91; European Community, 161, 165, 166-167; in Gulf Cooperation Council, 7, 107, 109, 111, 118; and Iran, 215, g; and Japan, 177, 178; military, 71, 78-81; military threats to, 100-101; oil policies, 18-19, 23, 86-87, 112, 113, 163, 194; oil production in, 215-216, 4, 5, 21-22; political threats to, 93-97; politics of, 91-93, 103-105; stability of, 98-100; and United States, 102-103, 125; worldview, 97-98
Saudi-Bahrain causeway, 216
Sea Island terminal, 216-217
Sea Isle City, 216
Secession, 144
Security: energy, 201-207; of Gulf Cooperation Council, 113-115, 128(n25); regional, 149, 192, 210; Soviet, 134-135, 136, 137, 138-139, 140-141, 146-147
Separatism, 59
Shari'at, Ali, 30
Shari'at Madari, Ayatollah, 34, 39
Sharjah, 117, 132
Shatt al-Arab, 213, 56, 62
Sheffield Forgemasters, 219
Shell, 21
Shevardnadze, Eduard, 218, 139
Shiites, 47(n13), 70, 128(n18), 204; in Bahrain, 211, 8; and Gulf Cooperation Council, 122-123; in Iraq, 4, 56, 58-59; in Saudi Arabia, 95, 98
Shipping, 216, 217, 1
Shirazi, Abdollah, 32
Shraihan, Ahmad, 219
Socialism, 94, 96, 98
Somalia, 100
Southeast Anatolian Project, 53
South Korea. *See* Republic of Korea
South Yemen. *See* People's Democratic Republic of Yemen
Soviet Union, 215, 217, 1, 8-9, 38, 71, 82, 133, 145, 195, 209; arms sales, 214, 77, 114, 168; and Gulf Cooperation Council, 125-126; and Iran, 212, 216, 218, 219, 64, 77, 135-136; and Iraq, 216, 66-67, 74, 75; Islam in, 140-141; and Japan, 174, 179; oil policy of, 24(n1), 141-142; as regional power, 136-137; and Saudi Arabia, 80-81, 100, 104; security of, 134-135, 136, 137, 138-139; and United States, 131-132, 142-144, 146-147, 148-150, 196-197, 206
Spain, 154, 156, 159, 161

Index

SPR. *See* Strategic petroleum reserve
Sri Lanka, 71
Stark, USS, 216
Strategic petroleum reserve (SPR), 20, 21, 24
Students, 29
Sultan, Prince, 94
Sunnis, 58, 59, 70
Superpowers, 72-73, 168, 197
Syria: as regional power, 61, 71, 96, 193, 194, 196, 207

Tabataba'i-Qomi, Hassan, 32, 39
Taiwan, 178
Tajiks, 71
Talabani, Jalal, 59
Tavassoli, Resa, 37, 46-47(n6)
Taxation: on gasoline, 14
Taymiyya, Taqi al-Din Ahmad, 92, 94
Technocrats: Saudi, 93
Technology: access to, 55
Territory: disputes over, 117-119
Terrorism, 214, 215, 216, 9, 122-123, 144
Texaco, 21-22
Tikritis, 58
Trade, 218, 121, 125; embargoes, 212, g; with European Community, 154, 160, 161; with Iran, 215, 10; with Japan, 176-180, 181-183, 187(n12)
Treaty of Military Cooperation, 212
Trucial Oman Scouts, 120
Tudeh party, 135
Turkey, 211, 214, 46(n1), 51, 53, 61, 132, 144, 169, 193; economy of, 215, 180

UAE. *See* United Arab Emirates
UK. *See* United Kingdom
Umm Qasr, 62, 63
Unified Economic Agreement, 109, 110, 112
United Arab Emirates (UAE), 213, 215, 25(n7), 63, 122, 123, 124, 125, 136, 193, 194; Gulf Cooperation Council, 7, 8, 107, 111, 112, 113, 116, 117; and Japan, 177, 178; oil production in, 18, 19; ruling families in, 119, 120
United Kingdom (UK), 211, 219, 10, 144, 166, 171(n2), 192; arms sales, 215, 79, 167, 168, 169-170; Gulf interests, 153-154, 155, 165; Iran, 218, 160; Kuwait, 3, 167; military, 132, 155-156, 165; oil production, 23, 157, 159, 163
United Nations, 49, 138, 181; Iran-Iraq war, 216, 217, 115; Resolution 598, 116-117, 136; Security Council, 155, 156, 163, 185
United States, 213, 214, 1, 3, 9, 133, 137, 140, 162, 181, 189, 192, 209; arms sales, 114, 168; and European Community, 164-165; and Gulf Cooperation Council, 125-127, 128-129(n27); and Iran, 211, 212, 216, 43-44, 45-46, 64, 78; and Iraq, 218, 61, 65, 66, 67; and Japan, 173-174, 175-176, 178, 182-183, 186; military, 216, 217, 69, 82, 136, 145-146, 204, 208; oil dependence of, 13-14, 17-18, 190-191; oil policy of, 20-25, 202-203; regional influence of, 197-198; and Saudi Arabia, 218-xi, 78-79, 91, 96, 99, 102-103, 104, 105; and Soviet Union, 131-132, 138, 142-144, 146-147, 148-150, 196-197, 206
Urbanization: in Iraq, 53-54
USSR. *See* Soviet Union
Uzbekistan, 71
Uzbeks, 71

Va'ez-e-Tabasi, Hojjat al-Eslam, 31-32
Venezuela, 18, 21-22, 23, 157, 159
Venice Declaration, 162
Vincennes, USS, 217

Wahhab, Mohammad Ibn Abd al-, 92
Wahhabism, 92, 94
War. *See* Iran-Iraq war
Warbah Island, 63
Weapons, 114, 179; biological, 65; chemical, 217, 219, 6, 52, 59, 65, 66, 70, 74, 75-76, 139, 199, 205; Iraqi, 69-70; nuclear, 213, 65, 67(n6), 75, 76, 139, 194; suppliers of, 6-7. *See also* Arms control; Arms race; Arms sales
Weinberger, Caspar, 136
West Germany. *See* Federal Republic of Germany
Wright, Jim, 216

Yamani, Ahmad Zaki, 215, 93

Yazdi, Ibrahim, 211, 212, 37, 44, 46(n6), 47(n8)
Yemen, 64, 75, 79, 80, 104, 108, 115. *See also* People's Democratic Republic of Yemen; Yemen Arab Republic
Yemen Arab Republic, 145

Zayid, Sheikh, 119, 120
Zionism, 98